For Ed & Jan,
who live in it.

With affection,

Leroy

THE WORLD OF MUSIC

LEROY OSTRANSKY

Professor of Music
and Composer in Residence
University of Puget Sound

the
world
of
MUSIC

Prentice-Hall Inc., Englewood Cliffs, N.J.

to Sonya

PRENTICE-HALL INTERNATIONAL, INC., *London*
PRENTICE-HALL OF AUSTRALIA, PTY. LTD., *Sydney*
PRENTICE-HALL OF CANADA, LTD., *Toronto*
PRENTICE-HALL OF INDIA PRIVATE LTD., *New Delhi*
PRENTICE-HALL OF JAPAN, INC., *Tokyo*

Current printing (last digit):

10 9 8 7 6 5 4 3 2 1

© 1969 by
Leroy Ostransky

Library of Congress Catalog card number 69-12823
Printed in the United States of America

THE WORLD OF MUSIC by Leroy Ostransky

Foreword

THIS COLLECTION OF WRITINGS ON MUSIC IS IN-tended for college students who elect a two-semester music course as part of an Arts or a Humanities requirement. The majority of these students enter into this course with little or no formal musical training. The course—often called "Introduction to Music Literature" or "Survey of Music" or "Music 101" or something else similar to these titles—is frequently the student's first encounter with a college music course and (according to the way in which his curriculum is planned) is likely to be a terminal course as well.

It is with this knowledge in mind, and with the experience that comes from twenty years of teaching such a course to non-music majors, that these writings were brought together. Although each contributing writer is a specialist with his own particular musical discipline—Aaron Copland, composer; Leonard Bernstein, composer and conductor; Frederick Dorian, teacher and historian; to mention but a few—there is one factor that binds them together. Each of these professional musicians makes a strong plea to the non-professional musician, the layman, to try to understand what music is about.

It is safe to assume that a certain number of beginning students will have had some experience with, and enjoyment of, various phases of serious music and will continue to do so throughout their lives. For these students this collection offers the kind of information that we believe will lead not only to a better understanding, but also we trust, to an even greater enjoyment of all music.

The special value of this collection, however, lies in the way it can be made to fascinate and interest the intelligent student with a minimum of experience in serious music. Our collection starts where the student is; it does not assume knowledge and experience that the student is not likely to have. The writings explain clearly and lucidly, and, for the most part, in non-technical language, the ramifications of music in a way calculated to draw the student to the great music itself.

It is our belief that each instructor prefers to explain such things as scale construction, chord construction, note values, and other fundamentals in his own way and in his own time, if he wishes to discuss these questions at all. For this reason we have excluded our own explanation of these matters. Again, we cannot presume to suggest that one particular symphony—the *Jupiter*, for example—is a more useful or more valuable musical illustration for the section on *the symphony*, than, say, Beethoven's *First*. The instructor will no doubt introduce his favorite pieces of music to coincide with the appropriate essay, and that is as it should be.

Although some of the essays are historically oriented, it has not been our intention in collecting these essays to provide a history of music. It has been our intention, rather, to take the student logically from one aspect of music to another aspect of music, according to his current frame of reference.

For example, we believe that the subject of *program music* may be introduced to the class without first discussing the question of *form* in music. Most program music, as we know, may be followed intelligently and understood by simply making the student aware of the composer's program. On the other hand, it is difficult to make students understand the special appeals of *absolute music* without first presenting them with the elements of form. Therefore, it seemed logical to present these three subjects in this order: program music; form; absolute music.

To look back for a moment: Since the orchestra is the principal medium for performing program music, it seemed logical to have the subject of *the orchestra* precede program music. The section on absolute music is given to chamber music, because this kind of music—absolute music—is the principal province of the small chamber ensemble. The transition from absolute music to the symphony is an easy one; the most significant example of absolute music for orchestra is the symphony. The origins of opera must be sought in the music of the church, and here, we confess, it seemed as logical to have the church music precede opera as to follow it. The final choice will no doubt remain with the individual instructor.

At this stage in the student's training, we have found it useful to provide him with a degree of historical perspective. To this end, we have selected essays characterizing the musical life of the chief historical periods—the Middle Ages, the Renaissance, the Baroque Era, the Classical Period, the Romantic Period, and the Twentieth Century—through their composers. These essays may either be used in the order we have presented them or individually as the necessity presents itself.

We have concluded with essays on musical comedy and jazz—types of music with which the student has had wide experience and with which he is at once familiar. We believe that the intelligent student will now be able to place these familiar types of music, as well as all music, in their proper context.

Each essay is preceded by a short introduction giving the background and information necessary to an understanding of the essay's intention. Each essay is then followed by a series of what we believe to be interesting and provocative questions of a serious nature. These questions may be used for class discussion, as subjects for short papers, or as examination questions. Wherever possible, the questions have been phrased in concrete terms and deal with ideas on which students feel capable of expressing themselves.

Finally, in selecting the various essays, we have tried to point out that music exists because human beings have composed music for others who have performed it for others who have listened, and that this vital, essential activity is still going on.   L.O.

Acknowledgments

I WISH TO ACKNOWLEDGE THE ASSISTANCE OF Warren Perry, librarian of the University of Puget Sound, and his associates, Elspeth Pope and Desmond Taylor. My deepest thanks I owe to my wife, who suffered through the selection of each essay, except my own.

I wish to express my appreciation for permission to use the following materials:

HOW WE LISTEN, with permission of the publishers, from *What to Listen for in Music* by Aaron Copland. Copyright © 1939, 1957 by the McGraw-Hill Book Company, Inc.

IMAGE PROCESSES AND CONNOTATION, reprinted from *Emotion and Meaning in Music* by Leonard B. Meyer by the permission of the University of Chicago Press. Copyright 1956 by the University of Chicago Press.

THE NATIONAL SCHOOLS, reprinted from *Symphonic Music* by Homer Ulrich by permission of the Columbia University Press. Copyright 1952 by the Columbia University Press.

THE MEANING OF FORM from *The Musical Workshop* by Frederick Dorian, pp. 245–246, 249–251, 253–259, 267–269, 271–273. Copyright 1947 by Harper & Row Publishers, Incorporated. Reprinted by permission of Harper & Row, Publishers.

CHAMBER MUSIC by Donald Francis Tovey, reprinted from *Cobbett's Cyclopedic Survey of Chamber Music*, Volume 1, by permission of the publishers, the Oxford University Press, Inc. Copyright 1929–1930 by Oxford University Press, Inc.

THE HEYDAY OF OPERA, reprinted from *Going to the Opera* by Lionel Salter, by permission of Lionel Salter. Copyright 1955 by Phoenix House Ltd.

THE CHORALE IN THE CHURCH SERVICE, reprinted with the permission of The Macmillan Company from *J. S. Bach* by Albert Schweitzer, Volume 1, tr. by Ernest Newman. First published in English in 1911 by Breitkopf and Härtel. Permission outside the United States of America by A. & C. Black Ltd.

BACH, from: *The Stream of Music* by Richard Anthony Leonard. Copyright 1943 by Richard Anthony Leonard. Reprinted by permission of Doubleday and Company, Inc.

THE WEATHER AT MOZART'S FUNERAL by Nicolas Slonimsky, from *The Musical Quarterly*, January, 1960. Copyright 1960 by G. Schirmer, Inc. Reprinted by permission.

THE IMPRESSIONISTS, from *Music of the World* by Kurt Pahlen. Copyright 1949 by Crown Publishers, Inc. Used by permission of the publisher.

BARTÓK IN AMERICA, reprinted from *The Life and Music of Béla Bartók* by Halsey Stevens, by permission of the publishers, the Oxford University Press, Inc. Copyright 1953 by the Oxford University Press, Inc.

THE PROOF OF THE NOTATION from *Twentieth Century Music* by Peter Yates. Reprinted by permission of Random House, Inc. Copyright 1967 by Random House, Inc., Publishers. Permission outside the United States of America and Canada by George Allen & Unwin Ltd.

WHATEVER HAPPENED TO THAT GREAT AMERICAN SYMPHONY? from *The Joy of Music* by Leonard Bernstein. Reprinted by permission of Simon and Schuster, Inc. Copyright © 1954–1959 by Leonard Bernstein. Permission in the British Commonwealth and Empire by M/s George Weidenfeld and Nicolson Ltd.

JAZZ: SOME EARLY DIFFICULTIES, reprinted from *The Anatomy of Jazz* by Leroy Ostransky, by permission of the University of Washington Press. Copyright © 1960 by the University of Washington Press.

Table of Contents

THE SYMPHONY

THE OPERA

THE CHURCH

COMPOSERS IN THEIR TIMES

MUSIC OF SHOW BUSINESS

THE MEANING OF MUSIC

*Aaron Copland was born in Brooklyn, New York, in
1900, and is one of America's best known composers of
serious music. Among his most popular works are*
Appalachian Spring, *the ballet* Billy the Kid, *and* El
Salón México. *A tireless and devoted teacher and
lecturer, Copland has written many articles on music
for the layman. Concerned with raising the level of
musical understanding of the average listener, he wrote
his book,* What to Listen for in Music. *However, before
we can know what to listen for, we must first know
how to listen; Copland's essay deals with that subject.*

how we listen

AARON COPLAND

WE ALL LISTEN TO MUSIC ACCORDING TO OUR separate capacities. But, for the sake of analysis, the whole listening process may become clearer if we break it up into its component parts, so to speak. In a certain sense we all listen to music on three separate planes. For lack of a better terminology, one might name these: (1) the sensuous plane, (2) the expressive plane, (3) the sheerly musical plane. The only advantage to be gained from mechanically splitting up the listening process into these hypothetical planes is the clearer view to be had of the way in which we listen.

The simplest way of listening to music is to listen for the sheer pleasure of the musical sound itself. That is the sensuous plane. It is the plane on which we hear music without thinking, without considering it in any way. One turns on the radio while doing something else and absent-mindedly bathes in the sound. A kind of brainless but attractive state of mind is engendered by the mere sound appeal of the music.

You may be sitting in a room reading this book. Imagine one note struck on the piano. Immediately that one note is enough to change the atmosphere of the room—proving that the sound element in music is a powerful and mysterious agent, which it would be foolish to deride or belittle.

The surprising thing is that many people who consider themselves qualified music lovers abuse that plane in listening. They go to concerts in order to lose themselves. They use music as a consolation or an escape. They enter an ideal world where one doesn't have to think of the realities of everyday life. Of course they aren't thinking about the music either. Music allows them to leave it, and they go off to a place to dream, dreaming because of and apropos of the music yet never quite listening to it.

Yes, the sound appeal of music is a potent and primitive force, but you must not allow it to usurp a disproportionate share of your interest. The sensuous plane is an important one in music, a very important one, but it does not constitute the whole story.

There is no need to digress further on the sensuous plane. Its appeal to every normal human being is self-evident. There is, however, such a thing as becoming more sensitive to the different kinds of sound stuff as used by various composers. For all composers do not use that sound stuff in the same way. Don't get the idea that the value of music is

HOW WE LISTEN from *What to Listen for in Music* by Aaron Copland; copyright 1939, 1957 by the McGraw-Hill Book Company, Inc. Reprinted by permission.

The Meaning of Music / Copland

commensurate with its sensuous appeal or that the loveliest sounding music is made by the greatest composer. If that were so, Ravel would be a greater creator than Beethoven. The point is that the sound element varies with each composer, that his usage of sound forms an integral part of his style and must be taken into account when listening. The reader can see, therefore, that a more conscious approach is valuable even on this primary plane of music listening.

The second plane on which music exists is what I have called the expressive one. Here, immediately, we tread on controversial ground. Composers have a way of shying away from any discussion of music's expressive side. Did not Stravinsky himself proclaim that his music was an "object," a "thing," with a life of its own, and with no other meaning than its own purely musical existence? This intransigent attitude of Stravinsky's may be due to the fact that so many people have tried to read different meanings into so many pieces. Heaven knows it is difficult enough to say precisely what it is that a piece of music means, to say it definitely, to say it finally so that everyone is satisfied with your explanation. But that should not lead one to the other extreme of denying to music the right to be "expressive."

My own belief is that all music has an expressive power, some more and some less, but that all music has a certain meaning behind the notes and that that meaning behind the notes constitutes, after all, what the piece is saying, what the piece is about. This whole problem can be stated quite simply by asking, "Is there a meaning to music?" My answer to that would be "Yes." And "Can you state in so many words what the meaning is?" My answer to that would be, "No." Therein lies the difficulty.

Simple-minded souls will never be satisfied with the answer to the second of these questions. They always want music to have a meaning, and the more concrete it is the better they like it. The more the music reminds them of a train, a storm, a funeral, or any other familiar conception the more expressive it appears to be to them. This popular idea of music's meaning—stimulated and abetted by the usual run of musical commentator—should be discouraged wherever and whenever it is met. One timid lady once confessed to me that she suspected something seriously lacking in her appreciation of music because of her inability to connect it with anything definite. That is getting the whole thing backward, of course.

Still, the question remains, How close should the intelligent music lover wish to come to pinning a definite meaning to any particular work? No closer than a general concept, I should say. Music expresses, at different moments, serenity or exuberance, regret or triumph, fury or delight. It expresses each of these moods, and many others, in a numberless variety of subtle shadings and differences. It may even express a state of meaning for which there exists no adequate word in any language. In that case, musicians often like to say that it has only a purely musical meaning. They sometimes go farther and say that *all* music has only a purely musical meaning. What they really mean is that no appropriate word can be found to express the music's meaning and that, even if it could, they do not feel the need of finding it.

But whatever the professional musician may hold, most musical novices still search for specific words with which to pin down their musical reactions. That is why they always find Tchaikovsky easier to "understand" than Beethoven. In the first place, it is easier to pin a meaning-word on a Tchaikovsky piece than on a Beethoven one. Much easier. Moreover, with the Russian composer, every time you come back to a piece of his it almost always says the same thing to you, whereas with Beethoven it is often quite difficult to put your finger right on what he is saying. And any musician will tell you that that is why Beethoven is the greater composer. Because music which always says the same thing to you will necessarily soon become dull music, but music whose meaning is slightly different with each hearing has a greater chance of remaining alive.

Listen, if you can, to the forty-eight fugue themes of Bach's *Well-Tempered Clavichord*. Listen to each theme, one after another. You will soon realize that each theme mirrors a different world of feeling. You will also soon realize that the more beautiful a theme seems to you the harder it is to find any word that will describe it to your complete satisfaction. Yes, you will certainly know whether it is a gay theme or a sad one. You will be able, in other words, in your own mind, to draw a frame of emotional feeling around your theme. Now study the sad one a little closer. Try to pin down the exact quality of its sadness. Is it pessimistically sad or resignedly sad; is it fatefully sad or smilingly sad?

Let us suppose that you are fortunate and can describe to your own satisfaction in so many words the exact meaning of your chosen theme. There is still no guarantee that anyone else will be satisfied. Nor need they be. The important thing is that each one feel for himself the specific expressive quality of a theme or, similarly, an entire piece of music. And if it is a great work of art, don't expect it to mean exactly the same thing to you each time you return to it.

Themes or pieces need not express only one emotion, of course. Take such a theme as the first main one of the *Ninth Symphony*, for example. It is clearly made up of different elements. It does not say only one thing. Yet anyone hearing it immediately gets a feeling of strength, a feeling of power. It isn't a power that comes simply because the theme

The Meaning of Music / Copland

is played loudly. It is a power inherent in the theme itself. The extraordinary strength and vigor of the theme results in the listener's receiving an impression that a forceful statement has been made. But one should never try to boil it down to "the fateful hammer of life." That is where the trouble begins. The musician, in his exasperation, says it means nothing but the notes themselves, whereas the nonprofessional is only too anxious to hang on to any explanation that gives him the illusion of getting closer to the music's meaning.

Now, perhaps, the reader will know better what I mean when I say that music does have an expressive meaning but that we cannot say in so many words what that meaning is.

The third plane on which music exists is the sheerly musical plane. Besides the pleasurable sound of music and the expressive feeling that it gives off, music does exist in terms of the notes themselves and of their manipulation. Most listeners are not sufficiently conscious of this third plane.

Professional musicians, on the other hand, are, if anything, too conscious of the mere notes themselves. They often fall into the error of becoming so engrossed with their arpeggios and staccatos that they forget the deeper aspects of the music they are performing. But from the layman's standpoint, it is not so much a matter of getting over bad habits on the sheerly musical plane as of increasing one's awareness of what is going on, in so far as the notes are concerned.

When the man in the street listens to the "notes themselves" with any degree of concentration, he is most likely to make some mention of the melody. Either he hears a pretty melody or he does not, and he generally lets it go at that. Rhythm is likely to gain his attention next, particularly if it seems exciting. But harmony and tone color are generally taken for granted, if they are thought of consciously at all. As for music's having a definite form of some kind, that idea seems never to have occurred to him.

It is very important for all of us to become more alive to music on its sheerly musical plane. After all, an actual musical material is being used. The intelligent listener must be prepared to increase his awareness of the musical material and what happens to it. He must hear the melodies, the rhythms, the harmonies, the tone colors in a more conscious fashion. But above all he must, in order to follow the line of the composer's thought, know something of the principles of musical form. Listening to all of these elements is listening on the sheerly musical plane.

Let me repeat that I have split up mechanically the three separate planes on which we listen merely for the sake of greater clarity. Actually, we never listen on one or the other of these planes. What we do is to correlate them—listening in all three ways at the same time. It takes no mental effort, for we do it instinctively.

Perhaps an analogy with what happens to us when we visit the theater will make this instinctive correlation clearer. In the theater, you are aware of the actors and actresses, costumes and sets, sounds and movements. All these give one the sense that the theater is a pleasant place to be in. They constitute the sensuous plane in our theatrical reactions.

The expressive plane in the theater would be derived from the feeling that you get from what is happening on the stage. You are moved to pity, excitement, or gaiety. It is this general feeling, generated aside from the particular words being spoken, a certain emotional something which exists on the stage, that is analogous to the expressive quality in music.

The plot and plot development is equivalent to our sheerly musical plane. The playwright creates and develops a character in just the same way that a composer creates and develops a theme. According to the degree of your awareness of the way in which the artist in either field handles his material will you become a more intelligent listener.

It is easy enough to see that the theatergoer never is conscious of any of these elements separately. He is aware of them all at the same time. The same is true of music listening. We simultaneously and without thinking listen on all three planes.

In a sense, the ideal listener is both inside and outside the music at the same moment, judging it and enjoying it, wishing it would go one way and watching it go another—almost like the composer at the moment he composes it; because in order to write his music, the composer must also be inside and outside his music, carried away by it and yet coldly critical of it. A subjective and objective attitude is implied in both creating and listening to music.

What the reader should strive for, then, is a more *active* kind of listening. Whether you listen to Mozart or Duke Ellington, you can deepen your understanding of music only by being a more conscious and aware listener—not someone who is just listening, but someone who is listening *for* something.

QUESTIONS

1. When you play a record or turn your radio on while studying, on what level are you listening to the music? Are you listening at all? What do you hear?

2. Which would you say has a more sensuous appeal: a piano playing, a trumpet playing, an orchestra playing? Why? What are your reasons? What are the contributing factors?

3. Name a piece of music that expresses something special for you. Do you think other people find the same expressiveness, the same meaning in the music as you do? Why?

4. Is it necessary to understand a piece of music in order to enjoy it? On what listening level is "understanding?" On what level is pure "enjoyment?"

5. Why is the life of an average popular hit song only about three months? What, exactly, makes a standard work standard?

THE MUSICAL EXPERIENCE

The meaning of a musical composition depends on the individual listener, his education, his tastes, his experience, his memory. Leonard Meyer, *who teaches music at the University of Chicago and has done considerable research and writing on the effect of music on people, presents us with some interesting points of view.* In his authoritative book, Emotion and Meaning in Music, *Meyer tells us that music sets up images in the listener's mind; the music we hear evokes moods and memories, which then arouse these images. The following essay helps us to understand how music moves us, how it affects our feeling toward music, and why we may prefer certain kinds of music.*

Image processes and connotation

LEONARD B. MEYER

THE AFFECTIVE EXPERIENCES THUS FAR DISCUSSED
result from a direct interaction between a series of musical stimuli
and an individual who understands the style of the work being heard.
Because the forces shaping such an experience are exclusively musical,
the form of the affective experience will be similar to the form of the
musical work which brought it into being.

Not all affective experiences are as direct as this. Often music arouses
affect through the mediation of conscious connotation or unconscious
image processes. A sight, a sound, or a fragrance evokes half-forgotten
thoughts of persons, places, and experiences; stirs up dreams "mixing
memory with desire"; or awakens conscious connotations of referential
things. These imaginings, whether conscious or unconscious, are the
stimuli to which the affective response is really made. In short, music
may give rise to images and trains of thought which, because of their
relation to the inner life of the particular individual, may eventually
culminate in affect.

But if such image processes are really unconscious, we can never
know them. . . . Only feeling penetrates into awareness, a feeling
aroused by something of which the subject is quite ignorant. Self-
conscious minds seem to have a repugnance for such isolated disembodied mental phenomena: they are felt to be morbid and eerie. Consequently a process of rationalization is undertaken at once. Whatever is
in the focus of attention at the moment when the affect arises is held to
be the direct cause of it. Thus many affective experiences attributed
directly to musical stimuli may in point of fact be the products of
unconscious image processes. Because neither we nor the subject himself can know anything about such unconscious image processes any
discussion of such an experience is clearly impossible.

Often, however, image processes are conscious. The listener is aware
of the associations which he makes while listening. Conscious image
processes may be either private, relating only to the peculiar experiences
of a particular individual, or they may be collective, in the sense that
they are common to a whole group of individuals within a culture. The
image processes of a whole community will be referred to here as
connotations.

Private images, even when they are brought to consciousness with-

IMAGE PROCESSES AND CONNOTATION from *Emotion and Meaning in Music* by
Leonard B. Meyer; copyright 1956 by the University of Chicago Press. Reprinted
by permission.

out psychic distortion, are problematical because it is almost impossible to trace the relationships existing either between the musical stimulus and the image processes aroused or between the image processes and the resultant affect. The peculiar experience of an individual may, for example, cause a "happy" tune to be associated with images of a sad occasion.

Even where the original association appears to be relevant and appropriate to the character of the music being played, affective experience may be a result of the private meaning which the image has for the particular listener. For example, the image of a triumphal procession might within a given culture be relevant to the character of a piece of music; but the association might for private reasons arouse feelings of humiliation or defeat. Thus while the image itself is relevant to the music, the significance which it has for the particular individual is purely personal.

Image processes, whether private or collective, are tremendous temptations toward extramusical diversion. For an image, even though originally relevant to a particular passage, may itself initiate further image processes. The development and proliferation of these may, however, proceed without reference to the subsequent successions of musical stimuli. That is, one image may follow another, not because of the associations which obtain between the images and the progress of the music, but because of the associations in the mind of the listener between the images themselves.

Neither the form nor the referential content of such experiences, however affective they may be, have any necessary relationship to the form and content of the musical work which presumably activated them. The real stimulus is not the progressive unfolding of the musical structure but the subjective content of the listener's mind.

Yet, in spite of the many and cogent objections which can be leveled against the relevance of such responses, it seems probable that conscious or unconscious image processes play a role of great importance in the musical affective experiences of many listeners. Indeed, it is often difficult for even the most disciplined and experienced listeners to escape the deepseated power of memory over affective experience.

It should be noted in this connection that not only do memories frequently result in affective experience but affective experiences themselves tend to evoke memories and arouse image processes appropriate to the character of the affective experience, whether sad or gay, noble or tender, as determined by the objective situation. In other words, even the most purely musical affective experiences may give rise to image processes which, developing their own series of associations, may become independent of the musical succession itself.

By connotations, as distinguished from image processes, are meant those associations which are shared in common by a group of individuals within the culture. Connotations are the result of the associations made between some aspect of the musical organization and extramusical experience. Since they are interpersonal, not only must the mechanism of association be common to the given cultural group, but the concept or image must have the same significance for all the members of the group. The concept must be one that is to some extent standardized in cultural thinking; it must be a class concept that has the same meaning for, and produces the same attitudes in, all the members of the group. In the West, for example, death is usually depicted by slow tempi and low ranges, while in certain African tribes it is portrayed in frenzied musical activity; yet this results from difference in attitudes toward death rather than from differences in the associative processes of the human mind. The particular way in which a connotation is realized or represented in music cannot be understood apart from the beliefs and attitudes of the culture in question.

Some connotations are entirely traditional. Association is by contiguity; i.e., some aspect of the musical materials and their organization becomes linked, by dint of repetition, to a referential image. Certain instruments become associated with special concepts and states of mind. The organ, for example, is associated for Western listeners with the church and through this with piety and religious beliefs and attitudes. The gong is linked by contiguity to the Orient and often connotes the mysterious and the exotic. In fact, even where this association does not seem intended, as in Varèse's *Ionisation,* it tends to modify our response to this music. Certain modes of tonal organization may awaken connotations. The pentatonic mode, for example, is used in the nineteenth century to represent things pastoral. Certain intervals may be used to indicate special concepts or states of mind. For instance, the diminished fifth was closely associated with expressions of grief and anguish during the baroque period. Or specific tunes may be employed to evoke concepts, memories, or image processes. This is a frequent device in the music of Charles Ives.

As a rule such associations are used in combination so that each reinforces the other. If the composer wishes to evoke connotations of piety and those connected with religious beliefs, he will not only employ the appropriate instrument but he will also use techniques of composition —modality, polyphony, and so forth—that have the same associations.

Notice that all these associations are intracultural. The gong will not have a special exotic meaning for the oriental in whose music it is common, though it may have other different associations for him. Nor will the pentatonic mode connote things pastoral to peoples who use this mode for all kinds of music, for cultivated art music as well as for folk music.

Because such associations are completely cultural and in no sense necessary, they are subject to change. Old associations die and new ones come into being. In Western music, for example, the harp is no longer associated, as it was in the Middle Ages, with religious subjects. Because of its use in French music of the late nineteenth century, it is much more likely to be associated with a certain tender vagueness.

A particular epoch may develop quite an elaborate system of connotations in which certain melodic, rhythmic, or harmonic practices become signs of certain states of mind or are used to designate specific emotional states. The composers of the baroque period developed such a system of connotations. Other composers, notably Wagner, have invented their own systems of connotative symbols, in which a specific melody, not just a more or less general figure, indicates and symbolizes a specific idea, concept, or individual.

If our responses to such special systems of connotative or designative symbols are to be really effective, they must become habitual and automatic. This requires time and repeated encounters with a given association. We do not need to learn that an oboe is traditionally a pastoral instrument. By hearing it used in this context time and time again, by reading about pipes and shepherds in literature, and by seeing such instruments depicted in paintings of Pan or Marsyas, we gradually build up a set of powerful associations. Once such an association has become firmly established, our response to it will be just as direct and forceful as if the response were natural.

However important associations made by contiguity may be, they constitute but a small fraction of the total group of connotations evoked by music. Most of the connotations which music arouses are based upon similarities which exist between our experience of the materials of music and their organization, on the one hand, and our experience of the nonmusical world of concepts, images, objects, qualities, and states of mind, on the other.

There is a great deal of evidence, some of it intercultural, which indicates that our experience of musical stimuli is not a separate, special category of experience but that it is continuous with and similar to our experiences of other kinds of stimuli.

Both music and life are experienced as dynamic processes of growth and decay, activity and rest, tension and release. These processes are differentiated, not only by the course and shape of the motions involved in them, but also by the quality of the motion. For instance, a motion may be fast or slow, calm or violent, continuous or sporadic, precisely articulated or vague in outline. Almost all modes of experience, even those in which motion is not directly involved, are somehow associated qualitatively with activity. Spring, revolution, darkness, the pyramids, a circle—each, depending upon our current opinion of it, is experienced as having a characteristic motion. If connotations are to be aroused at all, there will be a tendency to associate the musical motion in question with a referential concept or image that is felt to exhibit a similar quality of motion.

The unity of perceptual experience, regardless of the particular sense employed, is also demonstrated by the fact that in experience even single musical tones tend to become associated with qualities generally attributed to non-aural modes of sense perception. This tendency is apparent not only in Western culture but in the culture of the Orient and in many primitive cultures. In Western culture, for example, tones are characterized with respect to size (large or small), color value (light or dark), position (e.g., a large object is generally associated with a low position), and both size and position are associated with color.

Through such visual and tactile qualities, which are themselves a part of almost all referential experience, tones become associated with our experience of the world. Thus, the associations, if any, evoked by a low tone will be limited, though not defined, by the fact that in Western culture such tones are generally associated with dark colors, low position, large size, and slower motion.

Often referential experiences are themselves partly aural. A city, the wind, solitude, or the expressions of the human voice—all have a peculiar quality of sound which music can imitate with varying success. Such imitation will tend to awaken connotations similar in some respects at least to the experiences which originally conditioned the musical organization.

To what extent the associations arising from similarities between our experience of music and our experience of the nonmusical world are products of cultural conditioning and to what extent they are in some sense natural is difficult to say. The many studies made by psychologists, although they present ample evidence of associative consistency within Western culture, throw little light upon the problem of the naturalness of these responses; for the subjects in such experiments have, almost without exception, already been saturated with the beliefs and attitudes of Western culture.

Evidence from primitive and non-Western cultures is not conclusive. Frequently the associations formed are ones which appear natural to us. But sometimes a connotation strikes us as odd or unusual. In the latter case, however, it must be remembered that the association evoked by a given musical passage depends upon the attitude of the culture toward the concept as well as upon the mechanism of association. In other words, although in a given culture one attitude toward an object or process will usually be dominant, others are possible. For example, although in our culture death is generally considered to be a solemn, fearful, and majestic summoner, it has also been viewed as an old friend or as the sardonic mocker of human pretensions. And obviously each of these attitudes would become associated with very different types of musical presentation.

This much, however, is clear: (1) In most cultures there is a powerful tendency to associate musical experience with extramusical experience. The many musical cosmologies of the Orient, the practice of most primitive cultures, and the writings and practices of many Western composers are striking evidence of this fact. (2) No particular connotation is an inevitable product of a given musical organization, since the association of a specific musical organization with a particular referential experience depends upon the beliefs and attitudes of the culture toward the experience. However, once the beliefs of the culture are understood, most associations appear to possess a certain naturalness because the experiences associated are in some sense similar. (3) No matter how natural a connotation may seem to be, it undoubtedly acquires force and immediacy through cultural experience.

Obviously a complex and subtle connotation is not defined by any single element of the sound organization. Taken individually any one aspect of the musical organization is a necessary but by no means a sufficient cause for defining a given connotation. For instance, while it would not be possible in Western culture to depict the joys of youth in the lowest ranges of the bassoon, high ranges alone would not assure such an association either. Other aspects of the musical organization, such as tempo, dynamics, rhythmic character, and texture, would have to play a part in defining such a connotation.

But the degree of specificity attained in association, the degree to which a given musical disposition will evoke the same or similar connotations in all listeners within the cultural group, is not merely the function of the number of elements defining the connotation. All the elements of music are always present if there is any music at all. That is, there is always texture, whether it be that of a single melodic line or that of a complex polyphonic web; there is always dynamic level, whether it be that of a striking fortissimo or that of a mezzoforte.

The specificity of a connotation depends upon the divergence of the elements of sound from a neutral state. A tempo may be neither fast nor slow; a sound may be neither loud nor soft; a pitch may seem neither high nor low, relative either to over-all range or the range of a particular instrument or voice. From the standpoint of connotation these are neutral states. Connotation becomes specified only if some of the elements of sound diverge from such neutral states.

The elements of sound are interdependent with respect to neutrality and divergence. For instance, changes in pitch are generally accompanied by changes in dynamics, timbre, and sometimes tempo. The relationship is physical as well as psychological. If a 33⅓ r.p.m. phonograph record is played at 78 r.p.m., pitch will get higher, dynamics louder, and timbre more piercing. Thus it is possible to build one divergence upon another. For instance, if tempo is fast and pitches are high, very soft dynamics will be experienced as a divergence, not only from the neutral state of moderate loudness, but also from the "contingent neutrality" in which a rapid tempo and high pitches are generally accompanied by loud dynamics.

In general, the more markedly the elements of a sound pattern diverge from neutrality the more likely they are to evoke connotations and the more specific those connotations are liable to be. Note that this accounts for the fact that many musical works arouse a wide variety of connotations. For the connotations aroused by a piece of music which, on the whole, employs normal ranges, moderate tempi, and so forth will be determined more by the disposition and susceptibility of the particular listener than by the nature of the musical organization itself.

But even where the most complex disposition of the musical materials and the most effective deviations are presented in a piece of music, they function only as necessary causes for the particular connotative experience aroused.

In the first place, unlike literature or the plastic arts, which generally speaking cannot be understood apart from the designative symbols they employ, most musical experience is meaningful without any reference to the extramusical world. Whether a piece of music arouses connotations depends to a great extent upon the disposition and training of the individual listener and upon the presence of cues, either musical or extramusical, which tend to activate connotative responses.

In the second place, unlike verbal symbols or the iconic signs used in the plastic arts, musical sounds are not, save in a few isolated instances, explicit in their denotation. They limit and define the associations possible but, in the absence of either a specific musical symbolism, such as Wagner's, or a definite program furnished by the composer, they cannot particularize connotation. The musical materials and their organization are the necessary causes for a given connotation but, since no summation of necessary causes can ever amount to a sufficient cause, the sufficient cause of any connotation experienced must be supplied by the listener.

The fact that music cannot specify and particularize the connotations which it arouses has frequently been cited as a basic difficulty with any attempt to theorize about the connotative meanings of music. Yet from one point of view, this flexibility of connotation is a virtue. For it enables music to express what might be called the disembodied essence of myth, the essence of experiences which are central to and vital in human existence.

The human mind has an uncanny power of recognizing symbolic forms; and most readily, of course, will it seize upon those which are presented again and again without aberration. The eternal regularities of nature, the heavenly motions, the alternation of night and day on earth, the tides of the ocean, are the most insistent repetitious forms outside our own behavior patterns. . . . They are the most obvious metaphors to convey the dawning concepts of life-functions—birth, growth, decadence, and death.

What music presents is not any given one of these metaphorical events but rather that which is common to all of them, that which enables them to become metaphors for one another. Music presents a generic event, a "connotative complex," which then becomes particularized in the experience of the individual listener.

Music does not, for example, present the concept or image of death itself. Rather it connotes that rich realm of experience in which death and darkness, night and cold, winter and sleep and silence are all combined and consolidated into a single connotative complex.

The interassociations which give rise to such a connotative complex are fundamental in human experience. They are found again and again, not only in the myths and legends of many cultures, but also in the several arts. For example, the connotative complex discussed above is made explicit in Shelley's *Ode to the West Wind*:

> O thou,
> Who chariotest to their dark wintry bed
> The winged seeds, where they lie cold and low
> Each like a corpse within its grave. . . .

Connotative complexes may be more and less specific. Additional divergences in timbre, dynamic level, and so forth may help to limit the quality of the complex. Association by contiguity or the imitation of actual sound processes heard in the extramusical world may also play a part in defining the extent of connotation. Finally, connotation may be specified by the presence of a text, a plot, or a program established by the composer.

Ultimately it is the listener who must make connotation concrete. In so doing the listener may draw upon his stock of culturally established images, including those derived from literature and mythology, or he may relate the connotative complex to his own particular and peculiar experiences. But in either case there is a causal connection between the musical materials and their organization and the connotations evoked. Had the musical organization been different, the connotation would also have been different.

Since, however, connotations are not necessary concomitants of musical experience, a potentially connotative passage may fail to evoke any concrete images whatsoever. Instead the listener may become aware of how the musical passage "feels" in relation to his own designative emotional experiences and the observed emotional behavior of others. The music may, in short, be experienced as mood or sentiment. For not only are connotations themselves intimately associated with moods, in the sense that youth or spring, for instance, are traditionally considered to be times of exuberant and carefree gaiety, but the same psychological and musical processes which arouse specific connotations also evoke definite, though perhaps less specific, mood responses.

In a discussion of the communication of moods and sentiments two important considerations must be kept in mind.

1. The moods and sentiments with which music becomes associated are not those natural spontaneous emotional reactions which are often diffuse and characterless. Rather music depicts those modes of behavior, conventionalized for the sake of more efficient communication, which were called "designative emotional behavior." In Western culture, for example, grief is communicated by a special type of behavior: physical gestures and motor behavior tend to minimal; facial expression reflects the cultural picture of sorrow; the range of vocal expression is confined and often sporadic; weeping is customary; and dress, too, serves as a behavioral sign. It is this special, culturally sanctioned picture of grief which is communicated in Western music. But such designative emotional behavior is not the only possible way of denoting grief. Were the standardized expression of grief in Western culture different, were it, for instance, that of an incessant and violent wailing and moaning, then the "expression" of grief in Western music would be different.

This is important because it allows for and accounts for variation in mood expression between the music of different cultures. That is, different cultures may communicate moods and sentiments in very different ways, not because the psychological mechanism of association is different but because the behavior patterns denoting mood and emotional states are different.

2. Just as communicative behavior tends to become conventionalized for the sake of more efficient communication, so the musical communication of moods and sentiments tends to become standardized. Thus

particular musical devices—melodic figure, harmonic progressions, or rhythmic relationships—become formulas which indicate a culturally codified mood or sentiment. For those who are familiar with them, such signs may be powerful factors in conditioning responses.

Association by contiguity plays a considerable role in the musical definition of mood. A melodic figure, a set of modal relationships, or a harmonic progression is experienced time and time again in conjunction with texts, programs, or extramusical experiences which either designate the mood directly or imply it. In oriental music, for instance, a particular mode or even a particular pitch may become associated with a specific sentiment or humor as well as with connotative concepts such as winter, night, and blackness. Once such associations become habitual, the presence of the proper musical stimulus will, as a rule, automatically evoke the customary mood response. In Western music of the baroque period, to cite only one example, melodic formulas, conventionalized for the sake of communication, attain precision and force through contiguity with texts and programs which fix their meanings within the culture and style.

Mood association by similarity depends upon a likeness between the individual's experiences of moods and his experience of music. Emotional behavior is a kind of composite gesture, a motion whose peculiar qualities are largely defined in terms of energy, direction, tension, continuity, and so forth. Since music also involves motions differentiated by the same qualities, "musical mood gestures" may be similar to behavioral mood gestures. In fact, because moods and sentiments attain their most precise articulation through vocal inflection, it is possible for music to imitate the sounds of emotional behavior with some precision. Finally, since motor behavior plays a considerable role in both designative emotional behavior and in musical experience, a similarity between the motor behavior of designative gestures and that of musical gestures will inforce the feeling of similarity between the two types of experience.

Like connotation, mood or sentiment depend for their definition upon divergence. If the elements of sound are neutral, then the mood characterization, if any, will depend largely upon the disposition of the individual listener. That is, there will be no consistency in the responses of various listeners. But, and this is of paramount importance, the fact that the mood is indefinite does not mean that affect is not aroused. For a lack of divergence in the elements of sound does not preclude significant deviation in those dynamic processes which form our affective responses to music.

It was observed earlier that image processes, whether conscious or unconscious, and connotations often result in affective experience.

Whether mood responses can eventuate in affect is doubtful. Merely because the musical designation of a mood or sentiment is comprehended by the listener does not mean that the listener responds affectively. It is perfectly possible to be aware of the meaning of behavior without responding as though the behavior were our own. But even an empathetic response to the materials delineating mood or sentiment does not require a resultant affective experience. We may sympathize with the mood of another individual without having an emotional experience ourselves. In fact, although such empathetic behavior may create a psycho-physiological condition in which affect is likely to arise, it is difficult to see what direct causal connection could exist between mood and affect. It appears more likely that mood eventuates in affect only through the mediation of image processes or connotations. That is, a mood arouses image processes already associated in the experience of the individual with the particular mood response, and these image processes are the stimuli which actually give rise to affect.

QUESTIONS

1. Have you ever noticed that the background music for all villains in TV Westerns is essentially the same—low sounds, low plucked chords? Why do you suppose the composers of this music all use the same musical ideas?

2. On what wind instrument is an "Oriental" solo usually played? Why? Would the effect be the same on another instrument? Why?

3. When you hear an unaccompanied drum solo, what does it make you think of? Is it the rhythmic pattern that sets your imagination working? Are you moved one way or another simply because it is a drum? Would you feel the same if the rhythmic pattern was repeated on a violin, or a clarinet?

4. Listen to the instructor play several low chords. Of what do these sounds remind you, if anything? Why? Listen to the instructor play high chords. Of what do these remind you, if anything? Listen to ascending and descending scales, and ask yourself the same questions.

5. Do you believe that "sad" music is usually in a minor key? Can you name a "sad" piece of music? Can you name a "gay" piece? Why do you think so?

THE ORCHESTRA   *Hector Berlioz (1803-1869) was one of the master orchestrators of all time. In a period when most composers were still struggling to conquer the normal-sized orchestra, Berlioz was composing works to be performed by thousands. The ideal large orchestra conceived by Berlioz was not a mere fantastic notion; his grasp of the principles of composing for outsized ensembles has still to be matched. In 1884 he wrote his monumental* Traité d'instrumentation et d'orchestration modernes, *a work eventually translated into all European languages. Berlioz's major contributions to music in particular and to the nineteenth century in general are exhaustively treated in Jacques Barzun's two-volume* Berlioz and the Romantic Century.

THE ORCHESTRA
&
THE CONDUCTOR

HECTOR BERLIOZ

T HE ORCHESTRA MAY BE CONSIDERED AS A LARGE
instrument capable of uttering at once or successively a multitude
of sounds of different kinds; and of which the power is mediocre or
colossal according as those means are well or ill chosen and placed in
acoustic conditions more or less favorable.

The performers of all kinds whose assemblage constitutes it thus
seem to be its strings, its tubes, its pipes, its planes of wood or metal;
machines, intelligent it is true, but subject to the action of an immense
key-board, played upon by the conductor under the direction of the
composer.

I believe I have already said that it seemed to me impossible to indicate how fine orchestral effects are to be found; and that this faculty
—developed doubtless by practice and rational observation—is like the
faculties of melody, of expression, and even of harmony; and belongs to
the number of those precious gifts which the musician-poet, the inspired
inventor, must receive from nature herself.

But certainly it is easy to demonstrate, in a manner almost exact, the
art of *making orchestras* fit to give a faithful rendering of compositions
of all shapes and dimensions.

Theatrical orchestras and concert orchestras should be distinguished
the one from the other. The former, in certain respects, are generally
inferior to the latter.

The place occupied by the musicians, their disposal on a horizontal
plane or on an inclined plane, in an enclosed space with three sides,
or in the very centre of a room, with reverberators formed by hard
bodies fit for sending back the sound, or soft bodies which absorb and
interrupt the vibrations, and more or less near to the performers, are
points of great importance. *Reverberators* are indispensable; they are
to be found variously situated in all enclosed spaces. The nearer they
are to the point whence the sounds proceed, the more potent is their
influence.

This is why there is *no such thing* as music in the open air. The
most enormous orchestra placed in the middle of an extensive garden
open on all sides—like that of the Tuileries—would produce no effect.
The reverberation from the palace walls even, were it placed against
them, is insufficient; the sound instantaneously losing itself on all the
other sides. An orchestra of a thousand wind instruments, with a chorus

THE ORCHESTRA & THE CONDUCTOR from *A Treatise on Modern Instrumentation
and Orchestration* by Hector Berlioz; Novello and Co. Ltd.; 1907.

of two thousand voices, placed in a plain, would not have a twentieth part of the musical action that an ordinary orchestra of eighty players with a chorus of a hundred voices would have if well disposed in the concert-room at the Conservatoire. The brilliant effect produced by military bands in the streets of great towns comes in support of this statement, which it seems to contradict. But the music is not then in the *open air;* the walls of high houses skirting the streets right and left, avenues of trees, the fronts of grand palaces, neighbouring monuments, all serve as reverberators; the sound revolves and circulates freely in the circumscribed space thus surrounding it, before escaping by the points left open; but let the military band, pursuing its march, and continuing to play, leave the large street for a plain devoid of trees and habitations, and the diffusion of its sounds is immediate, the orchestra vanishes, there is no more music.

The best way of disposing the performers, in a room with dimensions proportioned to their number, is to raise them one above another by a series of steps, arranged in such a way that each row may send out its sounds to the hearer without any intermediate obstacle.

All well-organised concert orchestras should be thus arranged in steps. If the orchestra be erected in a theatre, the stage should be completely closed in at the back, at the sides both right and left, and above, by an enclosure of wooden planks.

If, on the contrary, it be erected in a room dedicated to the purpose, or in a church where it occupies one of the extremities, and if, as it frequently happens in such cases, the back of this space be formed of massive building which reflects with too much force and hardness the sound of the instruments placed against it, the force of the reverberation—and consequently the too great resounding—may easily be mitigated, by hanging up a certain number of draperies, and by bringing together at this point such bodies as will break the motion of the waves of sound.

Owing to the construction of our theatres, and to the exigencies of dramatic representation, this amphitheatrical disposal is not possible for orchestras intended for the performance of operas. The instrumentalists brought together in lyric theatres, in the lowest central point of the building, before the footlights, and on a horizontal plane, are deprived of the majority of the advantages resulting from the arrangement I have just indicated for a concert orchestra; hence, what lost effects, what unperceived delicate gradations in opera bands, in spite of the most admirable execution! The difference is such that composers are almost compelled to bear it in mind, and not to instrument their dramatic scores quite in the same way as symphonies, masses, or oratorios, intended for concert-rooms and churches.

Opera orchestras were always formerly composed of a number of stringed instruments proportioned to the mass of other instruments; but this has not been the case for many years. A comic opera orchestra in which there were only two flutes, two hautboys, two clarinets, two horns, two bassoons, rarely two trumpets, and hardly ever any kettledrums, was balanced then with nine first violins, eight second violins, six violas, seven violoncellos, and six double-basses; but as four horns, three trombones, two trumpets, a long drum, and cymbals figure there nowadays, without the number of stringed instruments having been increased, the balance is destroyed, the violins are scarcely to be heard, and the result of the whole is detestable. The orchestra of the Grand-Opéra, where there are, besides the wind instruments already named, two cornets-à-pistons and an ophicleide, the instruments of percussion, and sometimes six or eight harps—is not balanced either with twelve first violins, eleven second violins, eight violas, ten violoncellos, and eight double-basses; it should have at least fifteen first violins, fourteen second violins, ten violas, and twelve violoncellos, the extra instruments being left unused in those pieces where the accompaniments are very soft.

The proportions of a comic opera orchestra would suffice for a concert orchestra intended for the performance of Haydn's and Mozart's symphonies.

A larger number of stringed instruments would even be, sometimes, too much for the delicate effects which these masters have usually assigned to the flutes, hautboys, and bassoons.

For Beethoven's symphonies, Weber's overtures, and modern compositions conceived in the grand and impassioned style, there needs, on the contrary, the mass of violins, violas, and basses which I have just indicated for the grand opera.

But the finest concert orchestra, for a room scarcely larger than that of the Conservatoire—the most complete, the richest in gradations, in varieties of tone, the most majestic, the most powerful, and at the same time the most soft and smooth, would be an orchestra thus composed:

21 First Violins.
20 Second do.
18 Violas.
 8 First Violoncellos.
 7 Second do.
10 Double-Basses.
 4 Harps.
 2 Piccolo Flutes.
 2 Large Flutes.
 2 Hautboys.
 1 Corno Inglese.
 2 Clarinets.
 1 Corno di Bassetto, or one Bass-Clarinet.

4 Bassoons.
4 Horns with Cylinders.
2 Trumpets with Cylinders.
2 Cornets à Pistons (or with Cylinders).
3 Trombones—1 Alto, 2 Tenors; or 3 Tenors.
1 Great Bass Trombone.
1 Ophicleide in B♭ (or a Bass-Tuba).
2 Pairs of Kettle-Drums, and 4 Drummers.
1 Long Drum.
1 Pair of Cymbals.

If a choral composition were to be executed, such an orchestra would require:

46 Sopranos—Firsts and Seconds.
40 Tenors—Firsts and Seconds.
40 Basses—Firsts and Seconds.

By doubling or tripling this mass of performers, in the same proportions, and in the same order, a magnificent Festival orchestra might doubtless be obtained. But it is erroneous to believe that all orchestras should be constituted according to a system based on the predominance of stringed instruments; very admirable results may be obtained from a contrary plan. The stringed instruments—too weak to prevail over masses of clarinets and brass instruments—then serve as a harmonious link with the thrilling sounds of the wind instruments; softening their brilliancy in some cases, and animating their effect in others, by means of the tremolo, which, by blending with them, renders musical even the roll of the drums.

Common sense tells the composer—unless he be compelled to a different course by any particular form of orchestra—that he should combine his mass of performers according to the style and character of the work he brings forth, and according to the nature of the principal effects which the subject demands. Thus, in a *Requiem,* and in order to deliver musically the grand images of this *hymn of the dead,* I have employed four small orchestras of brass instruments (trumpets, trombones, cornets, and ophicleides), placed apart from each other, at the four corners of the main orchestra, formed of an imposing body of stringed instruments, of all the other wind instruments doubled and tripled, and of ten drummers playing on eight pairs of kettle-drums tuned in different keys. It is quite certain that the particular effects obtained by this novel form of orchestra were absolutely unattainable by any other.

Here we have an opportunity to remark upon the importance of the various *points of procedure of the sounds.* Certain parts of an orchestra are intended by the composer to interrogate and answer each other; now, this intention can only be made manifest and of fine effect by causing the groups between which the dialogue occurs to be placed at a sufficient distance from one another. The composer should, therefore, in his score, indicate for them the disposition which he judges proper.

The drums, long drums, cymbals, and kettle-drums, if employed to strike certain rhythms all at once—after the common mode of proceeding—may remain together; but if they have to execute an interlocutory rhythm, of which one fragment is struck by the long drums and cymbals, and the other by the kettle-drums and drums, there is no doubt the effect will be made incomparably better, finer, and more interesting, by placing the two masses of instruments of percussion at the extremities of the orchestra, and consequently at a sufficient distance from one another. The constant uniformity of the executive masses is one of the great obstacles to the production of sterling and really new works; it besets composers more from old custom, routine, laziness, and want of reflection than from motives of economy—motives unfortunately but too important, in France especially, where Music is so far from forming a part of the moral being of the nation, where the government does everything for theatres, and nothing at all for music properly so called, where capitalists are ready to give 50,000f. and more for some great master's picture, *because that represents an intrinsic value,* yet would not lay out 5of. to render feasible, once a year, some solemnity worthy of a nation like ours, and fitted to display the very numerous musical resources which it really possesses without the capability of making them of use.

It would nevertheless be curious to try for once, in a composition written *ad hoc,* the simultaneous employment of all the musical forces which might be gathered together in Paris. Supposing that a master had these at his disposal, in a vast space adapted for the purpose by an architect who should be well versed in acoustics and a good musician, he ought, before writing, to determine with precision the plan and arrangement of his immense orchestra, and then to keep them always present to his mind while writing. It is obvious that it would be of the highest importance, in the employment of so enormous a musical mass, to take account of the distance or the nearness of the different groups which compose it. This condition is one of the most essential to deriving the utmost advantage from it, and in calculating with certainty the scope of its effects. Until now, at the Festivals, merely the ordinary orchestra and chorus have been heard, quadrupled or quintupled in their several parts, according to the greater or less number of the performers; but in the case proposed it would be quite another affair; and the composer who should attempt exhibiting all the prodigious and innumerable resources of such an *instrument,* would assuredly have to achieve an entirely new task.

The Orchestra / Berlioz

Here, then, is how—with time, care, and the necessary *outlay*—it could be effected in Paris. The disposal of the groups would remain at the will, and subject to the particular intentions, of the composer; the instruments of percussion, which exercise an irresistible influence on the rhythm, and which always lag when they are far from the conductor, should be placed sufficiently near him to be able instantaneously and strictly to obey the slightest variations of movement and measure:

120 Violins, divided into two, or three, and four parts.
 40 Violas, divided or not into firsts and seconds; and of which ten at least
      should be ready to play, when needed, the Viole d'amour.
 45 Violoncellos, divided or not into firsts and seconds.
 18 Double-Basses with 3 strings, tuned in fifths (G, D, A).
 15 other Double-Basses with 4 strings, tuned in fourths (E, A, D, G).
  4 Octo-Basses.
  6 Large Flutes.
  4 Third-Flutes (in Eb), improperly called in F.
  2 Octave Piccolo Flutes.
  2 Piccolo Flutes (in Db), improperly called in Eb.
  6 Hautboys.
  6 Corni Inglesi.
  5 Saxophones.
  4 Bassons-Quinte.
 12 Bassoons.
  4 Small Clarinets (in Eb).
  8 Clarinets (in C, or in Bb, or in A).
  3 Bass-Clarinets (in Bb).
 16 Horns (of which six should be with pistons).
  8 Trumpets.
  6 Cornets à Pistons.
  4 Alto-Trombones.
  6 Tenor-Trombones.
  2 Great Bass-Trombones.
  1 Ophicleide in C.
  2 Ophicleides in Bb
  2 Bass-Tubas.
 30 Harps.
 30 Pianofortes.
  1 very low Organ, provided with stops of at least 16 feet.
  8 Pairs of Kettle-Drums (10 Drummers).
  6 Drums.
  3 Long Drums.
  4 Pairs of Cymbals.
  6 Triangles.
  6 Sets of Bells.
 12 Pairs of Ancient Cymbals (in different keys).
  2 very low Great Bells.
  2 Gongs.
  4 *Pavillons Chinois.*
___
467 Instrumentalists.

40	Children Sopranos (firsts and seconds)
100	Women Sopranos (firsts and seconds).
100	Tenors (firsts and seconds).
120	Basses (firsts and seconds).
360	Chorus-singers.

It will be perceived that in this aggregate of 827 performers the chorus-singers do not predominate; and even thus, there would be much difficulty in collecting in Paris three hundred and sixty voices of any excellence, so little is the study of singing at present cultivated or advanced.

It would evidently be necessary to adopt a style of extraordinary breadth, each time the entire mass is put in action; reserving the delicate effects, the light and rapid movements, for small bands which the author could easily arrange, and make them discourse together in the midst of this musical multitude.

Beside the radiant colours which this myriad of different tone-qualities would give out at every moment, unheard-of *harmonic effects* would be deduced from them.

From the division of the 120 violins into eight or ten parts, aided by the 50 violas, in their high notes, the angelic aërial accent, and the *pianissimo* tint.

From the division of the violoncellos and double-basses below in slow movements, the melancholy religious accent, and the *mezzo forte* tint.

From the union, *in a small band,* of the very low notes of the clarinet family, the gloomy accent, and the *forte* and *mezzo forte* tints.

From the union, *in a small band,* of the low notes of the hautboys, corni inglesi, and bassons-quinte, mingled with the low notes of the large flutes, the religiously mournful accent, and the *piano* tint.

From the union, *in a small band,* of the low notes of the ophicleides, bass-tuba, and horns, mingled with the *pedals* of the tenor-trombones, and of the 16-foot stop (open flute) of the organ, profoundly grave, religious, and calm accents, and the *piano* tint.

From the union, *in a small band,* of the highest notes of the small clarinets, flutes, and piccolo flutes, the shrill accent, and the *forte* tint.

From the union, *in a small band,* of the horns, trumpets, cornets, trombones, and ophicleides, a pompous and brilliant accent, and the *forte* tint.

From the union, *in a large band,* of the 30 harps with the entire mass of bowed instruments playing *pizzicato,* and thus forming together another gigantic harp with *nine hundred and thirty-four* strings, graceful, brilliant, and voluptuous accents, in all tints and gradations.

From the union of the 30 pianofortes with the six sets of bells, the twelve pairs of ancient cymbals, the six triangles (which might be tuned, like the ancient cymbals, in different keys), and the four *pavil-lons chinois,* constituting a metallic *orchestra* of percussion, joyous and brilliant accents, and the *mezzo forte* tint.

From the union of the eight pairs of kettle-drums with the six drums, and the three long drums, forming a small *orchestra* of percussion, and almost exclusively *rhythmical,* the menacing accent, in all tints.

From the mixture of the two gongs, the two bells, and the three large cymbals, with certain chords of trombones, the lugubrious and sinister accent, in the *mezzo forte* tint.

How can I enumerate all the harmonic aspects under which each of these different groups, associated with other groups either sympathetic or antipathetic with them, would appear!

There might be grand duets between the band of wind instruments and the stringed band; between one of these two bands and the chorus; or between the chorus and the harps and pianofortes only.

A grand trio between the chorus in unison and in octave, the wind instruments in unison and in octave, and the violins, violas, and violoncellos also in unison and in octave.

This trio might be accompanied by a rhythmical form designed by all the instruments of percussion, the double-basses, the harps, and the pianofortes.

A simple chorus, double or triple, without accompaniment.

An air for violins, violas, and violoncellos *together,* or for wooden wind instruments *together,* or for brass instruments *together,* accompanied by a *vocal band.*

An air for sopranos, or tenors, or basses, or all the voices in octave, accompanied by an *instrumental band.*

A small choir singing, accompanied by the large choir, and by some instruments.

A small band playing, accompanied by the large orchestra, and by some voices.

A grand deep melody, executed by all the bowed basses; and accompanied above by the violins divided, and the harps and pianofortes.

A grand deep melody, executed by all the wind basses and the organ; and accompanied above by the flutes, hautboys, clarinets, and the violins divided.

Et cetera, et cetera, et cetera.

The system of rehearsals requisite for this colossal orchestra cannot be doubtful; it is that which must be adopted whenever there is an intention to get up a work of grand dimensions, the plan of which is complex, and certain parts or the whole of which offer difficulties in performance; it is the system of partial rehearsals. This is how the conductor will have to proceed in his analytical operation.

I take for granted that he knows *thoroughly, and in its minutest details,* the score which he is about to have performed. He will first appoint two subconductors, who should—marking the beats of the bar in the general rehearsals—keep their eyes continually upon him, in order to communicate the movement to the masses too far removed from the centre. He will then select rehearsers for each of the vocal and instrumental groups.

He will first make them rehearse themselves, that they may be well instructed in the way in which they will have to direct the portion of study allotted to them.

The first rehearser will rehearse separately the first sopranos, then the seconds, and then the firsts and seconds together.

The second rehearser will practice in the same way the first and second tenors.

The third rehearser will do the same by the basses. After which, three choirs, each composed of a third of the total mass, will be formed; and then lastly, the whole chorus will be practised together.

As an accompaniment to these choral studies, either an organ, or a pianoforte may be used; assisted by a few wind instruments, violins and basses.

The sub-conductors and the orchestral rehearsers will practice separately in the same way:

1stly. The first and second violins separately; then all the violins together.

2ndly. The violas, violoncellos, and double-basses separately; then all together.

3rdly. The entire mass of bowed instruments.

4thly. The harps alone.

5thly. The pianofortes alone.

6thly. The harps and pianofortes together.

7thly. The wooden wind instruments alone.

8thly. The brass wind instruments alone.

9thly. All the wind instruments together.

10thly. The instruments of percussion alone, particularly teaching the kettle-drummers to tune their kettle-drums well.

11thly. The instruments of percussion joined with the wind instruments.

12thly. Lastly, the whole vocal and instrumental mass united, under the direction of the conductor himself.

This method of proceeding will have the result of securing, first, an excellence of execution that never could be obtained under the old system of collective study; and next, of requiring from each performer but four rehearsals at most. It should not be forgotten to have a profusion of tuningforks of the exact pitch among the members of the orchestra; it is the sole means by which the accurate tuning of this crowd of instruments of such various nature and temperament can be ensured.

Vulgar prejudice stigmatizes large orchestras as *noisy:* but if they be well constituted, well practised, and well conducted; if they perform sterling music, they should be called *powerful;* and certainly, nothing is more dissimilar than these two expressions. A trumpery little vaudeville orchestra may be *noisy,* when a large body of musicians properly employed shall be of extreme softness; and shall produce—even in their loudest effects—sounds the most beautiful. Three ill-placed trombones will seem *noisy,* insufferable; and the instant after, in the same room, twelve trombones will strike the public by their noble and *powerful* harmony.

Moreover, unisons acquire real value only when multiplied beyond a certain number. Thus, four violins of first-rate skill playing together the same part will produce but a very poor—nay, perhaps, even detestable effect; while fifteen violins of ordinary talent shall be excellent. This is why small orchestras—whatever the merit of the performers who compose them—have so little effect, and consequently so little value.

But in the thousand combinations practicable with the vast orchestra we have just described would dwell a wealth of harmony, a variety of tone qualities, a succession of contrasts, which can be compared to nothing hitherto achieved in Art; and above all, an incalculable melodic, expressive, and rhythmical power, a penetrating force of unparalleled strength, a prodigious sensitiveness for gradations in aggregate and in detail. Its repose would be majestic as the slumber of ocean; its agitations would recall the tempest of the tropics; its explosions, the outbursts of volcanos; therein would be heard the plaints, the murmurs, the mysterious sounds of primeval forests; the clamours, the prayers, the songs of triumph or of mourning of a people with expansive soul, ardent heart, and fiery passions; its silence would inspire awe by its solemnity; and organizations the most rebellious would shudder to behold its *crescendo* spread roaringly, like a stupendous conflagration!

The Orchestral Conductor

Music appears to be the most exacting of all the Arts, the most difficult to cultivate, and that of which the productions are most rarely presented in a condition which permits an appreciation of their real value, a clear view of their physiognomy, or discernment of their real meaning and true character. Of producing artists, the composer is almost the only one, in fact, who depends upon a multitude of intermediate agents between the public and himself; intermediate agents, either intelligent or stupid, devoted or hostile, active or inert, capable—from first to last—of contributing to the brilliancy of his work, or of disfiguring it, misrepresenting it, and even destroying it completely.

Singers have often been accused of forming the most dangerous of these intermediate agents; but, in my opinion, without justice. The most formidable, to my thinking, is the conductor of the orchestra. A bad singer can spoil only his own part; while an incapable or malevolent conductor ruins all. Happy, also, may that composer esteem himself when the conductor into whose hands he has fallen is not at once incapable and inimical. For nothing can resist the pernicious influence of this person. The most admirable orchestra is then paralysed, the most excellent singers are perplexed and rendered dull; there is no longer any vigour or unity; under such direction the noblest daring of the author appears extravagance, enthusiasm beholds its soaring flight checked, inspiration is violently brought down to earth, the angel's wings are broken, the man of genius passes for a madman or an idiot, the divine statue is precipitated from its pedestal and dragged in the mud. And, what is worse, the public, and even auditors endowed with the highest musical intelligence, are reduced to the impossibility (if a new work be in question, and they are hearing it for the first time) of recognising the ravages perpetrated by the orchestral conductor—of discovering the follies, faults, and crimes he commits. If they clearly perceive certain defects of execution, not he, but his victims, are in such cases made responsible. If he have caused the chorus-singers to fail in taking up a point in a finale, if he have allowed a discordant wavering to take place between the choir and the orchestra, or between the extreme sides of the instrumental body, if he have absurdly hurried a movement, if he have allowed it to linger unduly, if he have interrupted a singer before the end of a phrase, they exclaim: "The singers are detestable! The orchestra has no firmness; the violins have disfigured the principal design; everybody has been wanting in vigour and animation; the tenor was quite out, he did not know his part; the harmony is confused; the author is no accompanist; the voices are . . ." etc., etc., etc.

Except in listening to great works already known and esteemed, intelligent hearers can hardly distinguish the true culprit, and allot to him his due share of blame; but the number of these is still so limited that their judgment has little weight; and the bad conductor—in presence of the public who would pitilessly hiss a *vocal accident* of a good singer—reigns, with all the calm of a bad conscience, in his baseness and inefficiency. Fortunately, I here attack an exception; for the malevolent orchestral conductor—whether capable or not—is very rare.

The orchestral conductor full of goodwill, but incapable, is, on the contrary, very common. Without speaking of innumerable mediocrities directing artists who, frequently, are much their superiors, an author, for example, can scarcely be accused of conspiring against his own works. Yet how many are there who, fancying they are able to conduct, innocently injure their best scores!

Beethoven, it is said, more than once ruined the performance of his symphonies; which he would conduct, even at the time when his deafness had become almost complete. The musicians, in order to keep together, agreed at length to follow the slight indications of time which the concertmeister (first violin-player) gave them; and not to attend to Beethoven's conducting-stick. Moreover, it should be observed, that conducting a symphony, an overture, or any other composition whose movements remain continuous, vary little, and contain few nice gradations, is child's play in comparison with conducting an opera, or like work, where there are recitatives, airs, and numerous orchestral designs preceded by pauses of irregular length.

The example of Beethoven, which I have just cited, leads me at once to say that if the direction of an orchestra appear to me very difficult for a blind man, it is indisputably impossible to a deaf one, whatever may have been his technical talent before losing his sense of hearing.

The orchestral conductor should *see* and *hear;* he should be *active* and *vigorous,* should know the *composition* and the *nature* and *compass* of the instruments, should be able to *read* the score, and possess—besides the especial talent of which we shall presently endeavour to explain the constituent qualities—other almost indefinable gifts, without which an invisible link cannot establish itself between him and those he directs; the faculty of transmitting to them his feeling is denied him, and thence power, empire, and guiding influence completely fail him. He is then no longer a conductor, a director, but a simple beater of the time—supposing he knows how to beat it, and divide it, regularly.

The performers should feel that he feels, comprehends, and is moved: then his emotion communicates itself to those whom he directs, his inward fire warms them, his electric glow animates them, his force of impulse excites them; he throws around him the vital irradiations of musical art. If he be inert and frozen, on the contrary, he paralyses all about him, like those floating masses of the polar seas, the approach of which is perceived through the sudden cooling of the atmosphere.

His task is a complicated one. He has not only to conduct, in the spirit of the author's intentions, a work with which the performers have already become acquainted, but he has also to give them this acquaintance when the work in question is new to them. He has to criticize the errors and defects of each during the rehearsals, and to organise the resources at his disposal in such a way as to make the best use he can of them with the utmost promptitude. For, in the majority of European cities nowadays, musical artisanship is so ill distributed, performers so ill paid, and the necessity of study so little understood, that *economy of time* should be reckoned among the most imperative requisites of the orchestral conductor's art.

Let us now see what constitutes the mechanical part of this art.

The power of *beating the time,* without demanding very high musical attainments, is nevertheless sufficiently difficult to secure, and very few persons really possess it. The signs that the conductor should make—although generally very simple—nevertheless become complicated, under certain circumstances, by the division and even the subdivision of the time of the bar.

The conductor is, above all, bound to possess a clear idea of the principal points and character of the work of which he is about to superintend the performance or study; in order that he may, without hesitation or mistake, at once determine the time of each movement desired by the composer. If he have not had the opportunity of receiving his instructions directly from the composer, or if the *times* have not been transmitted to him by tradition, he must have recourse to the indications of the metronome, and study them well; the majority of composers, nowadays, taking the precaution to write them at the head, and in the course of, their pieces. I do not mean to say by this that it is necessary to imitate the mathematical regularity of the metronome; all music so performed would become of freezing stiffness, and I even doubt whether it would be possible to observe so flat a uniformity during a certain number of bars. But the metronome is none the less excellent to consult in order to know the original time, and its chief alterations.

If the conductor possesses neither the author's instructions, tradition, nor metronome indications—which frequently happens in the ancient masterpieces, written at a period when the metronome was not invented—he has no other guide than the vague terms employed to designate the time to be taken, and his own instinct, his feeling—more or less distinguishing, more or less just—of the author's style. We are compelled to admit that these guides are too often insufficient and delusive. Of this we have proof in seeing how old operas are given in towns where the traditional mode of performance no longer exists. In ten different kinds of time, there will always be at least four taken wrongly. I once heard a chorus of *Iphigenia in Tauride* performed in a German theatre *allegro assai, two in the bar,* instead of *allegro non troppo, four in the bar;* that is to say exactly twice too fast. Examples might be multiplied of such disasters, occasioned either by the ignorance or the carelessness of conductors of orchestras; or else by the real difficulty which exists for even the best-gifted and most careful men to discover the precise meaning of the Italian terms used as indications of the time to be taken. Of course no one can be at a loss to distinguish a largo from a presto. If the presto be two in a bar, a tolerably sagacious conductor, from inspection of the passages and melodic designs contained in the piece, will be able to discern the degree of quickness intended by the author. But if the largo be four in a bar, of simple melodic structure, and containing but few notes in each bar, what means has the hapless conductor of discovering the true time? And in how many ways might he not be deceived? The different degrees of slowness that might be assigned to the performance of such a largo are very numerous; the individual feeling of the orchestral conductor must then become the sole authority; and, after all, it is the author's feeling, not his, which is in question. Composers therefore ought not to neglect placing metronome indications in their works; and orchestral conductors are bound to study them closely. The neglect of this study on the part of the latter, is an act of dishonesty.

I will now suppose the conductor to be perfectly well acquainted with the times of the different movements in the work of which he is about to conduct the performance or rehearsals; he wishes to impart to the musicians acting under his orders the rhythmical feeling within him, to decide the duration of each bar, and to cause the uniform observance of this duration by all the performers. Now, this precision and this uniformity can only be established in the more or less numerous assemblage of band and chorus by means of certain signs made by their conductor.

These signs indicate the principal divisions, the accents of the bar, and, in many cases, the subdivisions, and the half-accents. I need hardly here explain what is meant by the 'accents' (accented and unaccented parts of a bar); I am pre-supposing that I address musicians.

The orchestral conductor generally uses a small light stick, of about a foot in length, and rather whitish than of a dark colour (it is seen better), which he holds in his right hand, to make clearly distinct his mode of marking the commencement, the interior division, and the close of each bar. The bow, employed by some violinist-conductors (leaders), is less suitable than the stick. It is somewhat flexible, and this want of rigidity, together with the slight resistance it offers to the air, on account of its appendage of hair, renders its indications less precise.

The simplest of all times—two in a bar—is beaten simply.

The arm and the stick of the conductor being raised, so that his hand is on a level with his head, he marks the first beat, by dropping the point of his stick perpendicularly (*bending his wrist* as much as possible; and not lowering the whole arm), and the second beat by raising the stick by a contrary gesture.

The time one in a bar being in reality, and particularly for the conductor, but the time of an extremely rapid two in a bar, should be beaten like the preceding. As the conductor is obliged to raise the point of his stick, after having lowered it, he necessarily divides this into two portions.

In the time four in a bar, the first gesture, or down beat, is universally adopted for marking the first accented part, the commencement of the bar.

The second movement made by the conducting-stick, from right to left, rising, indicates the second beat (first unaccented part). A third, transversely, from left to right, indicates the third beat (second accented part); and a fourth, obliquely, from down to up, indicates the fourth beat (second unaccented part).

It is of importance that the conductor, in thus delivering his different directions, should not move his arm much; and consequently, not allow his stick to pass over much space; for each of these gestures should operate nearly instantaneously; or at least take but so slight a movement as to be imperceptible. If the movement become perceptible, on the contrary, and multiplied by the number of times that the gesture is repeated, it ends by throwing the conductor behind in the time he is beating, and by giving to his conducting a tardiness that proves injurious. This defect, moreover, has the result of needlessly fatiguing the conductor, and of producing exaggerated evolutions, verging on the ridiculous, which attract the spectators' attention and become very disagreeable to witness.

In the time three in a bar, the first gesture made, from up to down, is likewise universally adopted for marking the first beat; but there are two ways of marking the second. The majority of orchestral conductors indicate it by a gesture from left to right. Some German Kapellmeisters do the contrary; and carry the stick from right to left.

This way has the disadvantage—when the conductor turns his back to the orchestra, as in theatres—of permitting only a small number of musicians to perceive the very important indication of the second beat; the body of the conductor then hiding the movement of his arm. The other method of proceeding is preferable; since the conductor stretches his arm *outwards*, withdrawing it from his chest; and his stick, which he takes care to raise slightly above the level of his shoulder, remains perfectly visible to all eyes. When the conductor faces the players, it is immaterial whether he mark the second beat to the right, or to the left.

However that may be, the third beat of the time, three in a bar, is always marked like the last of the time, four in a bar; by an oblique movement upwards.

The times five and seven in a bar would be more comprehensible for the performers, if, instead of indicating them by a particular series of gestures, they were treated as though the one were composed of three and two in a bar, and the other composed of four and three.

These different times, in order to be divided in this way, are assumed to belong to movements of moderate measure. The advice would not hold good, if their measure were either very quick or very slow.

The time two in a bar, I have already signified, cannot be beaten otherwise than as we have before seen—whatever its degree of rapidity. But if, as an exception, it should be very slow, the conductor ought to subdivide it.

A very rapid four in a bar, on the contrary, should be beaten two in a bar; the four accustomed gestures of a moderate movement becoming then so hurried as to present nothing decided to the eye, and serving only to confuse the performer instead of giving him confidence. Moreover—and this is of much more consequence—the conductor, by uselessly making these four gestures in a quick movement, renders the pace of the rhythm awkward, and loses the freedom of gesture, which a simple division of the time into its half, would leave him.

Generally speaking, composers are wrong to write, in such a case, the indication of the time as four in a bar. When the movement is very brisk, they should never write any other than the sign for 2/2, and not that for 4/4, which might lead the conductor into error.

It is exactly the same for the time three in a bar, fast 3/4, or 3/8. Then the conductor must omit the gesture of the second beat, and, by remaining the period of a beat longer on the first, only raise the stick at the third.

It would be absurd to attempt to beat the three in a bar of one of Beethoven's scherzos.

In slow movements the rule for these two times is like that for two in a bar. If the movement be very slow, each time must be divided; and consequently eight gestures must be made for the time four in a bar, and six for the time three in a bar, repeating (and shortening) each of the principal gestures we have before instanced.

The arm should take no part in the little supplementary gesture indicating the subdivision of the bar; merely the wrist causing the stick to move.

This division of the different times is intended to prevent the rhythmical divergences which might easily take place among the performers during the interval which separates one beat from the other. The conductor not indicating anything during this period (rendered somewhat considerable by the extreme slowness of the movement), the players are then entirely left to themselves, *without conductor;* and as the rhythmical feeling is not the same with all, it follows that some hurry, while others slacken, and unity is soon destroyed. The only exception possible to this rule is that of a first-rate orchestra, composed of performers who are well acquainted with each other, are accustomed to play together, and know almost by heart the work they are executing. Even then, the inattention of a single player may occasion an accident. Why incur its possibility? I know that certain artists feel their self-love hurt when thus kept in leading-strings (like children, they say); but with a conductor who has no other view than the excellence of the ultimate result, this consideration can have no weight. Even in a quartet, it is seldom that the individual feeling of the players can be left entirely free to follow its own dictates. In a symphony, that of the conductor must rule. The art of comprehending it, and fulfilling it with unanimity, constitutes the perfection of execution; and individual wills —which can never agree one with another—should never be permitted to manifest themselves. . . .

We will now speak of the conductor's method of beating in recitatives. Here, as the singer or the instrumentalist is reciting, and no longer subject to the regular division of the bar, it is requisite, while following him attentively, to make the orchestra strike, simultaneously and with precision, the chords or instrumental passages with which the recitative is intermingled; and to make the harmony change at the proper instant, when the recitative is accompanied either by holding-notes or by a tremolo in several parts, of which the least apparent, occasionally, is that which the conductor must most regard, since upon its motion depends the change of chord.

Many conductors have the habit, when directing the orchestra in recitatives, of paying no heed to the written division of the bar, and of marking an up beat before that whereon a brief orchestral chord occurs, even when this chord comes on an unaccented part of the bar.

In a passage such as this, they raise the arm at the rest which commences the bar, and lower it at the time of the chord.

I cannot approve such a method, which nothing justifies, and which may frequently occasion accidents in the execution. Neither do I see why, in recitatives, the bar should not be divided regularly, and the real beats be marked in their place, as in music beaten in time. I therefore advise that the first beat should be made down, as usual, and the stick carried to the left for striking the chord upon the second beat; and so on for analogous cases; always dividing the bar regularly. It is very important, moreover, to divide it according to the time previously indicated by the author, and not to forget, if this time be *allegro* or *maestoso*, and if the reciting part have been some time reciting unaccompanied, to give to all the beats, when the orchestra comes in again, the value of those of an allegro or of a maestoso. For when the orchestra plays alone, it does so generally in time; it plays without measured time only when it accompanies a voice or instrument in recitative.

In the exceptional case where the recitative is written for the orchestra itself, or for the chorus, or for a portion of either orchestra or chorus, it being then requisite to keep together, whether in unison or in harmony, but without regular time, a certain number of performers, *the conductor himself becomes the real reciter*, and gives to each beat of the bar the duration he judges fit. According to the form of the phrase, he divides and subdivides the beats, now marks the accents, now the semiquavers, if there be any, and, in short, indicates with his stick the melodic form of the recitative.

It is an understood thing that the performers, knowing their parts almost by heart, keep their eye constantly upon him, otherwise, neither security nor unity can be obtained.

In general, even for timed music, the conductor should require the players he directs to look towards him as often as possible.

An orchestra which does not watch the conducting-stick has no conductor. Often, after a pedal-point for instance, the conductor is obliged to refrain from marking the decisive gesture which is to determine the coming in of the orchestra until he sees the eyes of all the performers fixed upon him. It is the duty of the conductor, during rehearsal, to accustom them to look towards him simultaneously at the important moment.

If the rule just indicated were not observed, the passage could not be uttered with firmness and unity; the players, not watching the conductor's stick, could not know when he decides the second beat and resumes the movement suspended by the pedal-point.

The obligation upon the performers to look at their conductor necessarily implies an equal obligation on his part to let himself be well seen by them. He should, whatever may be the disposal of the orchestra, whether on rows of steps, or on a horizontal plane, place himself so as to form the centre of all surrounding eyes.

To place him well in sight, a conductor requires an especial platform, elevated in proportion as the number of performers is large and occupies much space. His desk should not be so high as that the portion sustaining the score shall hide his face. For the expression of his countenance has much to do with the influence he exercises, and if there be no conductor for an orchestra that does not and will not watch him, neither is there any if he cannot be well seen.

As to the employment of noises of any kind whatever, produced by the stick of the conductor upon his desk, or by his foot upon the platform, they call for no other than unreserved reprehension. It is worse than a bad method; it is a barbarism. In a theatre, however, when the stage evolutions prevent the chorus-singers from seeing the conducting-stick, the conductor is compelled—to ensure, after a pause, the taking up a point by the chorus—to indicate this point by marking the beat which precedes it by a slight tap of his stick upon the desk. This exceptional circumstance is the only one which can warrant the employment of an *indicating noise,* and even then it is to be regretted that recourse must be had to it.

While speaking of chorus-singers, and of their operations in theatres, it may here be observed that chorus-masters often allow themselves to beat time at the side-scenes, without seeing the conductor's stick, frequently even without hearing the orchestra. The result is that this time, beaten more or less ill, and not corresponding with that of the conductor, inevitably induces a rhythmical discordance between the choral and instrumental bodies, and subverts all unity instead of tending to maintain it.

Another traditional barbarism lies within the province of an intelligent and active conductor to abolish. If a choral or instrumental piece be performed behind the scenes, without accompaniment from the principal orchestra, another conductor is absolutely essential. If the orchestra accompany this portion, the first conductor, who hears the distant music, is then strictly bound to *let himself be guided* by the second, and to follow his time *by ear.* But if—as frequently happens in modern music—the sound of the chief orchestra hinders the conductor from hearing that which is being performed at a distance from him, the intervention of a special conducting mechanism becomes indispensable, in order to establish instantaneous communication between him and the distant performers. Many attempts, more or less ingenious, have been made of this kind, the result of which has not everywhere answered expectations. That of Covent Garden Theatre, in London, moved by the conductor's foot, acts tolerably well. But the *electric metronome,* set up by Mr. Van Bruge in the Brussels Theatre, leaves nothing to be desired. It consists of an apparatus of copper ribbons, leading from a Voltaic battery placed beneath the stage, attached to the conductor's desk, and terminating in a movable stick fastened at one end on a pivot before a board at a certain distance from the orchestral conductor. To this latter's desk is affixed a key of copper, something like the ivory key of a pianoforte; it is elastic, and provided on the interior side with a protuberance of about a quarter of an inch long. Immediately beneath this protuberance is a little cup, also of copper, filled with quicksilver. At the instant when the orchestral conductor, desiring to mark any particular beat of a bar, presses the copper key with the forefinger of his left hand (his right being occupied in holding, as usual, the conducting-stick) this key is lowered, the protuberance passes into the cup filled with quicksilver, a slight electric spark is emitted, and the stick placed at the other extremity of the copper ribbon makes an oscillation before its board. The communication of the fluid and the movement are quite simultaneous, whatever be the distance traversed.

The performers being grouped behind the scenes, their eyes fixed upon the stick of the electric metronome, are thus directly subject to the conductor, who could, were it needful, conduct, from the middle of the Opera orchestra in Paris, a piece of music performed at Versailles.

It is merely requisite to agree beforehand with the chorus-singers, or with their conductor (if, as an additional precaution, they have one), the way in which the orchestral conductor beats the time—whether he mark all the principal beats, or only the first of the bar—since the oscillations of the stick, moved by electricity, being always from right to left, indicate nothing precise in this respect.

When I first used, at Brussels, the valuable instrument I have just endeavoured to describe, its action presented one objection. Each time that the copper key of my desk underwent the pressure of my left forefinger, it struck, underneath, another plate of copper, and, notwith-standing the delicacy of the contact, produced a little sharp noise, which, during the pauses of the orchestra, attracted the attention of the audience, to the detriment of the musical effect.

I pointed out the fault to Mr. Van Bruge, who substituted for the lower plate of copper the little cup filled with quicksilver, previously mentioned. Into this the protuberance so entered as to establish the electric current without causing the slightest noise.

Nothing remains now, as regards the use of this mechanism, but the crackling of the spark at the moment of its emission. This, however, is too slight to be heard by the public.

The metronome is not expensive to put up; it costs £16 at the most. Large lyric theatres, churches, and concert-rooms should long ago have been provided with one. Yet, save at the Brussels Theatre, it is nowhere to be found. This would appear incredible, were it not that the care-lessness of the majority of directors of institutions where music forms a feature is well known; as are their instinctive aversion from whatever disturbs old-established customs, their indifference to the interests of art, their parsimony wherever an outlay for music is needed, and the utter ignorance of the principles of our art among those in whose hands rests the ordering of its destiny.

I have not yet said all on the subject of those dangerous auxiliaries named chorus-masters. Very few of them are sufficiently versed in the art to conduct a musical performance, or so that the orchestral conductor can depend upon them. He cannot therefore watch them too closely when compelled to submit to their coadjutorship.

The most to be dreaded are those whom age has deprived of activity and energy. The maintenance of vivacious times is an impossibility to them. Whatever may be the degree of quickness indicated at the head of a piece confided to their conducting, little by little they slacken its pace, until the rhythm is reduced to a certain medium slowness, that seems to harmonize with the speed at which their blood flows, and the general feebleness of their organization.

It must in truth be added, that old men are not the only ones with whom composers run this risk. There are men in the prime of life, of a lymphatic temperament, whose blood seems to circulate *moderato*. If they have to conduct an allegro assai, they gradually slacken it to *moderato*; if, on the contrary, it be a largo or an andante sostenuto, provided the piece be prolonged, they will, by dint of progressive animation, attain a *moderato* long before the end. The *moderato* is their natural pace, and they recur to it as infallibly as would a pendulum after having been a moment hurried or slackened in its oscillations.

These people are the born enemies of all characteristic music, and the greatest destroyers of style. May Fate preserve the orchestral conductor at any cost from their co-operation.

Once, in a large town (which I will not name), there was to be performed behind the scenes a very simple chorus, written in 6/8, allegretto. The aid of the chorus-master became necessary. He was an old man.

The time in which this chorus was to be taken having been first agreed upon by the orchestra, our Nestor followed it pretty decently during the first few bars; but, soon after, the slackening became such that there was no continuing without rendering the piece perfectly ridiculous. It was recommended twice, thrice, four times; a full half-hour was occupied in ever-increasingly vexatious efforts, but always with the same result. The preservation of allegretto time was absolutely impossible to the worthy man. At last the orchestral conductor, out of all patience, came and begged him not to conduct at all; he had hit upon an expedient: He caused the chorus-singers to simulate a march-movement, raising each foot alternately, without moving on. This movement, being in exactly the same time as the dual rhythm of the 6/8 bar, allegretto, the chorus-singers, who were no longer hindered by their director, at once performed the piece as though they had sung marching; with no less unity than regularity, and without slackening the time.

I acknowledge, however, that many chorus-masters, or sub-conductors of orchestras, are sometimes of real utility, and even indispensable for the maintenance of unity among very large masses of performers. When these masses are obliged to be so disposed as that one portion of the players or chorus-singers turn their back on the conductor, he needs a certain number of sub-beaters of the time, placed before those of the performers who cannot see him and charged with repeating all his signals. In order that this repetition shall be precise, the sub-conductors must be careful never to take their eyes off the chief conductor's stick for a single instant. If, in order to look at their score, they cease to watch him for only three bars, a discrepancy arises immediately between their time and his, and all is lost.

In a festival where 1200 performers were assembled under my direction, at Paris, I had to employ four chorus-masters, stationed at the four corners of the vocal mass, and two sub-conductors, one of whom directed the wind-instruments, and the other the instruments of percussion. I had earnestly besought them to look towards me incessantly; they did not omit to do so, and our eight sticks, rising and falling without the slightest discrepancy of rhythm, established amidst our 1200 performers the most perfect unity ever witnessed.

With one or more electric metronomes, it seems no longer necessary to have recourse to this means. One might, in fact, thus easily conduct chorus-singers who turn their back towards the chief conductor; but attentive and intelligent sub-conductors are always preferable to a machine. They have not only to beat the time, like the metronomic staff, but they have also to speak to the groups around them, to call their attention to nice shades of execution, and, after bar-rests, to remind them when the moment of their re-entry comes.

In a space arranged as a semicircular amphitheatre, the orchestral conductor may conduct a considerable number of performers alone, all eyes then being able to look towards him. Nevertheless, the employment of a certain number of sub-conductors appears to me preferable to individual direction, on account of the great distance between the chief conductor and the extreme points of the vocal and instrumental body.

The more distant the orchestral conductor is from the performers he directs, the more his influence over them is diminished.

The best way would be to have several sub-conductors, with several electric metronomes beating before their eyes the principal beats of the bar.

And now, should the orchestral conductor give the time standing or sitting down?

If, in theatres where they perform scores of immense length, it be very difficult to endure the fatigue of remaining on foot the whole evening, it is none the less true that the orchestral conductor, when seated, loses a portion of his power and cannot give free course to his animation, if he possess any.

Then, should he conduct reading from a full score or from a first violin part (leader's copy), as is customary in some theatres? It is evident that he should have before him a full score. Conducting by means of a part containing only the principal instrumental cues, the bass, and the melody, demands a needless effort of memory from a conductor; and moreover, if he happen to tell one of the performers, whose part he cannot examine, that he is wrong, exposes him to the chance of the reply: "How do you know?"

The disposal and grouping of the players and chorus-singers come also within the province of the orchestral conductor; particularly for concerts. It is impossible to indicate arbitrarily the best method of grouping the performers in a theatre or concert-room; the shape and arrangement of the interior of these places necessarily influence the course to be taken in such a case. Let us add that it depends, moreover, upon the number of performers requiring to be grouped; and, on some occasions, upon the style of composition adopted by the author whose work is to be performed.

In general, for concerts, the following disposal of the orchestra seems best: An amphitheatre of eight, or at least, five rows is indispensable. The semicircular form is the best for the amphitheatre. If it be large enough to contain the whole orchestra, the entire mass of instrumentalists will be disposed of along these rows; the first violins in front on the right, facing the public; the second violins in front on the left; the violas, in the middle, between the two groups of violins; the flutes, hautboys, clarinets, horns, and bassoons behind the first violins; a double rank of violoncellos and double-basses behind the second violins; the trumpets, cornets, trombones, and tubas behind the violas; the rest of the violoncellos and double-basses behind the wooden wind instruments; the harps in the foreground, close to the orchestral conductor; the kettle-drums, and other instruments of percussion behind or in the centre of the brass instruments; the orchestral conductor, turning his back to the public, at the base of the orchestra, and near to the foremost desks of the first and second violins.

There should be a horizontal flooring, or stage, more or less wide, extending in front of the first rows of the amphitheatre. On this flooring the chorus-singers should be placed, in form of a fan turned three-quarters towards the public, so that all shall be able easily to see the motions of the orchestral conductor. The grouping of the chorus-singers, in consonance with their respective order of voice, will differ according as the author has written in three, four, or six parts. At any rate, the women—sopranos and contraltos—should be in front, seated; the tenors standing behind the contraltos; and the basses standing behind the sopranos.

The solo-singers should occupy the centre, and foremost, part of the front stage, and should always place themselves in such a way as to be able, by slightly turning the head, to see the conducting-stick.

For the rest, I repeat, these indications can be but approximate; they may be, for many reasons, modified in various ways.

At the Conservatoire, in Paris, where the amphitheatre is composed of only four or five rows, not circular, and cannot therefore contain the whole orchestra, the violins and violas are on the stage; while the basses and wind instruments alone occupy the rows; the chorus is seated on the front of the stage, facing the public, and the women, sopranos and contraltos, turning their backs directly upon the orchestral conductor, are utterly unable to see his motions. The arrangement is very inconvenient for this portion of the chorus.

It is everywhere of the greatest consequence that the chorus-singers placed on the front of the stage shall occupy a plane somewhat lower than that of the violins; otherwise they would considerably deaden the sound of these instruments.

For the same reason, if there are not other rows for the choir in front of the orchestra, it is absolutely needful that the women should be seated, and the men remain standing up; in order that the voices of the tenors and basses, proceeding from a more elevated point than those of the sopranos and contraltos, may come forth freely and be neither stifled nor intercepted.

When the presence of the chorus-singers in front of the orchestra is not necessary, the conductor will take care to send them away; since this large number of human bodies injures the sonority of the instruments. A symphony, performed by an orchestra thus more or less stifled, loses much of its effect.

There are yet other precautions, relative especially to the orchestra, which the conductor may also take, to avoid certain defects in performance. The instruments of percussion, placed, as I have indicated, upon one of the last rows of the orchestra, have a tendency to modify the rhythm, and slacken the time. A series of strokes on the long drum struck at regular intervals in a quick movement will sometimes lead to the complete destruction of a fine rhythmical progression, by checking the onward bound of the rest of the orchestra, and destroying the unity. Almost always, the long drum player, through not observing the original time given by the conductor, is somewhat behindhand in striking his first stroke. This retardment, multiplied by the number of strokes which follow the first one, soon produces—as may be imagined—a rhythmical discrepancy of the most fatal effect. The conductor, all whose efforts to re-establish unanimity are then in vain, has only one thing left to do; which is, to insist that the long drum player shall count beforehand the number of strokes to be given in the passage in question, and that, knowing his part, he shall no longer look at his copy, but keep his eyes constantly fixed upon the conducting-stick; by which means he will follow the time without the slightest want of precision.

When a long *accelerando, little by little,* is indicated by the composer, for passing from an allegro moderato to a presto, the majority of orchestral conductors hurry the time *by jerks,* instead of quickening it equally throughout, by an insensible onward rate. This should be carefully avoided.

The same remark applies to the converse proposition. It is even more difficult to slacken a quick time smoothly, and without checks, so as to transform it little by little into a slow time. Often, from a desire to testify zeal, or from defect of delivery in his musical feeling, a conductor demands from his players *an exaggeration of nice gradations.* He comprehends neither the character nor the style of the piece. The gradations then become so many blemishes; the accents, yells; the intentions of the poor composer are totally disfigured and perverted; while those of the orchestral conductor—however politely meant they may be—are none the less injurious: like the caresses of the Ass in the fable, who crushed his master while fondling him.

And now let us instance many deplorable abuses that have obtained in almost all the orchestras of Europe—abuses which reduce composers to despair, and which it is the duty of conductors to abolish as soon as possible.

Performers playing stringed instruments will rarely give themselves the trouble to play a tremolo; they substitute for this very characteristic effect, a tame repetition of the note, half, and sometimes three-quarters slower than the one whence results the tremolo: instead of demisemiquavers, they make triple or double ones; and in lieu of producing sixty-four notes in a bar in four-time (adagio), they produce only thirty-two, or even sixteen. The action of the arm necessary for producing a true tremolo demands from them too great an effort. This idleness is intolerable.

Many double-bass players permit themselves—from idleness, also, or from a dread of being unable to achieve certain difficulties—to simplify their part. This race of simplifiers, be it said, has existed for forty years; but it cannot endure any longer. In ancient works, the double-bass parts were extremely simple; therefore there can be no reason to impoverish them still more: those in modern scores are rather more difficult, it is true; but, with very few exceptions, there is nothing in them impossible of execution; composers, masters of their art, write them with care, and as they ought to be executed. If it be from idleness that the simplifiers pervert them, the energetic orchestral conductor is armed with the necessary authority to compel the fulfilment of their duty. If it be from incapacity, let him dismiss them. It is his best interest to rid himself of instrumentalists who cannot play their instrument.

Flute players, accustomed to be above the other wind instruments, and not admitting that their part can be written below that of clarinets or hautboys, frequently transpose entire passages an octave higher. The conductor, if he do not carefully peruse his score, if he be not thoroughly acquainted with the work he is conducting, or if his ear lack keenness, will not perceive the strange liberty thus taken. Nevertheless, multitudes of such instances occur, and care should be taken to banish them entirely.

It happens everywhere (I do not say in some orchestras only)—it happens everywhere, I repeat, that violinists, who have, as is well known, to play—ten, fifteen, twenty of them—the same part in unison, do not count their bars' rest; each, always from idleness, relying on the others doing it. Whence it follows that scarcely the half of them come in again at the right moment; while the rest still hold their instrument under their left arm, and look about them. Thus the point is greatly weakened, if not entirely missed. I invoke the attention and rigour of orchestral conductors to this insufferable habit. It is, however, so rooted that they will only ensure its extirpation by making a large number of violinists amenable for the fault of a single player; by inflicting a fine, for example, upon a whole row, if one of them misses coming in. Even were this fine no more than half-a-crown, I will answer for it that each of the violinists would count his rests, and keep watch that his neighbours did the same, since it might be inflicted five or six times upon the same individuals in the course of one performance.

An orchestra, the instruments of which are not in tune individually, and with each other, is a monstrosity; the conductor, therefore, should take the greatest care that the musicians tune accurately. But this operation should not be performed in presence of the public; and, moreover, every instrumental noise—every kind of preluding between the acts—constitutes a real offence to all civilized auditors. The bad training of an orchestra, and its musical mediocrity is to be inferred from the impertinent noise it makes during the periods of quiet at an Opera or Concert.

It is also imperative for a conductor not to allow clarinet-players to use always the same instrument (the clarinet in Bb), without regard to the author's indications; just as if the different clarinets—those in D and in A, particularly—had not a special character of their own, of which the intelligent composer knows the exact value.

A habit as vicious, and still more baneful, has crept into many orchestras since the introduction of horns with cylinders and pistons: it is that of playing *in open sounds,* by means of the new mechanism adapted to the instrument, those notes intended by the composer to be produced *in closed sounds,* by means of the right hand within the bell. Moreover, the horn players nowadays, on account of the facility afforded by the pistons or cylinders for putting their instrument into different keys, use only the *horn in F,* whatever may be the key indicated by the author. This custom gives rise to a host of inconveniences, from which the conductor should use all his efforts to preserve the works of composers *who know how to write.* As to those of others, it must be confessed, the disaster is of much less consequence.

He should also set his face against the economical fashion adopted by certain theatres—called lyric—of causing the cymbals and the long drum to be played by the same performer. The sound of the cymbals when attached to the long drum—as they must be to render this economy feasible—is an ignoble noise, fit only for bands at tea-gardens. This custom, moreover, leads mediocre composers into the habit of never employing one of these instruments without the other, and of considering their use as solely confined to forcibly marking the accented parts of the bar. This is an idea fruitful in noisy platitudes; and one that has brought upon us the ridiculous excesses beneath which, if a stop be not put to them, dramatic music will sooner or later sink.

I conclude by expressing sincere regret at beholding choral and orchestral studies still so badly organized. Everywhere, for grand choral and instrumental compositions, the system of rehearsals in the mass is maintained. They make all the chorus-singers study at once, on the one hand; and all the instrumentalists at once, on the other. Deplorable errors, innumerable mistakes, are thus committed—particularly in the intermediate parts—errors which the chorus-master and the conductor do not perceive. Once established, these errors degenerate into habits, and become part and parcel of the execution.

The hapless chorus-singers, moreover, are by far the worst treated of all the performers during their studies, such as they are. Instead of giving them *a good conductor,* knowing the times of the different movements accurately, and proficient in the art of singing, to beat the time and make critical observations: *a good pianist,* playing *from a well-arranged pianoforte score,* upon *a good piano;* and *a violinist,* to play in unison or in octave with the voices as each part is learned alone—instead of these three *indispensable artists,* they commit them (in two-thirds of the lyric theatres of Europe) to the superintendence of a single man, who has no more idea of the art of conducting than of that of singing, who is generally a poor musician, selected from among the worst pianists to be found, or who cannot play the pianoforte at all— some old superannuated individual, who, seated before a battered out-of-tune instrument, tries to decipher a dislocated score which he does not know, strikes false chords, major when they are minor, or vice-versa, and, under the pretext of conducting and of accompanying by himself, employs his right hand in setting the chorus-singers wrong in their time, and his left hand in setting them wrong in their tune.

One might believe oneself in the Dark Ages, on witnessing such an exhibition of barbarism for the sake of economy.

A faithful, well-coloured, clever interpretation of a modern work, even when confided to artists of a higher order, can only be obtained, I firmly believe, by partial rehearsals. Each part of a chorus should be studied singly until it be thoroughly known, before combining it with the others. The same step should be taken with regard to the orchestra, for a symphony at all complicated. The violins should first be practised alone; the violas and basses by themselves; the wooden wind instruments (with a small band of stringed instruments, to fill in the rests, and accustom the wind instruments to the points of re-entrance) and the brass instruments the same; and very often it is necessary to practise the instruments of percussion alone; and lastly, the harps, if they be numerous. The studies in combination are then far more profitable, and more rapid; and there is then good hope of attaining fidelity of interpretation, now, alas, but too rare.

The performances obtained by the old method of study are merely *approaches* to achievement; beneath which so very many masterpieces have succumbed. The superintending conductor, after the butchering of a master, none the less serenely lays down his stick with a satisfied smile; and if some few misgivings remain with him as to the mode in which he has fulfilled his task, should no one venture at the close to dispute its accomplishment, he murmurs aside: *"Bah! vae victis!"* (So what! Losers weepers!)

QUESTIONS

1. In a music dictionary look up *hautboy* and *ophicleide*. What sort of instruments are these? How have they been replaced in the modern orchestra?

2. Why do you suppose orchestras have so many stringed instruments in

comparison to wind instruments? Show the proportion of stringed instruments, woodwinds, brass, and percussion, according to Berlioz's idea of the ideal orchestra. How does his orchestra compare with the modern orchestra?

3. Discuss Berlioz's "points of procedure of the sound," and his disposition of percussion instruments in the orchestra. Do you think this foreshadows the principles of stereophonic sound? How?

4. Berlioz indicates that, in his time, people with money "are ready to give 50,000 francs and more" for a great painting; yet would not give 50 francs to help produce, once a year, an important musical work. What do you think accounts for this? Has this practice changed any in our time?

5. How does one study to become a conductor? Does studying any particular instrument help? Look up some famous conductors and list the instruments they studied. Have they anything in common? What did Toscanini play? Berlioz? Bernstein? Koussevitsky? Ormandy? Stokowski?

PROGRAM MUSIC *Nationalist music has been called the people's popular serious music. Practically every composer has tried his hand at nationalist music, some devoting most of their compositional efforts toward this end. Nationalist music (as a type of serious music) makes a special appeal to those who have difficulty in grasping the spirit and nature of music that is essentially abstract. Music with a "national" program is strongly akin to program music in general and may, in fact, be considered as program music. Homer Ulrich, musicologist and head of the music department at the University of Maryland, is the author of five books on music. He is not only a scholar but also a practicing musician, having played bassoon with the Chicago and San Antonio symphony orchestras.*

The National Schools

HOMER ULRICH

$\mathcal{T}$HE ART OF MUSIC IS IN A CERTAIN SENSE analogous to a language; indeed, it has often been called a "universal language." Two closely related possibilities of furthering the analogy may be noted: a language may be spoken with personal or regional accents, or even with different dialects; and out of its dialects new languages may be formed—somewhat in the way that the several Romance languages developed out of Latin. A glance at music history reveals how the first of these possibilities was realized. Composers from Haydn to Schumann "spoke" with a German accent, so to say, but remained within the language through the universal appeal of their utterances. At the same time such diverse composers as Rameau, Rossini, and Chopin "spoke" respectively with French, Italian, and even Polish idioms and inflections, yet remained universal. The music of these composers recaptured in an intangible way something of the national characteristics, spiritual sense, and personal aspirations of their respective people.

In the second half of the nineteenth century other groups of composers went some distance on the path of the second possibility, namely that of creating regional languages out of the universal tongue. Their method was to make overt use of their own folk songs, idioms, dances, and legends and to transform the universal aspects of the language to fit the new expressive material. These composers, unlike those of the first group, were active in geographical areas where political oppression or personal subjection were the order of the day—notably Russia and Bohemia. This tendency to employ indigenous materials is called "nationalistic" in music. Nationalism represents in a sense the pugnacious, self-assertive denial of a cultural inferiority; it is a form of artistic self-consciousness.

Certain necessary preliminaries to the formation of musical nationalism took place in earlier decades. The urge, in the late eighteenth and early nineteenth centuries, to preserve folk songs on a national basis had resulted in many collections of source material. The composers of that time had shown how the material might be used. Haydn and Schubert had turned in a few works, for example, to Hungarian Gypsy idioms; Beethoven had on occasion quoted Russian tunes; and both Haydn and Beethoven had interested themselves in folk songs

---

THE NATIONAL SCHOOLS from *Symphonic Music* by Homer Ulrich; copyright 1952 by the Columbia University Press. Reprinted by permission.

Program Music / Ulrich

of the British Isles. And now the nationally minded composers in the period after about 1860 found it necessary to consider the musical worth of their own material in order to utilize and exploit their respective folk heritages. This was doubly desirable; for many composers of the time, faced with the tremendous accomplishments of Haydn, Mozart, and especially Beethoven, and unable to meet those giants on their own terms, were thus forced to express themselves on a smaller, more intimate scale.

A national music does not come into being as soon as folk materials are employed, however; for an essential part of national self-expression consists of unveiling the nation's soul in the music. This requires a composer of genius who, if he is to write music that will hold its own upon the universal scene, must present a universally significant content even though it is couched in national idioms and, perhaps, in national forms and color. The earliest of such composers were Michael Ivanovich Glinka (1804-1857) among the Russians and Bedřich Smetana (1824-1884) among the Czechs. Glinka in his operas, *A Life for the Tsar* (1836) and *Russlan and Ludmilla* (1842), introduced Russian, Polish, and oriental colors, painted a succession of brilliant nationalistic pictures, and made liberal use of Russian melodic and rhythmic idioms. The overture to *Russlan and Ludmilla* has survived on the concert stage. It is, however, not typical of the opera itself; its Italian brightness and energy as well as its universal humor and melodiousness are scarcely representative of Glinka's essential nationalism. Truly Russian orchestral music did not emerge until later in the century; it will be discussed in due course.

Smetana, on the other hand, was active in the orchestral field and was the creator of a Czech national music. His earliest works in the field, however, gave only faint promise of that accomplishment: the three symphonic poems written between 1858 and 1861 were inspired by western European literature and reflected the composer's admiration for the music and methods of Liszt. Theme transformation and a quantity of sequence repetition characterize these forgotten works. From 1863, after several years spent in Gothenburg, Smetana lived in Prague and was active in supplying the Czech National Theater with repertoire material. In eight operas, among them the well-known *Bartered Bride* (1866), he disclosed his fondness for Czech legend and literature and placed a great variety of folk songs and dances upon the operatic stage. More importantly, however, he revealed the Czech temperament in all its rhythm, color, and emotional vitality. These operas are nationalistic even when they do not embody folk songs. Yet at the same time the universal appeal of *The Bartered Bride*, for instance, is felt keenly; its characters are human beings, and a close relationship exists between Smetana's style and the lyric style of the Viennese masters, particularly Schubert.

His great contribution to symphonic literature is the cycle of six symphonic poems with the collective title *Má vlast* ("My Country"), written between 1874 and 1879 in spite of his complete loss of hearing. Here Smetana strove to recapture the spirit of Bohemia itself. The cycle is compounded of legend (*Vyšehrad* and *Šárka*), history (*Tábor* and *Blaník*), and description of landscape (*The Moldau* and *From Bohemia's Fields and Groves*). The Vyšehrad motive, quoted at the beginning of the cycle, is employed throughout the first poem and is mentioned in the second as well as the sixth; it plays little part in the thematic materials of the others, for one may do no more than trace a faint resemblance (based upon a sequence of falling intervals) between the motive and subsequent themes.

All six poems of the cycle are devoted to revealing the glories of the Czech heritage; it is this poetic idea rather than the Vyšehrad motive which unifies the cycle. Within each of the six symphonic poems, faint echoes of Liszt's practices are heard; a considerable amount of theme transformation is undeniable, and each work is divided into several sections which are often marked by contrasting tempos. Yet the sections of each work constitute in effect a four-movement connected symphony; and the harmony, the melodic and rhythmic elements, and the general color of the cycle are Smetana's own and hence stand for the Czech national style. Polkas and other dances appear on occasion—but also, notably in the love scene of *Šárka*, a breadth of melody that is closely akin to Wagner and has little in common with Czech idioms.

Smetana, like many others who adhered to the ideals of the neo-German party, depended upon poetic stimulus for his musical inspiration. Without relying upon realistic description or departing from clear, well-organized forms, he yet remained faithful to his programmatic ideas. Never obscure, always melodious or rhythmically alive, Smetana was content to remain on a somewhat local, intimate level. He showed little interest in posing problems of universal emotional significance and solving them musically. Thus he cannot be reckoned among the Promethean composers whose music benefits a larger group. It is perhaps inevitable that outside his own country *The Moldau* is the only work of the *Má vlast* cycle to have survived in the standard repertoire.

Antonín Dvořák (1841-1904) was far more prolific in the orchestral field and composed in a greater variety of forms and styles than Smetana. Influenced in turn by virtually all the great composers of the nineteenth century, he consistently returned to a fresh, problem-free expression and a love for his Czech homeland after each digression. In nine symphonies, five symphonic poems, several concertos, and almost two dozen miscellaneous works for orchestra, Dvořák disclosed a gift for pure melody and a grasp of the relationships between form and content unequaled by his nationalistically minded contemporaries.

Dvořák's nationalism is not outwardly as perceptible as that of Smetana—at least not in the orchestral works; nor was his interest in literary stimulus and programmatic content as consistent. The majority of his symphonies are in the sphere of abstract music. They are dedicated to presenting attractive, forceful, and contrasting melodies in forms which are basically those of the early nineteenth century. Occasionally a symphonic movement suggests dance rhythms or is an outspoken dance form—notably the *furiant* which serves in place of a scherzo in the so-called "first" symphony. But actual quotation of folk songs is held to a minimum. It is rather the Czech spirit, with all its impulsive alternation between gaiety and gloom, with its rhythmic vitality and physical energy, that comes to expression.

The first four of Dvořák's symphonies were not published during his lifetime; the remaining five, along with many works in other categories, were arbitrarily treated as to chronological order and opus number by his publishers. Thus one ordinarily gains a distorted view of Dvořák's development as a composer. The great maturity and considerable technical mastery revealed by the first symphony, for example, are truly astonishing—unless one realizes that it is actually his sixth work in the form.

Early works—insofar as they are available, and including categories other than the symphonic—reveal a Dvořák who was greatly attracted to the style of Wagner. Free, expansive forms and long, flowing melodies set in a rhapsodic manner are typical. A period in the late 1870's saw him greatly concerned with Czech folk materials; this phase is seen in the four *Slavonic Rhapsodies* and in the first set of *Slavonic Dances* (originally for piano four-hands, but later orchestrated), all of which were written between 1874 and 1878. The F-major symphony of 1875 makes lesser use of national elements, it is true; yet its slow movement is closely allied to the Slavonic and melancholy *dumka*.

About 1877 Dvořák was befriended by Brahms and became, in a sense, the latter's *protégé*. Thereupon he tended to shake off the earlier influences, develop his own style, and follow a musical ideal which in many ways resembles that of his great contemporary. The D-major symphony gives evidence of the program-free, eloquent, and logical manner of Dvořák in the 1880s; it is a joyous, sparkling work. And yet the A-minor violin concerto of about the same years reveals a free, rhapsodic expression combined with unmistakably nationalistic elements in a form which owes much to Liszt. Conversely, the *Scherzo capriccioso* of 1883 represents Dvořák at his imaginative and formal best. Cast in the form of a scherzo with trio, but containing long developments and brilliant transitions, it is a breathless, effective—and difficult—movement for large orchestra. The work deserves to be restored to the high place in the repertoire it once enjoyed.

With the D-minor symphony of 1884-1885 Dvořák reached new heights. Here is a "universal" work, as opposed to a national or purely personal one; the emotional scale of this symphony is far above any other of his orchestral compositions. From a technical point of view, he revealed himself here to be a master of thematic manipulation devoted to intense emotional expression; only Brahms among his contemporaries could write more concisely and logically. It is unfortunate that the D-minor symphony is not as well known as the ever-popular "New World."

The G-Major symphony of 1889 marks a complete contrast to the foregoing. For here is an easygoing collection of unrelated material, developed without any great emotional compulsion. Enjoyable in the manner of virtually all of Dvořák's music and containing a few enchanting passages, it cannot compare with the symphonies which precede and follow it. A cycle of three related pieces from 1891-1892 may be mentioned here. At first united under the title, "Nature, Life, and Love," the pieces were later issued as overtures with separate titles: *In Nature's Realm, Carnival,* and *Othello.* Bound together by a pastoral motive which appears at appropriate moments in the works, they mark a return of the programmatic element to Dvořák's music. The *Carnival,* especially, has retained its place in the repertoire; it brings to expression the composer's exuberant spirit and mastery of orchestration.

The E-minor symphony, the ninth of his works in this form, was written in 1893 during the first year of Dvořák's stay in the United States; its subtitle, "From the New World," is thus justified. As he had done elsewhere, he expressed the spirit of a people—this time the American people instead of the Czech, of course, but American as reflected in the life of the Czech community of Spillville, Iowa—without quoting folk melodies. A deliberately naïve air pervades the themes of this work; its melodies are not so much developed as repeated, and sequence repetitions and routine climaxes play a larger part here than in any other of his major works. This type of treatment is perhaps made necessary by the shape and content of the themes; the latter are in the main scarcely adapted to true symphonic treatment, and one may be sure that Dvořák was aware of this. For, almost as if to compensate for this type of theme elaboration, he makes a bow to sophisticated cyclical form: themes from the first movement appear in the second and in the

Program Music / Ulrich

third, and the coda of the fourth quotes liberally from all three preceding movements. The symphony as a whole is a brilliant, effective, and satisfying work; but it is not the most significant of Dvořák's compositions.

The B-minor cello concerto of 1894-1895 also belongs to the American stay; but his third year in the United States found Dvořák homesick. One may surmise a loss of interest in the American scene, and this is reflected in the romantic, somewhat melancholy tone which predominates in the concerto. A colorful, rhapsodic work resulted, one which exploits the solo instrument's technical possibilities without exceeding the bounds of good taste. It remains one of the most attractive works in the cello repertoire.

Dvořák's interest in program music was revived after his return to Prague. In 1896 and 1897 he wrote no fewer than five symphonic poems. The immediate stimulus was a collection of folk ballads. Terror, death, and fantasy are characteristic of the ballads he selected, yet he exercised great restraint and thematic economy in setting them to music. These works have not held their place in the repertoire; they are mentioned here only to give evidence of Dvořák's uncertainty as to his true mission as a composer.

An eloquent melodic quality shines through all of his works; in a sense, his lyric gifts were akin to Schubert's. His instinct for form and proportion was as highly developed as his melodic sense, and he possessed a technical ability and an imagination which allowed him at all times to balance these opposites. Extreme contrasts, embracing abrupt changes from dark melancholy to wild joy, are typical of his music; yet such contrasts are usually justified by the contexts in which they appear. Seldom did he allow mediocre passages to remain in his works; his self-critical sense was almost as keen as Brahms's. It is only by comparison with the very greatest—with a Beethoven or a Mozart, say—that the personal, subjective nature of his emotional palette is revealed. In all respects save those of profundity and eternal significance, Dvořák must be ranked among the finest of nineteenth-century composers.

To express Russian life and feeling, following the work of Glinka and Alexander Dargomijsky (1813-1869), became the underlying purpose of a group of enthusiastic musical amateurs who came under the influence of Mili Balakirev (1837-1910). The latter, together with Alexander Borodin (1833-1887), César Cui (1835-1918), Modest Moussorgsky (1839-1881), and Nicholas Rimsky-Korsakov (1844-1908), formed the nucleus (called "The Five") of a nationalistic school which exercised a great influence upon later generations of Russian composers.

The technical training and musical abilities of this loosely knit group were so varied, however, and their central purpose was so vaguely stated, that little solid, systematic work came from their respective pens.

Balakirev, largely self-taught, became interested in teaching and conducting; his compositions are few, and his function was principally that of acting as a gadfly to the others. Only Rimsky-Korsakov felt it necessary to pursue organized musical study later in life. The main preoccupation of the others seems to have been the composition of operas; and it is in the operatic field that their true worth as nationalists and musicians is to be measured. In every case, the quantity and quality of their purely orchestral works falls below their operas. Since none of Cui's works have survived in the repertoire, the following discussion will concern itself only with Borodin, Moussorgsky, and Rimsky-Korsakov.

In Borodin one encounters an element which runs through much Russian music: economy of thematic material, and with it, deliberate, monotonous repetition of melodic fragments. We have seen this in Tchaikovsky. This trait is not to be looked upon as a weakness in Borodin, but as the expression of an aesthetic creed different from that of German composers since Haydn. Borodin had demonstrated his ability to write along Classical lines and to develop themes in the German manner in his first symphony, in E-flat major, composed in 1862-1867. In the second, however, the repetitive method is fully revealed. The symphony is in B minor, was written between 1872 and 1876, and is his most important orchestral work.

A striking motive heard at the very outset impresses itself upon virtually the entire first movement. The few bits of contrasting melody that are introduced play little part in the structure of the whole; rather is there a constant dwelling upon or reflecting upon the first motive. Outwardly in sonata-form, in that the principal divisions of that form are well marked, the movement develops little thematic conflict. The scherzo is an orchestral tour de force in which themes are of minor importance; a few melodic fragments do appear, but they become lost in the rich, kaleidoscopic orchestral color. The slow movement is more orthodox and expresses something of a melancholy, quasi-oriental character that has, since Borodin, been taken to reflect the Russian temperament. The finale is a series of vivid, exciting episodes, based in part on contrasting themes but unified by the unfailing brilliance of the orchestral sound. Harmonies are free throughout the symphony, and a typical alternation of barbaric and intimate moods gives the work much of its national character. A third symphony was left incomplete at Borodin's death.

It is remarkable that the second symphony should be so closely knit both in structure and intention; for it was written across a four-year interval, was interrupted by work on other compositions and by Borodin's scientific studies and medical-administrative duties. There is a certain similarity in all of his works, it is true, in that his melodies are generally of folk-song type and tinged with oriental color, and that constant repetition with changed orchestration is the chief organizing principle. This basic similarity may be seen when two other orchestral works are compared to the symphony: the ever-popular set of "Polovtzian Dances" from the unfinished opera, *Prince Igor,* and a small symphonic poem, *On the Steppes of Central Asia,* the latter written in 1880.

Moussorgsky is even more sparsely represented in the orchestral literature than Borodin. A single composition, *A Night on the Bare Mountain,* is his principal representative. It was designed originally (1860) as incidental music for a lurid drama called *The Witches;* it suffered many modifications at the composer's hands (including one version for piano and orchestra, and a place in two operas) and, about 1882, at Rimsky-Korsakov's. Its present form as a symphonic poem is largely the work of the latter. The thematic material of the work is unified by a harsh, macabre quality which goes far toward carrying out the implied program—an orgy of witches and grisly apparitions, finally dispersed by the chimes of the village bells. The material and framework are Moussorgsky's, the sequence and arrangement Rimsky-Korsakov's. But the fantastic nature of the composition, its dramatic transitions, and its sheer excitement are undeniable, regardless of the author. *A Night on the Bare Mountain* is not, strictly speaking, within the body of nationalistic music. It does, however, testify to Moussorgsky's interest in Russian legendary subjects, an interest which animates the greater part of his operas.

Pictures from an Exhibition was originally a set of piano pieces composed in 1874; it was orchestrated about 1922 by Maurice Ravel, and in its new dress has added considerable luster to Moussorgsky's name. The ten pieces are descriptive sketches, and several of them are connected by a "promenade," a short interlude which represents the composer moving from one picture to the next. Quite apart from Ravel's masterly orchestration, the set reveals the depth of Moussorgsky's insight, his vivid imagination, and his forward-looking harmonic sense.

Rimsky-Korsakov, the youngest of "The Five," served a double function. As musical executor of Moussorgsky's fragments and unfinished works he prepared a number of compositions for practical performance; and as the most industrious and best-trained musician in the group he wrote more systematically and in greater quantity than his colleagues. About a dozen Russian historical and legendary subjects were made into operas and performed during his lifetime. But more than a dozen orchestral works were written also; several hold respected places in today's symphonic repertoire. One of them, *Antar,* began its career as Rimsky-Korsakov's second symphony in 1868, was revised and reorchestrated several times, and emerged finally in 1903 as a symphonic suite of four movements. It is constructed somewhat on the Berlioz model: it is a programmatic work, it contains a basic motive or *idée fixe* which appears in each movement, and it brings to expression four episodes in the adventures of the legendary Antar, an Arabian poet and desert hero. The movements describe Antar's encounter with the queen of the fairies, and his moods of revenge, power, and love, respectively.

Three compositions of 1887-1888, however, are the works upon which Rimsky-Korsakov's orchestral fame is most largely founded. A *Capriccio espagnol* was at first planned as a fantasy on Spanish themes for violin and orchestra—perhaps to serve as a companion piece to the *Fantasy on Russian Themes* for the same instrumental combination, completed in 1886. That plan was discarded, and the *Capriccio* was composed as a virtuosic set of five movements for orchestra. The composer was careful to point out that the brilliance of the work lay in the structure of the themes and in the piece itself: "It is the very essence of the composition, not its garb or orchestration." His considerable knowledge of instrumental idioms and technical possibilities, gained in part as an inspector of naval bands, stood him in good stead; he knew the difficulties and inmost nature of the instruments as perhaps no composer before him. As a result, the many gay, wild, or sentimental tunes in the *Capriccio* are well adapted to form an orchestral work of the greatest effectiveness.

The symphonic suite, *Scheherazade,* followed directly upon the *Capriccio.* For its literary subject-matter Rimsky-Korsakov turned again, as he had done for *Antar,* to the *Arabian Nights.* The suite is based upon the story of the sultan Schahriar, who is diverted from his habit of murdering one of his wives each night by the charm and narrative ability of Scheherazade. The movements are entitled "The Sea and Sinbad's Ship," "The Tale of the Kalendar Prince," "The Young Prince and Princess," and "Festival at Bagdad." Two themes run through the suite: a hard, brutal one, carried by full orchestra and symbolizing the sultan; and a suave, florid cadenza for violin and harp, representing Scheherazade. The themes appear in the manner of Berlioz's *idée fixe,* either to introduce the various movements or at significant moments within. It may be pointed out that the transformation of the sultan's theme in the course of the work represents the gradual weakening of his murderous resolve; the composer has written character sketches of the two protagonists rather than drawn simply a series of brilliant, fanciful oriental pictures.

The richness of color and orchestral mastery which characterize all of Rimsky-Korsakov's larger works are nowhere so clearly revealed as in

Program Music / Ulrich

Scheherazade. An orchestra of standard, pre-Wagnerian dimensions sufficed him; yet he achieved a great variety of sonorous, delicate, massive, and even overwhelming effects. Like his contemporaries, he was much given to thematic reiteration and showed little interest in developing themes to provide closely knit forms; but the monotony dangerously inherent in this practice is avoided by the flexibility of his orchestration. Indeed, the virtuosity he revealed in this respect became something of a weakness. One becomes surfeited with the constant change of color and sound, one realizes that in Rimsky-Korsakov such elements are ends in themselves. Of all the Russian nationalists, he was perhaps the most effective in a superficial sense, yet his dramatic ability did not compare with Moussorgsky's, for example, or his perception of form and proportion with Borodin's. He possessed a full measure of sentimental and lyric qualities; yet these are often overlooked because of the exciting, forceful expression which is seldom absent from his music.

The remaining composition of 1888, called *Easter Overture* and *Russian Easter* among other variants, is essentially a fantasy on Russian liturgical themes and is designed to contrast the gloom of the days preceding Easter with the joy and merriment of Easter Sunday itself. A slow and somber introduction, in which a chantlike theme is presented in company with florid cadenzas for a solo violin, leads directly into an allegro that is brilliant, dark, and majestic in turn. Several themes, all suggestive of liturgical moments, are treated in Rimsky-Korsakov's usual manner: fragmentary repetition with changed orchestration. A large percussion section in which bells are featured adds to the festive mood of the final portion, and the composer's purpose of depicting the rejoicing on Easter is well achieved. The *Russian Easter* is a satisfying composition.

The type of symphonic suite introduced by Rimsky-Korsakov is found in the works of many Russian composers of a later generation. One of these is by Michael Ippolitov-Ivanov (1859-1935), a pupil of the former and for some years a conductor in Tiflis, the chief city of Transcaucasia. His familiarity with the music and topography of the region came to expression in the *Caucasian Sketches*, a suite of four descriptive movements. An array of Georgian (hence, partly oriental) melodies gives pictures of the mountains, villages, and mosques of the area, and a pleasant but scarcely significant work results.

The movement toward musical nationalism in the Scandinavian countries was neither as vigorous nor as productive of lasting results as in Russia and Bohemia. Further, leading Scandinavian composers were usually sent to Germany for their education; there they came under the influence of the German Romantic tradition and remained largely in its thrall. Niels Gade (1817-1890), the foremost Danish composer of his time, was typical in this respect. He became essentially a transplanted Mendelssohn "speaking" with a mild Danish accent. Sweet sentiment, a graceful style, and a narrow emotional range characterize many of his works—eight symphonies and several overtures among them. But an essential lack of virility and an avoidance of dramatic conflicts in those works have doomed them to virtual oblivion.

Edvard Grieg (1843-1907) was alone successful among Norwegian composers in impressing his individual yet nationalistic style upon the international concert stage. Two orchestral suites, arranged from music composed for Ibsen's play, *Peer Gynt,* about 1874-1875, have become universally popular. They reveal Grieg's full mastery of smaller forms and disclose the lyricism which was his outstanding characteristic; the eight pieces which constitute the suites are filled with charming melodies set to colorful and piquant harmonies. Grieg was primarily a composer of mood pieces in which a faint air of melancholy predominates; such moods come to full expression in the *Peer Gynt* music as well as in the suite, *Aus Holbergs Zeit* (a set of piano pieces arranged for string orchestra), and in the incidental music to *Sigurd Jorsalfar.*

Grieg, like many other composers of his time, received his training at Leipzig; Schumann's poetic, short-breathed style remained of great influence upon him. The fresh, open-air, and rhapsodic aspects of that style left their mark principally upon the A-minor piano concerto, composed in 1868—the work which best represents Grieg in the repertoire of today and which is one of his very few compositions in large form.

The concerto is representative of nationalism in that it breathes the spirit of Norwegian folk music. Folk songs as such are not quoted; but the subtle, often modal harmonies, the melodic lines which have a contour all their own, plus the dark and melancholy moods which prevail—these are national in their color and effect. The restraint and economy typical of Grieg elsewhere are less evident in the concerto. Forceful, brilliant, and even exuberant passages abound, and the virtuosic solo part is in the best Romantic tradition. In common with nationalists of other lands, Grieg showed little interest in thematic development and structural logic. Sequence repetitions of the kind found in Czech and Russian music are found to an even greater degree here— the material so repeated being Norwegian rather than Slavic, of course.

The first and last movements of the concerto are vigorous and are compounded of many short melodic fragments; the middle movement is songful and is based largely upon a single melody. But regardless of tempo and type of treatment, warm lyric qualities are seldom absent. It was Grieg's great accomplishment to develop a unique, truly personal style; its basis is a type of melody that hovers about the fifth of the scale rather than the keynote, and a piquant harmonic system. These, together with his penchant for sequences and his fragmentary, episodic forms, give Grieg's music an individuality possessed by few other composers. It is that individuality of style plus the eloquent and attractive melodic material which raise the concerto to its high place as one of the best-liked concertos in the repertoire.

The Spanish folk-music heritage, perhaps the most colorful in western Europe, was even later in coming to the notice of significant orchestral composers than any of the foregoing. And it is ironic that three French composers were among the first to include Spanish idioms in their larger works. Bizet, in his opera, *Carmen* (1875), had recaptured the characteristic melodic patterns, the inexorable rhythms, and the intense expression of Spain. At about the same time, Edouard Lalo (1823-1892) introduced a synthetic Spanish quality in his *Symphonie espagnole*, a five-movement concerto for violin and orchestra. The vivid orchestral colors as well as the exotic themes and rhythms of this work provide it with a picturesque quality that justifies the title in part. In the finale of his D-minor cello concerto of 1876, Lalo quoted a Spanish folk song; and many passages in the two other movements are filled with a type of rhapsodic expression that suggests the same national temperament. And finally, Emmanuel Chabrier (1841-1894) composed *España*, a rhapsody for orchestra, in 1883; this work is overtly Spanish in all its rhythmic and melodic aspects.

To such composers, who appropriated a national idiom purely for its qualities as entertainment, one may scarcely attribute a desire to solidify or preserve Spanish folk culture. And the Spanish-flavored works of such composers are, with the exception of *Carmen*, purely occasional pieces. To this group we may add Rimsky-Korsakov's *Capriccio espagnol*, discussed above. Not until about 1885-1890, in the time of Isaac Albéniz (1860-1909), was the basis for a Spanish national school established. Albéniz was active primarily in the field of piano music, however; significant orchestral composition are not to be looked for before the end of the nineteenth century.

Nationally minded composers continued to appear in the years after 1900, both in the countries already spoken of in this chapter and in other regions even more remote from the larger cultural centers. Indeed, one of the striking facts about the early twentieth century is that national musical interests continued to be served no less strongly than they had been in the period after about 1860. The works of many such composers were purely of local interest; as such they cannot be discussed here. Other nationalistic compositions have won and held places in the standard repertoire. They give evidence that national and universal appeal are still as compatible as they were in the music of Dvořák, for example, and that national idioms and dialects had not, in the nineteenth century, reached the limits of their respective expressive possibilities.

QUESTIONS

1. What makes a "patriotic" piece of music patriotic, when the music has no words? Can you give several examples of such pieces?
2. Do you think there is any relation between folk music and the music discussed in the preceding essay? What do they have in common? What are the differences?
3. What does Ulrich mean when he says, "Nationalism represents in a sense the pugnacious, self-assertive denial of a cultural inferiority; it is a form of artistic self-consciousness." Paraphrase this sentence and discuss its implications.
4. Ulrich says that Dvořák's "New World" Symphony "is not the most significant of Dvořák's compositions." Yet in America it is undoubtedly one of his most performed, most popular work. Can you suggest any reasons for this seeming disparity?
5. Can you name any American nationalist composers? Do we have any works by Americans comparable to Smetana's *The Moldau*, or Moussorgsky's *A Night on Bare Mountain*, or Grieg's *Peer Gynt* suite?

FORM *The problem of form in music is perhaps
the most difficult for non-music students to grasp.
Definitions of various musical structures, like the
structures themselves, are frequently cast in abstract
terms. For this reason even the interested student often
sees these terms only as labels—words which mean
little to him except as the names of things. In his
book,* The Musical Workshop, *Frederick Dorian sets
out "to show how great composers of past centuries saw
their task and created their music." To do this, he
explores the minds of great composers as they search
for the total form and structure of their work. The
result gives us some insights into the broad aspects of
the creative process. Since 1936 Frederick Dorian
(1902—) has been Professor of Music at the
Carnegie Institute of Technology in Pittsburgh.*

THE MEANING
OF FORM

FREDERICK DORIAN

N ATURE CARRIES THE ARTIST TO AN INNER UNITY. Goethe came to this conclusion after a lifelong study of all the arts. The great creative artists were unifying natures, endowed with the power of synthesis—of that force which binds all separate elements of substance into the wholeness of the art work.

Every great composer is possessed with this inborn drive toward an entity. In the synthetic stage of composition, he eliminates all unessentials, closely links the factors of the art work and firmly organizes his music to the inner unity of its creative form.

Synthesis implies the act of composition in its most literal meaning: it is the putting of parts together, the tectonic combination of all details within the whole. It is the casting of the form, the total organization of all individual parts. Synthesis, as a synonym for the last stage of composition, pertains to all work following the previous stages of inventing and sketching. It also comprises the mere externalities of writing the manuscript in a final copy.

Creative synthesis is always the result of inner order. It succeeds only if a spiritual center had guided the organization of the tonal material. In this organization, the great composer clearly recognizes the principles of musical design. He balances all ideas included in the total score and tests their function. In this sense everything is teamwork; everything is co-operation to achieve the end purpose of form.

The idea of musical form has frequently been defined mechanically: theorists have shown the form of a fugue, sonata or song to be something like a prefixed pattern—like a form used for the casting of a chime or for a piece of sculpture. The shape of the tonal substance originates as though the composer would cast his form in a musical bell foundry. The soft tonal material is poured into a rigid, hard framework. It flows into given patterns, limiting the composer's inventiveness within a chosen, pre-established form-scheme. But if this were true, form in music could never be a freely swinging, released force, springing from the permutation of primary musical elements, from an expression which newly creates the form with every new work.

This notion of musical bell casting is disproved by the practice of composition in every era. The medieval and baroque working methods show how new forms readily emerged even if the composer employed previously existing form patterns. In the nineteenth century, Schumann rejected the claim of contemporary theorists that the fluid material of

THE MEANING OF FORM from *The Musical Workshop* by Frederick Dorian, pp. 245–246, 249–251, 253–259, 267–269, 271–273. Copyright 1947 by Harper and Row, Publishers, Incorporated. Reprinted by permission of Harper & Row, Publishers.

tones must be poured into traditional tonal forms: "... as though there were only one or two forms to which the spiritual features would have to be adjusted. As though not every idea would bring into the world its very own form by itself. As though not every art work must have a different content and therefore a different form." Schumann, schooled in the forms of the past and deeply admiring their design, still desired to free himself from the tyranny of ultraconservative formalists and lawmakers. . . .

The Blueprint as Germinating Force

"A GENUINELY artistic work of music," says Schumann, "always has a certain center of gravity toward which everything must tend, and from which the spiritual radius emerges. Many place it in the middle in the manner of Mozart, others to the end, as Beethoven. In any case, the total effect (of the work) depends on its forcefulness (of the ground-plan). If one has first listened to the music with tension and torture, then the moment must come when one can, for the first time, breathe freely. One has mounted to the peak—the view stretches brightly and contently forward and backward."

The point of gravity, or rather the spiritual center of the score decides, then, the distribution of all tonal balance—in the individual movement as well as in the cycle of an entire work. It is the crux of the design. It directs the whole course of the music. The chosen center is the magnet toward which all spiritual and tectonic elements of the music are drawn. Schumann, when referring to Beethoven's plans, thought of scores such as the Fifth Symphony: its curve from the dramatic opening to the liberating finale bears out perfectly Schumann's metaphor. The transition from the scherzo to the finale marks the point where, after the preceding tension, one can "breathe freely" again and serenely enjoy the outstretched view. Such an experience is typical of the classical cycle, which is one of a gradual loosening of tension. There is frequently a decrescendo of the expansive forces as the cycle unfolds from the opening to the last movement. Tonalities in minor lead to finales in major. The expression turns gradually from the serious to the light, from the problematic to the playful, from the closed to the open forms. Already the baroque suite with its austere beginning and its happy ending follows such a course. So do most sonata cycles of Haydn, Mozart and their contemporaries. By and large, this order continues until the revolutionary finale of Beethoven's Ninth Symphony.

Nottebohm justifiably divided Beethoven's sketches into one group in which the total form appears as the aim from the beginning, and another, in which thematic work predominates, with the form only distantly in mind. Psychologically, however, the origin of ideas is closely related, no matter how Beethoven elaborated upon them. A flash occurs and brings a motif, a harmony, or suggests an idea pertaining to form. Nevertheless, the various examples show the different function which such inspirational occurrences have in reference to the architecture of the finished music. The differences lie in the composer's evaluation of his tonal substance—where and how the various thoughts fit into the plan of a specific work.

The drafts for Beethoven's Fifth Piano Concerto in E-flat Major are stamped from their very beginning by a conception of forms rather than by a pursuit of melodic and other tectonic elements. Already in the initial sketches, the form idea unfolds itself. The piano introduces the concerto with a brilliant passage, without a pronouncement of the main theme. Along with this unusual opening, and likewise clear from the inception of the music, we observe its familiar harmonies. Yet the main theme of the concerto is not evident at all at this early stage of composition. Motifs come and go; they are accepted, rejected and newly cast. Obviously, they are of lesser importance for it was not a theme or rhythm which untied the flow of Beethoven's imagination. It was rather a definite idea of a form, given *a priori,* which inspired and remained the decisive factor throughout all stages in the composition of this movement.

An analogous procedure is shown in the sketches to the first movement of the Piano Sonata in D Minor, Op. 31, No. 2. Again, Beethoven is primarily concerned with the form. He envisions a recitative to be interpolated in the blueprint of the sonata movement at the recapitulation of its main thought. As in the case of the Fifth Piano Concerto, the melodic lines as such are only of secondary importance in relation to the pattern of form. In the early sketches, in which the usual form of this movement is already established, the thematic material itself is still in a problematic stage and shows little resemblance to its final shape. Without any decisions as to main or secondary themes, the form alone lives clearly in Beethoven's mind. He seeks and finds the blueprint first. In the piano concerto as well as in the sonata, the composition does not originate from thematic flashes. Waves of form decide their course.

A comparison of the different blueprints of Beethoven's work pertaining to the same genre proves the wealth and variety of his plans within the related form-scheme. How varied is the organization in the blueprints of the ten sonatas for violin and piano! Not two groundplans are identical. Of course, all of these sonatas are built on the basis of main themes. Yet the form that follows their initial statements, displays in each case striking differences of development. Again, all recapitulations in Beethoven's nine symphonies differ from each other in specific features. They differ here in the way the theme is reintroduced, there in instrumentation as in dynamics. Everywhere with Beethoven a high degree of newness is born with each new work. It is remarkable how Beethoven succeeds in accomplishing this variety, in spite of his emphasis on the classical sonata-scheme as a supreme guide.

In his synthetic work, Beethoven frequently utilizes previous ideas while he fuses new ones into his form: the old and the new attract each other in the playful teamwork of tectonics. The problem as to where to place an idea is often solvable only in later stages of creation. Thus, between work on the second and third movements of the Quartet in C Major, Op. 59, No. 3, there occur preliminary sketches for a highly characteristic theme. Had it at that time been intended for the quartet? We do not know. The theme disappeared for six years from the surface of traceable planning. Yet when Beethoven worked on the Seventh Symphony, he must have discovered that this forgotten idea functioned well in the framework of its allegretto: the melody of the elegiac A minor movement in the Seventh Symphony is nothing but the formerly discarded theme from the sketches of the C Major Quartet. . . .

. . . Generalizing, we can assume that nowhere in the development of great music can the tie-up between the total work plan and the details be ignored. In fact with many of Beethoven's scores, the first movements are commentaries on what happens in the first measures. No motif in any score in history incites the entire cyclic motion of an extended symphony as does the opening of Beethoven's Fifth. Like a turbine, the famous four notes generate the motion of the music. The structure of the inciting theme is one of utmost simplicity. It uses a design which is the favorite of all classical composers, consisting of tonic and dominant forms, reductions and cadential condensation. Yet as this scheme unfolds, we become aware of the unshakable logic of Beethoven's symphonic architecture.

As to the andante of the Fifth Symphony, we have traced the reasons which led to Beethoven's intense reworking of the theme: the onetime minuet had to be fused into the symphonic groundplan in its entirety. Even seemingly isolated ideas—striking modulations and unusual instrumentation in the Eighth Symphony, the various bird calls interpreting the voice of nature, the bubbling of the brook, lightning and thunder in the Pastoral—are all associatively inspired by the total idea. All these ideas are unthinkable detached from the fundamental plan.

The approach to the wholeness of work is again strikingly exemplified in Gluck's description of his creative procedure: "Once I am clear about the composition of the whole and about the characterization of the main parts, I consider the opera finished, although I have not yet written one single note." The whole composition occurs as a vision of the work in its totality, anticipating the total conception of the music drama. The pursuit of total ideas from memory also develops from inspiration through elaboration to synthesis. The difference lies in the fact that nothing is written down on paper. Gluck explained how the plan first fully matured in his mind and how the writing of the manuscript was but the after effect of an already completed mental elaboration:

First I go through each individual act, later through the whole work. The plan of the composition I sketch in my mind while sitting in the parterre (of the theater). Such a preparation usually takes one entire year and not rarely do I contract a severe disease upon such effort. Yet people call this composing light songs. . . .

Memory and Synthesis

MOZART HAS defined his approach to composition in words almost identical with those of Gluck: "Composed is everything, written not yet a single note." This remark, in the letter of December 30, 1780, turns up in all possible variations in Mozart's correspondence. As he explained, he became accustomed early to have "the whole in my head as it occurs in all parts." This type of brainwork remained his favorite mode of composing throughout his life. Leopold Mozart vehemently disapproved of his son's working procedure. Being a schoolmaster (though an excellent one and otherwise a pedagogue of the highest type), Leopold Mozart saw everything through the spectacles of a strict disciplinarian. Nagging, charging Wolfgang with "lack of industry," the systematic and precise father could see nothing but procrastination in such a method: no planning, hardly any sketching of the form. Nothing but the final manuscript!

But Wolfgang could not help it. His genius not only provided him with boundless inspiration but also dictated to him a specific and unchangeable approach to work. He did not, as his father complained, leave everything to the last minute. In reality, Wolfgang constantly composed. Thus he wrote to his father, July 31, 1778: "I am with music all the time, go around with it the whole day." Yet the mere final writing down into the score of already completed thoughts was to Mozart the least enjoyable part of composition. His phenomenal memory made it possible for him to postpone this job as long as possible. He felt that it was too mechanical, the least inspiring phase of his work. And what was worse, it consumed so much time—time which otherwise should have been available for new creative work. As Jahn shows in his biography, such aversion to writing down his works lasted throughout Mozart's life.

The technique of total planning and elaborating was obviously not a monopoly of the masters whose own comments we have just perused. Other composers developed their technique of work to the astonishing degree where they could not only write scores without the aid of preceding sketches, but could also put their music directly into the different parts without relying on a full score. This procedure accounts for many cases in which music has come down to us in the form of individual parts only. If full scores are missing, it does not necessarily mean that they have been lost. They may never have been written! A conductor's score was not considered indispensable at a time when the composer himself was, as a matter of routine, personally in charge of the performance of his music, frequently directing a symphony, an oratorio or an opera from the clavier. The composer knew his score; only parts for the individual instrumentalists or singers were necessary. The historic European libraries contain many manuscripts not written by the composers themselves but assembled to a full score (often at a later time) from the individual parts and by foreign hands.

Contrasts and Episodes

MUSIC HAPPENS in time. As the tonal events of the score unfold in sequence, the distribution of variety assumes added importance. Monotony is a mortal danger to the art work. The unbroken sameness of design, a similarity of acoustic experience decreases the listener's capacity for attention and may even kill his enjoyment of the music.

Variety then is an aesthetic postulate. Yet variety must not be superimposed or overdone. Too much diversity spoils the type of unity which is likewise an axiom of artistic planning. Too much of the best material leads to the unformed and chaotic. In every great art work, variety grows from its main features by way of logical development and organic contrast.

The composer achieves variety in his musical blueprint through the appropriate integration of contrasts and episodes. The painter distributes the chief contrasts of light and shadow on his canvas into the simultaneousness of visual form. But the composer must meet this problem of variety in a different manner: he has to apply his contrasts in time, placing them one after the other. In doing so, he employs contrasts to every feature of his composition.

Variety pertaining to the general organization of parts occupies the composer's attention at an early stage of synthesis. Such planning is concerned with contrast in the sequence of movements in a suite, sonata or symphony or with contrasts in the scenes and acts of an opera. Everywhere unity and variety are interdependent. They necessarily balance each other in a masterful blueprint.

Episodes are a chief means of obtaining the necessary contrast. This is so in the framework of every type of form. In contrast to the main theme, episodes are made up of material of lesser significance. They are transitory, leading from one section to another. In the fugue, the exposition of its theme is followed by an episodic transition to the next sequel of subject and answer. In dramatic music, the episodes are of particular necessity, taking on added meaning in the service of the stage action. Important episodes were often incorporated into the blueprint of an opera after the scheme had been designed in its main sections.

The order of contrasts and episodes may be firmly pre-established in the composer's mind. Yet the planned sequence of sections does not necessarily coincide with the order in which the composer actually proceeds with his score. Beethoven, by his own admission, wrote entirely out of order. Yet the result is one of unsurpassable unity. The finished score appears in a state of being one, leaving no trace of the multiple and separate attempts that led to the impressive singleness of form. Originally Beethoven concluded the scherzo of the Fifth Symphony with an authentic cadence, with a typical sequence of dominant and tonic chords in the last measures. But this version was not satisfactory: Beethoven desired a different transition through which the contrast of the oncoming finale and its tremendous strength would produce an overpowering effect. The sketches aim repeatedly at such a solution. But it was not until a late stage of work that he succeeded in finding the famous transition.

The homogeneity manifest in Mozart's opera scores would never betray the irregular procedure of composition to which they owe their existence. But the tightly knit sequence of such master scores as *Figaro*, *Don Giovanni*, *Magic Flute* came into being by the synthetic combination of independently written recitatives, arias and ensembles. The manuscript of *The Magic Flute* shows the role of instrumentation in the service of coloristic variety. Mozart had originally used trumpets and tympani not only in the overture but in the opening number of the first act as well. When he approached the composition of the brilliant scene in which the three Ladies-in-Waiting of the Queen of Night appear, Mozart desired the color of trumpets and tympani as a specific effect of splendor for this moment. He erased the respective brass and percussion parts in the preceding number, obviously to save the color of such festive instrumentation for its more fitting place. In the manuscript of *Don Giovanni*, Mozart originally employed tympani and trumpets in addition to the other instruments which accompany Leporello's Catalogue Aria. But Mozart, for reasons corresponding to those in *The Magic Flute*, later eliminated the tympani and trumpets. Neither Leporello's aria nor Tamino's opening number (in *The Magic Flute*) required these instruments. Mozart felt that they were more essential in later scenes of both works—to produce the instrumental contrast of added splendor. . . .

The Poetic Idea

WHEN BEETHOVEN, more than a century after these early essays in psychological program music, created for his Pastoral the style which he himself characterized as "more expression of feeling than painting," he was not altogether conquering new land. His chief contribution is a classical grasp of the material in which all programmatic elements are resolved in the great idea of nature. Everywhere in Beethoven's blueprints, form emerges as the central factor. Even the expansive forces of his poetic ideas are subjugated by the power and purity of his form ideal. The classical drama of the Eroica, the summer day dream of the Pastoral reveal such poetic ideas in forms of purest music. The ground-plans remain, at least in their fundamental conception, those of the classical symphony. Glorious conquests of poetic substance in the classical scheme are the piano sonata, Les Adieux, Op. 81, the three overtures to Leonore and the overtures to Coriolanus and Egmont. Beethoven's "Egmont" overture anticipates and fulfills prophetically the possibilities of dramatic expression within the blueprint of the sonata movement. Its features, kept in the iron bondage of form, concentrate on the very core of Goethe's five-act drama. The overture starts with the strong lament of the people of the Netherlands, oppressed and enslaved by foreign tyrants. In the allegro section, revolution rages. A coda of tumultuous rejoicing in liberation concludes the work. Beyond his overwhelming tonal imagination, Beethoven's greatness and guidance to posterity lies here in a self-imposed confinement. The symphonic plan reveals the sovereignty of music. The concise dramatic expression immortalized Egmont, the liberating hero.

The symphonic harvest of romantic seeds started in the autumn of classicism; the opening horn solo of Schubert's Seventh Symphony is an herald call of romanticism. The warm colors of an expressive brass, where even the trombones sing, the gentle romantic harmonies and their sighing suspensions and a slight loosening of form show the trend. The poetic factor becomes more and more entrenched, and the constructive factor loses its iron grip in the composer's workshop. In the romantic atmosphere, the purely abstract, the absolute conception of form is bound to assume a less important role. The composer's inspiration is nourished by extramusical sources in symphonic creation, too. Poetic ideas gradually take on more tangible content. Mendelssohn, Schumann, Weber and Spohr still tried to reconcile the romantic with the classical in their attempts to keep tone poetry behind the bars of traditional plans and cycles. The one-movement symphony and the four-movement symphony without break are typical products of the proverbial romantic conflict between form and content. Such works as Schumann's D Minor Symphony and Mendelssohn's Scotch Symphony preserve the traditional framework of a four-movement plan without interruption: "attaca" instructions at the end of the movements call for unbroken sequence of the main parts. Along with such steps toward a unification of the blueprint, there occur several changes in the symphonic structure such as alteration of the exposition and of the development. Mendelssohn blends the scherzo with the sonata form. In contrast to its vigorous predecessor (as Beethoven created it), the scherzo and other related types take on a sylphlike lightness. Pianissimo ensembles of woodwinds, embedded in tender brass sonorities, compete with the light and fast bowing of the strings in the irresistible spriteliness of romantic instrumentation—fairyland is entered through the middle movements of the symphony.

The scores of Weber and Spohr also show how tone poetry may benefit from the classical sonata-scheme. Still under disguising titles, a truly new form dawns—the symphonic poem. In the final romantic metamorphosis, the classical structure is overthrown. The tables are turned. Not the form, as in Beethoven's inner workshop, but the poetic content triumphs in romantic music.

Symphonic Drama Without Words

THE GREAT event in the evolution of orchestral program music during the early nineteenth century was the appearance of Berlioz's Symphonie Fantastique. It is a score incredibly audacious for 1830, the time of its completion—only three years after the death of Beethoven. In this work Berlioz blended the psychological and the naturalistic factors of program music into a unique style which he interpreted in his memoirs. A characteristic instance of his new approach is the third movement of the Fantastique, The Scene in the Country. Berlioz intended "to render the distant roll of the thunder in the middle of a peaceful atmosphere. This is not done in childish pleasure, aiming at imitation of the majestic noise. On the contary, the deep peacefulness (of this country scene) is more intensely emphasized by way of this contrast." In other words, the naturalistic imitation of the thunder on the tympani serves here only as a means to the poetic end of tranquillity and has no purpose in itself. The written word—the program attached to the score as verbal comment— fills the gap between the musical expression and the dramatic thought. As Berlioz admits, in reference to another of his program symphonies, Harold in Italy:

The author knows only too well that music cannot substitute for words or pictures. Hence, he never had the absurd idea to express (in tones) abstract or moral qualities, but only emotions or moods. He did not want to paint mountains—he simply wanted to suggest the style and the melodic form which pertains to the songs of their inhabitants or the impressions which the view of these important massives evoke.

The underlying "story" of a programmatic work may be derived from the composer's own imagination or it may stem entirely from a work of Arts and Letters. What is the influence of such a program on the ground-plan of the music? When Berlioz sketched his own scenario for the Symphonie Fantastique, he retained the classical frame for this score of hyper-romantic emotionalism and feverish dreams. His approach to the "instrumental dream without words" is based on *leit*-instruments and *leit*-melodies. Berlioz called the latter "idée fixe," by which he meant a thematic token calling for a fixed association of thoughts tied to a frequently recurring theme. Thus the "idée fixe" functions as a psychological signal—ready to direct the listener to a definite meaning within the tone poetic program.

Liszt later transplanted this symphonic-dramatic technique of Berlioz from France to Germany. What Liszt called the symphonic poem finally became the form par excellence of all orchestral program music. The blueprint of such scores as his Torquato Tasso is a typical example of a poetic program condensed into the one-movement form—with subdivisions suggested by the poem. The treatment of the *leit*-melody here shows how a principal theme lends itself to a constantly changing expression—ranging all the way from the hero's despair to his awakened hope and final triumph.

The drama of the symphony also speaks through the eternal symbols of tension and relaxation, tonally embodied in the cyclic curve. Such a symphonic curve may start in a dark and tragic minor mode, gradually leading up to the triumph and finale of a liberating major. The old Latin message, "per aspera ad astra," is the poetic connotation in works like Beethoven's Fifth and Ninth, Brahms' First, Tchaikovsky's Fourth, Liszt's Torquato Tasso and in many other romantic scores which all lead "through darkness to the stars." In the sense of Schumann's definition, these symphonies are finale symphonies. All threads of the preceding music lead to the last movements. This design also underlies the symphonies of Gustav Mahler. Here, too, the finale holds the key to the comprehension of the entire work. The message of the symphony emerges in retrospect, be it through the resurrection scene of the Second, the angelic idyll of the Fourth, the happy rondo of the Seventh or the "Farewell" in the Song of the Earth. . . .

Titles

FORM AND content of his music have guided the composer's search for the proper titles of his scores. Already a denomination such as sonata or symphony contains a certain characterization of the content of the work. Trio or quartet as titles of chamber music simultaneously indicate the performing ensemble as well as the number of participants. The same procedure prevails in vocal music. And the differentiation between terms such as duo and duet or trio and terzetto also points to differences in instrumental and vocal ensembles respectively. A trio is a chamber music work; a terzetto is a vocal number in an opera or an oratorio.

Yet in the specific tie-up with an underlying program (be it psychological or naturalistic) the choice of a title presents the imagination of the composer with a different kind of a problem. The nomenclature becomes, in a measure, also an exponent of the composer's style. It often gives away, anticipatingly, a taste of his creative approach.

Couperin points to the tie-up between the title and content in his Collection of Piano Pieces:

> In the composition of my pieces, I always had a definite objective before my eyes. The occasions . . . which suggested such an objective were of various natures, yet the titles of the pieces correspond to them. . . . The pieces pertaining to these titles were portrayals which were considered rather good likenesses, and most of the advantageous titles were to express the amiability of the originals rather than the success of my copies.

Couperin appears here as a champion of the pictorial, aphoristic and witty statement in tones. The inspiration of some of his pictures were the charming ladies of the French court, some of whom were his pupils. Other examples of Couperin's titles refer to abstract subjects such as the French national virtues and faults. Couperin's playful portrayal of concrete and abstract subjects on the keyboard points to a working method where, as the composer himself explained, the title determines the shaping of the music. The title guides the course of the work in the sense of an *a priori* given idea from which the composer approaches the total form and all details.

Frequently the situation is reversed: first the music and second the caption. The title may be only an afterthought which follows the completion of the score. The composer often finds himself in a conflict as to the proper formulation of titles:

> I have arranged the Nachtstücke—what do you think of calling them: No. 1, Funeral Procession; No. 2, Droll Company; No. 3, Nightly Carousel; No. 4, Round with Solo Voices? While I was composing I kept seeing funerals, coffins and unhappy despairing faces; and when I had finished and was trying to think of a title, the only one that occurred to me was Funeral Fantasia. I was so much moved by the composition that the tears came to my eyes.

Schumann, in these words to Clara, asks her advice concerning the choice of headings for his completed music. Elsewhere he explains, however, why he considers titles desirable at all: "There are secret states of the soul where a hint of the composer through words can lead to a faster understanding and must be gratefully accepted." Yet Schumann makes it unmistakably clear that no title can ever add to the quality of the music itself. And he suggests an easy test: one had only to leave out the titles in order to examine the effects and value of the musical product. Yet the programmatic intent of a considerable part of Schumann's music remains beyond doubt. Fanciful titles such as Carnival, Scenes from Childhood, Forest Scenes, Bird as Prophet, Kreisleriana point to Schumann's romantic brand of psychological program music. Often, as in Carnival, the program is hidden in mystification while the tonal play achieves an absolute beauty far beyond the need of a nomenclature. The stylistic position of Schumann as a composer of program music is idealistic: he creates his scores quite differently from the naturalistic musician who relentlessly unveils the essence of his program. This latter type is represented best by the programmatic works of Liszt and his scores of decorative realism. Liszt captures his content through the pictorial craft of naturalistic imitation and tonal suggestion.

The relationship between title and tonal content presents a specific problem in the workshop of the "absolute" musician. Due to his stylistic position, he will frequently consider a title a mere superimposition on his music—an extramusical association. But this contradicts the intent of the composer who wishes to remain "absolutely" free and sovereign in his play of beautiful tonal sensations. The composer of this type of music is apt to avoid all romantic nomenclature and resorts to headings which are mere generalities.

In the light of these observations, it is not surprising that Brahms, whenever confronted with the task of christening his music, found himself in a dilemma. Already as a young and romantic composer (1854), he wanted to give a work the long and involved tilte of Leaves from the Diary of a Musician Edited by the Young Kreisler. But Joachim convinced Brahms that such pseudonyms and mystifications had become hackneyed. As late as 1880 Brahms consulted with Elisabeth Herzogenberg: "Do you know a better title than Two Rhapsodies for the Pianoforte? The alternative would be Klavierstücke, a term which betrays nothing." The advice of the friend was to let it go with the "foggy dress" which Brahms gladly accepted. In the same year, Brahms asked his friends Deiters and Scholz for a more attractive name than Academic Festival Overture and a "prettier title" than the Tragic Overture. Yet, as we know, nothing "prettier" suited the heavy-hearted man. Referring to some of his latest works, the piano pieces, Op. 116 and 117, Brahms was "not clear whether to name them Monologues or Improvisations." He was finally persuaded to abandon both titles and chose Fantasias for

Op. 116 and Intermezzi for Op. 117. The scores, Op. 118 and 119, he called in a more neutral fashion, Klavierstücke. As always, Brahms preferred the understatement. He would rather say too little than too much in order not to steer the listener's imagination into any pictorial sidetracks.

QUESTIONS

1. What does Dorian mean by "thematic flashes"? How do these differ from "waves of form"? Try showing the relationship of these expressions to painting, poetry, architecture.
2. Listen to the first movement of Beethoven's Fifth Symphony. Can you count the number of times the opening four-note motive is repeated in this movement? Does the repetition become boring or interesting? Why?
3. Discuss the possibility that composing a musical work in your head (as Mozart and Gluck did) is much like composing a speech in your head. How do you plan a speech without writing anything down? Can it be done? How? What are the difficulties?
4. What does Dorian mean by "leit-instruments"? How do these differ from a "leit-motive"? How are they the same? Look up the term "leit-motive." With which composer's work is the term usually associated? Why?
5. Listen to a rondo. Can you grasp the structure of this work? Are you aware of some musical idea that keeps coming back? Look up the word "ritornello" and discuss its relation to the rondo.

ABSOLUTE MUSIC   *Sir Donald Francis*
Tovey (1875-1940), composer and teacher, is best
known for his excellent essays in musical analysis.
In 1914 he became Reid Professor of Music at the
University of Edinburgh, succeeding Frederick Niecks.
Tovey's musicianship and scolarship are impeccable.
In addition to the ten books he completed between
1931 and 1939, he contributed most of the articles on
music to the Encyclopaedia Britannica. *In the*
following essay Tovey, in his characteristically
warm style, discusses the principal chamber music
ensembles and the music written for them.

CHAMBER MUSIC

DONALD F. TOVEY

EVERY PECULIARITY OF THE PIANO IS IN KEEPING with the new and dramatic spirit which entered into all kinds of music from the operas of Gluck to the symphonies and string quartets of Haydn. To those who have in modern times been thrilled by the rediscovery of the organ-like richness of plain two-part writing on a harpsichord with 4-foot and 16-foot registers in play, nothing in the history of the sonata style is more surprising than the cheerfulness with which Mozart and Haydn accepted the renunciation of all attempts to apply such registers to the piano. Henceforth no written note was to represent more sounds than that of its own name and octave. The enrichment of harmony by doubling in octaves must be achieved by individual human fingers or players, and not by mechanical couplers. On the other hand, the sustaining of harmony was no longer exclusively the work of individual fingers; a pedal could prevent the dampers from stopping the sound when the fingers left the key, and so an arpeggio of single notes might leave behind a chord vibrating throughout four or five octaves with a rich and slowly evanescent sound transparent to all other instrumental tones. Thus the sonata ideals of chamber music and the style of the piano stimulated each other, and speedily determined the criteria which are valid from the time of Haydn to the present day. These classical criteria may be formulated under two headings, as follows:

I. Chamber music is music in large forms for a group of solo instruments on equivalent planes of tone and of equivalent musical capacity. The planes of tone need not be the same; on the contrary, the value of the piano in chamber music depends largely on its being inevitably on a different plane from all other instruments, but it has no difficulty in refraining from shattering the ensemble like a trumpet or a trombone, and the ear takes pleasure in low notes on a 'cello as a bass to full chords on the piano, the difference of plane being essential to the special effect. The introduction of the singing voice into the scheme, as in Schönberg's second string quartet and sextet, introduces a non-equivalent plane of tone, and accordingly goes beyond the classical criteria. A further step, both as to planes of tone and non-equivalence of musical resource, is shown in Schönberg's *Pierrot Lunaire*, where the singer is required to follow a prescribed rise and fall of pitch in a

CHAMBER MUSIC by Donald Francis Tovey from *Cobbett's Cyclopedic Survey of Chamber Music*, Volume 1; copyright 1929-30 by the Oxford University Press, Inc. Reprinted by permission.

Absolute Music / Tovey

speaking voice, carefully avoiding definite musical notes. In the opposite direction, Cyril Scott and Arthur Bliss use the singing voice without words in an instrumental ensemble.

The question of equivalent musical capacity was frequently raised in classical masterpieces by the use of the double-bass. In a mature style of chamber music this instrument, which, with the best of playing, cannot compete effectively with other stringed instruments in cantabile passages, justifies its existence as a support to large groups, especially such as contain wind instruments, as in Beethoven's septet and Schubert's octet. Even so, it associates itself naturally with the lighter and looser style of art typified by the serenades and divertimenti of Mozart. Early in the nineteenth century, Onslow, a prolific writer of chamber music, having occasion to use a double-bass as a makeshift for a 'cello, found the effect so satisfactory that he wrote numerous quintets for two violins, viola, 'cello, and double-bass. It is not clear from his notation in what octave he means the double-bass to play. Even in Dvořák's far more highly organized quintet in G, the double-bass does not seem quite at ease in the drawing-room, and its one shy cantabile remark in the minuet of Goetz's piano quintet is a pathetic triumph of unconscious humour.

Stravinsky's introduction of drums, trombones, and similar artillery into chamber music marks another new epoch with new criteria. What these criteria may be, we shall know when a propagandist arises who can convince us that a totally unprepared extemporization by a dozen players will not pass muster with him as a masterpiece of modern music. Stravinsky knows what he is doing; and experimental art is more important than experimental propaganda.

II. Chamber music requires no more than the number of players for whom individual parts are written; and every note written is intended to be heard. We have seen that chamber music before 1760 did not aim at this criterion; it was created with infinite labour by Haydn. The masters who may be taken as realizing it instinctively and imaginatively from first to last are Mozart, Beethoven, and Brahms. All who have attempted to write chamber music approximate to it at their best moments. But we may here profitably glance at some typical cases where music, otherwise beautiful and important, shows a defective sense of this criterion. It is interesting to note, by the way, that the criterion is never more severely maintained than in the most experimental works of the present day. Indeed, the desire to experiment with non-equivalent planes of tone and non-equivalent musical capacities goes naturally with the utmost sensitiveness to the individuality of each instrument. It is rather to the immediate successors of Beethoven that we must turn for examples of the confusion of thought natural to men who feel secure in a classical tradition not of their own making. Certain tremolo passages in the string quartets of Mendelssohn are often, and not unfairly, quoted as bad examples of orchestral writing in chamber music. But here we must beware of a worse confusion of thought than Mendelssohn's. There is no harm whatever in one kind of good music sounding like another kind, if it has the virtues of both kinds.

If any good orchestral sounds can be realized by a string quartet, so much the better for the quartet. What is wrong with Mendelssohn's tremolos is that they are conceived mechanically on the analogy of orchestral passages, and carried to lengths which only an orchestra could make acceptable. On paper the storm in the development of the first movement of Beethoven's quartet, op. 74, looks quite as coarse, but it would at the outset be far too thick for orchestral writing, and its wonderful diminuendo is all drawn exactly to scale in a quartet which, as a whole, is one of the most ethereal compositions ever written. The same praise is due to such apparently crude simplicities as the stiff minims with which the violins and 'cello accompany the viola solo in the second variation of the finale. Dante or Milton never surpassed that calm—

"They also serve who only stand and wait."

We are on less slippery ground in dealing with the integrity of the parts in classical chamber music. An honest violinist will be compelled to say that the second violin part of a Mendelssohn quartet is more interesting than that of one by Mozart. But this does not make Mendelssohn a better quartet-writer than Mozart. His work is on such a much larger scale that it often droops and fails, like the full-sized machine of an inventor who does not realize that its powers do not increase in the ratio of its bulk to that of the working model. The sympathetic but critical study of Schumann's chamber music will show more clearly where the criterion applies. With a full and sonorous piano style, he has even more than Haydn's curious inability to refrain from putting into the piano part all that the other parts have to say. Indeed, he has altogether lost the power of sorting out his material into its proper planes, and the exquisite first trio of the scherzo of the piano quartet is in such a tangle of useless and arbitrary doublings that it is impossible to discover the persons of the dialogue. Mozart, Beethoven, and Brahms would have delighted in making it stand out as a beautiful dialogue between five singing parts, the three strings and the pianist's right and left hand, with no confusion between these parts and the supporting chords to which each instrument would contribute between its own distinct entries with the themes. It is impossible to argue that there is aesthetic value in Schumann's unclarified scoring of this passage. The piano quartet is more highly organized than its delightful and popular brother the quintet. But the perversity of inattention to the integrity of parts can hardly be more clearly demonstrated than by the fact that, while the string parts of the quintet are such a primitive mass of harmony that there is no reason why they should not be arranged for quartet, sextet, or string orchestra, the opening of the piano quartet shows serious practical reasons why it should have been a quintet!

We must not confuse the criteria of mere part-writing with those of the treatment of an instrument as a whole. There is no reason why a string quartet should not, by means of double stops, produce a passage that effectively imitates an octet. But there is no excuse for making a string quartet play for pages together in such masses of double stops that there is no more evidence of four individual players than in a piano four-hand duet. It is no defence that such writing (as in Grieg's G minor quartet) is "effective"; to prolong it is to do a ridiculously easy thing at the expense of all higher possibilities. César Franck's string quartet is in this way a disappointment to every one who can appreciate the essential, if sometimes harmlessly orchestral, quintuplicity of his great piano quintet. The string quartet is full of excellent organ music, and it imitates the organ very skilfully. But, except for the scherzo, which is full of anybody's brilliance, there is strangely little evidence that it is a quartet at all.

These criteria are unquestionably correct, whatever disputes may arise as to their application. In conclusion, it may be as well to enumerate, and occasionally comment on, some of the principal combinations used in chamber music, beginning with Haydn.

I. Duets

(a) Two violins: magnificently exploited by Spohr, whom the severe discipline of this problem stimulated to his best work.

(b) Violin and viola, represented by two masterpieces of Mozart written to help Michael Haydn to complete the execution of a commission for six. The extra low fifth of the viola greatly eases the pressure on an imagination confined by the violin to a bass no lower than its open G.

(c) Two 'cellos: a magnificent medium, very sonorous in spite of its severe restrictions, and very little explored.

(d) Piano and violin. The most frequently attempted form of chamber music, and by far the most treacherous. The progress, from the use of the violin as a hardly necessary accompaniment to its perfect partnership in the ensemble, is beautifully shown in the works of Mozart's childhood, from his seventh year to his twelfth. There is a gap between these and his adult sonatas. With occasional lapses, his later sonatas, like Beethoven's, make severe but legitimate demands on the players' and listeners' capacity to focus the two planes of tone into one picture. For this reason duets for

(e) Piano and 'cello are much easier to write when it occurs to a composer to attempt them. There are far fewer 'cello sonatas of all kinds than violin sonatas in existence; but a much larger proportion of the former is good.

(f) Piano and a wind instrument. Here, as with other combinations, the horn and the clarinet have had the best chances, the flute being inconveniently weak for the piano, the oboe being apt to pall when not frequently relieved by other tones, and the bassoon being insufficiently appreciated except as a comedian, though Mozart wrote a sonata for 'cello and bassoon. Technical limitations, even when so severe as those of the natural horn, do not hamper the composer's imagination once it has been stirred, but he is absolutely inhibited by the suspicion of an incompatibility of tone.

II. Trios

(a) String trios for violin, viola, and 'cello are a rare tour de force not necessarily less valuable than string quartets. Mozart's divertimento— trio in E flat—is a marvel of euphony, and proceeds for pages together without a double stop. Beethoven's string trios are among the very greatest works of his first period.

(b) Trios for two violins and 'cello are mostly the aftermath of the continuo period.

(c) Trios for piano, violin, and 'cello. Of all combinations with piano this is the one that has stimulated composers to the finest results. Haydn's trios, imperfect as they are in point of integrity of parts, are full of his grandest forms and most pregnant ideas. Mozart sets the standard with his inevitable schematic accuracy. The autographs of his trios are written in a way that shows to the eye one of the important normal criteria of the style. He writes the violin above and the 'cello below the piano. And with all their rich subsequent developments of piano style, both Beethoven and Brahms retained the idea of the 'cello as an independent bass below the piano, but, like Mozart, giving it freedom to mount to its highest regions, and neglecting none of its possibilities.

The ordinary notation which puts the violin and 'cello together above the piano expresses another fact about the combination: viz. that when the piano is combined with two or more instruments, these tend to form a single antiphonal body of tone. This is equally the case when a wind instrument enters the combination; the three distinct planes of tone separate easily and naturally into two groups; namely, the piano and the other two instruments. Some of the combinations represented by important works are:

(d) Piano, clarinet, and violin (Mozart);
(e) Piano, clarinet, and violoncello (Brahms, Beethoven);
(f) Piano, violin, and horn (Brahms).

The piano and two wind instruments have also been successfully combined, the softest combination being with clarinet and horn. Publishers are reluctant to undertake the sale of such works unless alternative arrangements for more usual instruments are provided. When the composer executes these with freedom, the results are extremely instructive, both where they succeed and where they fail to give an adequate translation of the original.

(g) Among curious trio combinations mention should be made of Beethoven's tour de force for two oboes and cor anglais, a full-sized four-movement work within the compass of less than three octaves and with no possibility of a chord in more than three parts. His jocular serenade for flute, violin, and viola has inspired Reger to two essays in this slender combination.

III. *Quartets*

(a) In the string quartet for two violins, viola, and 'cello we have the purest and highest revelation of chamber music and perhaps of all music. Its criteria need no further discussion here.

(b) The flute and the oboe have each been deliciously combined with strings in short works by Mozart.

(c) Quartets for piano and strings are surprisingly rare considering the popularity of the existing classical examples. Mozart's two masterpieces should have belonged to a set of six. They show with the utmost clearness the principle of setting the strings in antiphonal mass against the piano, and are at the same time exquisitely polyphonic. Later publishers tried to atone for former errors by arranging Mozart's clarinet quintet, D major string quintet, and quintet for piano and wind, as piano quartets. Nothing can be learnt from these.

Apart from three juvenile essays, Beethoven's only piano quartet is an arrangement of his quintet for piano and wind, op. 16. The piano part is unchanged, but the string parts are full of excellent new detail inserted during the long rests of the wind instruments, these rests being unnecessary for string players.

Mendelssohn's three juvenile quartets are wonderful for a boy of thirteen, and the third, in B minor, has many intrinsic merits. After this there is nothing important, except the beautiful Schumann quartet, before the masterpieces of Brahms.

IV. Quintets

(a) String quintets differ little from quartets. The favourite extra instrument is a second viola, but, apart from the merely decorative works of the 'cellist Boccherini, the combination with a second 'cello is revealed as a majestic art form by Schubert in his great C major quintet.

(b) The clarinet makes a glorious combination with a string quartet, as has been shown by Mozart and Brahms. Mozart also wrote a charming little quintet for the curious combination of one violin, two violas, 'cello, and horn. His most unclassifiable quintet is the adagio and rondo for flute, oboe, viola, 'cello, and glass harmonica, evidently a most skilfully planned combination.

(c) Quintets for wind instruments present a peculiar problem, especially centred in the group of the five different members, flute, oboe, clarinet, horn, and bassoon. Even under the stimulus of a prize competition, nothing great has been achieved, though an extraordinary amount has been written for this combination. Towards the middle of the nineteenth century that ingenious calculating machine, Reicha, turned out an incredible number of such quintets. He was too sure of his ground either to fail in securing euphony or to show why he took all this trouble. The great composers have not been attracted by the problem of making coherent chords out of five utterly different timbres, and the only time Mozart combined the flute with another wind instrument in chamber music was when he also employed the glass harmonica. The term "wind quintet" suggests to lovers of classical music a work of very different calibre, namely, Mozart's glorious quintet for piano, oboe, clarinet, horn, and bassoon. Beethoven's early and easygoing imitation of this is also well known, especially in his above-mentioned arrangement as a quartet for piano and strings. With Mozart the oboe leads, and with Beethoven the clarinet.

(d) Piano quintets, i.e. quintets for piano and string quartet, differ in no important aesthetic point from piano quartets. It is surprising how few have been written, and how abnormal is the position of those that are known as classics. Schubert's comparatively early *Forellen* quintet is a voluminous and loose-knit serenade in five movements. Schumann's, the most popular of all, has, as already noted, no inner necessity to be written for a quintet rather than for a quartet or sextet or any larger combination. The masterpiece of Brahms, which sets a pure standard for the style, attained its final form only after a chequered existence, first as a quintet for strings with two 'cellos, and then as a sonata for two pianos.

V. Sextets, &c.

(a) The two glorious masterpieces of Brahms for two violins, two violas, and two 'cellos are unmistakably inspired by the example of Schubert's great string quintet. (b) Octets for strings, i.e. four violins, two violas, and two 'cellos have tendencies to top-heaviness and internal congestion. Spohr accordingly hit upon the device of double quartets, for two string quartet groups treated antiphonally. The genius of the boy Mendelssohn had, however, already discovered at the age of fifteen that two hundred and fifty odd antiphonal combinations are more interesting than Spohr's pair, and so he enjoyed himself without scruple in his octet, and communicated his enjoyment to others.

(c) Most of the larger combinations of chamber music result from the grouping of strings with more than one wind instrument. The effect is often said to be semi-orchestral, but this is a mere illusion arising from the fact that wind instruments are seldom heard outside the orchestra, which they therefore suggest to the hearer. As a criterion, it is on a level with that of the backwoods critic who regretted that so superior a composition as Beethoven's op. 59, no. 1, had not been played by a larger band. The character of works like Beethoven's septet and Schubert's glorification of the same scheme and combination as an octet (with the addition of a second violin) is neither orchestral nor hybrid, and in the one point where they differ from the purest chamber music, the introduction of the double-bass, the effect is essentially different from that of an orchestral bass. The style was perfectly understood by Mozart and Haydn, the serenades and divertimenti of Mozart being on every sort of scale, and sometimes for the queerest combinations. Such works are often voluminous, Beethoven's and Schubert's schemes of six movements with grand introductions to first movement and finale being typical, but the style is festive and the texture loose. In fact, the brilliant fixed contrasts of tone between the various instruments of these combinations go best with as light a style as the grand sonata forms will allow. The very terms serenade and divertimento suggest as much, and if the notion of chamber music is widened to tolerate the heavy-footed double bass, it may as well also allow the first violin to behave more like the solo instrument in a concerto than would be seemly in a string quartet.

(d) Compositions for wind instruments alone are most successful when pairs of each kind are taken; otherwise the balance of every chord is a tour de force. The greatest works in this line are Mozart's two octets for two oboes, two clarinets, two horns, and two bassoons. Both are entitled serenades (like all Mozart's works for wind instruments alone), but the one in C minor is a grand and pathetic work, full of wonderful counterpoint and a most un-serenade-like seriousness. It is led throughout by the oboes, the tone of which becomes very fatiguing to the ear even with the finest playing. Perhaps this is why Mozart afterwards arranged it as a string quintet, in which form it is well known. The other octet is led by the clarinets, and, though far slighter, can thus be far more easily produced. But the fact that Mozart is said to have first expanded it from a sextet by adding the oboes, and afterwards to have added two cors anglais, shows that we are leaving the region of a chamber music that tolerates no vagueness as to the number of players. The limit is reached in the same composer's glorious serenade for two oboes, two clarinets, two basset horns (alto clarinets), four horns, two bassoons, and contra-fagotto or double-bass.

Beethoven's works for wind instruments tell us only what he could learn from Mozart, and to pursue the subject into later times would be to lose our thread in a mass of detail.

QUESTIONS

1. What are the essential differences between the chamber music ensemble and the symphony orchestra? Does the size of the group affect the kind of music the group can play? How is it affected?
2. Is there such a thing as vocal chamber music? Can you name any vocal chamber works? What determines whether or not you have such a work?
3. Can you name any instruments that have not been used in chamber music ensembles? What accounts for an instrument being used, or not being used?
4. What does Tovey mean when he says that certain piano quartets should have been quintets? Why does he think there ought to be an additional player? What does he mean by "the integrity of the parts?"
5. Check up on the seating arrangements of various chamber groups: string trio, string quartet, piano trio, piano quartet. Can you suggest why the players sit in these positions? Would other seating arrangements do as well? Why?

THE SYMPHONY   *Between 1900 and
1921 Philip H. Goepp, a Philadelphia lawyer,
organist, teacher, and writer, wrote the program
notes for the Philadelphia Orchestra concerts. One
result of this employment was a series of books
by Goepp entitled Symphonies and their Meanings.
In this essay Goepp tried to show that the symphony
(characterized as music to be played rather than sung)
grew out of man's desire to express himself in tones as
well as in words. Though many writers on music may
not agree with Goepp's thesis, his essay is nonetheless
stimulating, strongly presenting one provocative view.*

INTRODUCTION TO
THE SYMPHONY

PHILIP H. GOEPP

ART, IT WOULD SEEM, BEGINS ITS CAREER, LIKE MAN, by leaning on another. Thus, sculpture was first subordinate to architecture. Painting, in turn, was the foster-child of sculpture, in the beginning merely tracing outlines and features, much like an infant writing with guided hand. Music in Greece followed slavishly the metre of the poetry. In the early church, before Gregory, the words of the liturgy were intoned with complete subservience to the rhythm of the verse, so that agreement of singing was possible only when the chorus followed the arbitrary leader.

It is most valuable to see clearly the final evolution of the independent art of absolute instrumental music as the latest link in this chain. Leaning on the words and story of the drama, music developed, on the stage of the opera, melody, and its accompaniment in tones colored by various blending and contrasting instruments. She was preparing her pallet. In the church, following the lead of the service, music was exploring all the possibilities of polyphonic combination and of architectural complexity by algebraic computation. But in neither church service nor in opera was she progressing unaided. Of course, walking with a cane is different from depending on a guiding parent. So differs the music of Palestrina from that of Ambrose. But even in the great Bach's works music had not thrown away all her supports. She first learned to tread her independent course, speaking her message purely in her own language of tones unaided by words, when she lisped the first sonata, which, in orchestral dress, is the symphony.

It must be remembered that the entire growth of the art of music, and what was really the slow manufacture of its elements and forms, was wrought within the Church. This development began when to the unison chant was added the servile accompaniment of a second voice, keeping always its unaltered respectful distance. It ended when all the changes of fugal counterpoint had been rung with mathematical ingenuity. But until modern centuries there had not been a thought of music without words, of unsung music. When the absurdly artificial forms were abandoned by mutinous singers, the organ took the place of the unwilling voice and invited further composition for its special performance.

But this had nothing in common with secular instrumental music

INTRODUCTION TO THE SYMPHONY from *Symphonies and Their Meanings* by Philip H. Goepp; J. B. Lippincott Co.; 1897.

The Symphony / Goepp

and its origin. For the elements, we must go back to the strange attempts at opera by Italian amateurs. The very convenient date of the first opera—1600—is an excellent landmark in gauging the growth of unsung secular music—the year when Peri's *Eurydice* was produced in Florence. It is in the formless preludes and interludes of the players that the germ of the symphony lies. The first conception of flowing *cantabile* melody, which is the very fibre and tissue of every movement, came in the early opera. (There is absolutely no kinship between this *melody* and the fugal *theme* of the church school.) With these the dance, of obscure origin, completes the foundation on which sonatas and symphonies were reared.

If we enter the forge in which these materials were being welded into the great forms of the symphony—in other words, if we study the precursors of the masters—we find, indeed, little promise of intellectual significance, or, for that matter, of pleasurable amusement. But, in art, periods of exclusively formal growth always lack imaginative power. It is like latent heat, when ice changes to water. Great men, it would seem, are content with the form they find, hiding the lines with their fulness of thought. Shallower minds, sensitive to popular demand, tinker at new devices of outward novelty. Thus, Sebastian Bach did not find the sonata sufficiently perfected. Haydn was the first master to approve. Therefore, in a review of the history of musical thought rather than of musical structure, it may fairly be said that the sonata and the whole school of secular instrumental music did not begin before Haydn.

The analogy between Bach and the secular masters is striking. In his earlier generation he found nothing but the strict forms of the church school. He gave them their essential artistic purpose; he crowned their development by endowing them with the highest expression of religious feeling. When a master thus reaches the greatest height, a lower level must be started in another direction, leading to a second master.

If we take a survey of this new stream of worldly composition— melodies with artificial accompaniment, digressions of rippling scales or tripping arpeggios and suddenly intruding crashes of full chords—and contrast it with what is found in the church school with its precise, dignified, and elaborate structure of voices, independent in melody, yet interdependent in harmony, the question comes, What new spirit moves here? How can there be, almost at the same time, two opposite phases of the same art, both honored by the greatest masters?

Clearly, here is the latest, though not the weakest, wave of the Renaissance pulse. The same rebellion against the all-absorbing intellectual domination of the Church, the same resistless wave of earthly feeling and its expression, apparent in painting and in the literatures of England, France, and Italy, is here manifest in the youngest of the arts.

Why the movement is so late in music need not be discussed beyond saying that the art was jealously and exclusively fostered by the Church. All its forms, its whole framework had been devised solely for worship. An entirely new garb must be created before it could venture from the cloister into the gay world without great awkwardness and stiffness. Much depth of feeling or intellectual emphasis must not be expected of the first century of this new phase. The early works show their reactionary origin by utter frivolity and shallowness. Until an actual fitting form was obtained, there was a constant striving after a satisfaction of this very need, a self-conscious kind of emphasis of mere sound; the composer sought to fill in as many black notes as possible.

The beginning of Haydn's career marks the final attainment of this form, and at the same time a sudden spring of true poetic feeling. The result was what is commonly called the sonata, which is really what we are considering; for a symphony is nothing else than a sonata written for the orchestra. In the light of the absolute newness of unsung music is seen the fitness of the name "sonata," that which is merely sounded, in contrast with that which is sung, the "cantata." Nowhere, I venture to say, in any phase of art, is the shock greater than of this burst from the sombre, confined, careful, intellectual process of the cloister to the free, irresponsible fancy dancing first over the meadows and in the forests, then into the life of men, the turmoil and the triumph of war, the romance and ecstasy of human affection.

It is clear, then, why the expected order—first of the less defined, second of the more clearly significant phase of the art—should be reversed. Within the cloister music had reached a high and complex power of expression of those feelings which were there sanctioned. Without, all was new and vague; there were no words or forms of expression for the new life. It must begin with the ABC of a new language. To condemn the first fruits of this stage for lack of definiteness of meaning would be to misunderstand the very purpose of all art. While definite language is not impossible to art, this is not its chief function; no more is mere beauty of outline. If a sentiment be expressed and transmitted, the medium of its transmission will be entitled to its place as an art of form. The language of prose has not the power thus to express and transmit all sentiment, though it may entitle its field in a rough sort of way. What prose cannot, the other arts must do, each in its peculiar region, not, perhaps, without encroaching mutually. Each art, beginning with primordial feelings, will translate more and more delicate shades in a constantly refining process, the form always reacting on the sentiment and suggesting an advance.

This must account for the vagueness of the earlier great works for instruments. But even in Haydn the pastoral element, the poetry of nature, discovered anew, is unmistakable, as is the peculiar playfulness of his humor. In fact, the appearance of humor of any kind in music in the eighteenth century is as absolutely new as anything can be under the sun. Imagine how utterly inconceivable it would have been to the long line, stretching through many centuries, of the worthy fosterers of music in the Church.

The sonata was said by a German critic to be intended by the earliest writers to show in the first movement what they could do, in the second what they could feel, in the last how glad they were to have finished. The simplicity of this interpretation—and no doubt it is accurate— emphasizes the vagueness of the real sentiment. In the hands of great men the form very soon attained a much more dignified plan.

In technicalities the essence is often lost. There is no value in analysis in itself. Yet a clear view of the general purpose is not dimmed by a glance at those elements which have in them more than mere technical value. The question is not merely what is the general purpose of the symphony, but what is the special value of the accepted model in carrying out this purpose. And, as has been said above, the first requisite in the listener is an intelligent grasp of the work.

In short, what is the essential of the much-mentioned sonata form; of the outline of the other movements; indeed, of the structure of the whole? A few relentless *wherefores* will bring us to the right point of attack. Nor can the answer lie in a technical statement of theme, of development, of tonality, and so on. But the one clear and grateful approach is by an historic view, where we see the need—the real *raison d'être*—of each cardinal element.

In the first place, the main stress of the symphony—indeed, of most absolute music—is centered on what is called the sonata form. It is the mould in which is cast the first movement: the serious burst of aspiring thought. The second, to be sure, is of no less dignity. But it is in complete contrast with the stress and strife, the stirring progress of the first. It is a calm lyric utterance from the high level to which the first mood has ascended. It does not need the discussion of the other. Simplicity of statement in the verses of a song is its natural utterance. Nowhere is the depth of genius of the highest master better shown than in the Andante—that profound, broad sympathy of Beethoven, distinct from the statuesque pathos of Haydn, or the stately grace of Mozart. Here was reflected Beethoven's highest trait, that which bound men to him most strongly. In the third phase the feeling of relaxation is undoubted, and, fittingly, the form, even in the highest flights, is based on the dance. The mood has passed from the spirit's stir and spring through pathos to humor. In its original conception this effect of relief, of restraint from the tension of the early movements, was continued in the last. A form peculiarly fitting for careless joy existed in the Rondo, where the melody appeared and vanished with graceful interludes, which later developed into lesser tunes. Discussion was supplanted by a constant, playful alternation of the various melodies. As the symphony grew a more serious utterance of poetic feeling, the last movement often rose to a second climax; and—here appears the meaning of form and of detail—the rondo yielded then to the Sonata type.

What, then, was this sonata form? What are the elements of its power for this new poetic expression?

Again, in the historic view, it is at once amusing, pathetic, and enlightening to see the struggles which preceded the great discovery. In Bach's time the approved form was the suite of dances, transplanted from the itinerant street-players to the new clavichord or newer pianoforte. At best this was a mere series of unrelated dances, idealized, to be sure, with expansion and polyphonic treatment. It was the holiday music of the learned musician, his only secular vent; and it afforded the special form for a kind of public tournament between rival players and composers. But, with the best intention to be worldly, there was over it the stern, ascetic, intellectual stamp of the Church spirit. What was the reaction of treatment which must answer the reaction of secular feeling?

The peculiar quality, as in the strict Church forms, was an unrelieved *monothemism*. Impressed with the traditional simple theme of counterpoint, men could not escape it; they lacked the artistic conception of the dual element, of balance, of contrast. The mystery, the strangeness, is that, not to speak of the eventual solution, the need itself was not clear. And unless we can see the very need, we cannot grasp the full meaning of the sonata and symphony.

In a general way, it was felt, there must be rebellion against the Church process—no more learned counterpoint; no textual theme frugally sounded without harmonic surroundings, like the verse of a sermon; no eternal ringing of its relentless burden, like the doom of dogma without a hint of repose, of cadence—on and on, the voices ever multiplying the warning phrase to a final massive climax of solemn architecture. Away with it all! There must be no taint of fugue in the new spirit. . . .

Now see the features of this new expression as they carry out this new feeling. There must be a better and simpler meaning for our technical big words. What seems the first, the most significant, the most potent, is a clear sense of harmonic residence, what the musicians call tonality, as against the gray color, in the fugue, of a key vague until the end. Again, it seems, there is the impulse to utter a sense of worldly repose, in defiance of the constant strife in the fugue, which knew no rest until the final end.

Nowhere is this constrast clearer than in the piano works of Sebastian Bach and of Domenico Scarlatti. They were contemporaries, almost to the year. But Scarlatti had caught the earthly spirit in sunny Italy, under the inspiration of his father Alessandro, the founder of the new *aria*. Bach, somehow, could never get clear of the shadow of the cloister. With the German his dance-moods are still o'ercast with the pale hue of meditation. He was glancing out of doors through the windows of his study. The Italian was roving with a firm foot in the fields; he was ringing out his tintinnabulations with clearest note of tonal serenity and certainty—still always the same one tune. He could have but a single idea at a time; no broad sense of balance, of contrast, of perspective. On such a basis there could never rise a structure of much serious dignity. But this is not all.

We must see, too, the strange alternative of the qualities of *Bach* and of *Scarlatti*: of vague reflections and of clear tonal simplicity. It seems that tonality must be at the expense of depth. The voices were borrowed for harmonic subservience, and must cease to discuss the theme. In a sense they were degraded from counsellors to train-bearers. So, in an ideal sense, there was a temporary loss of dignity. But this simplicity was after all a gain.

So far the elements are the same of the other secular moulds, of the song, the dance, and the rondo. We have not yet come to the final typical trait of the strict sonata. It was a reconciliation of the various needs: first, of this tonality, the sense of certain harmonic location; second, of relief from monotony of single melody, a sense of duality; finally, of a quality which had been too completely lost with the fugue.

And this very stirring search has shown what a peculiar place the fugue filled. Let us return, for a thought, before the days of unsung music. Our art is still walking hand in hand with her older sister Poetry, but unmanageable, restless. One day a master dreams his melody for the instrument alone. Now it is clear that music must somehow atone for the new want of words. A song deprived of words is and remains incomplete. The clear meaning is gone, there is mere vacant beauty. Here begins the stir for a definite language of pure tones. And this is significant, too: none of the older forms were the achievement of music itself, its self-found utterance. They are foreign; they belonged to poetry, like the song, or to the dance, like the minuet. See, therefore, how this new *sonata* form is actually the first proper mode of expression of the pure art of music. *It says something in mere tones.*

From another point of view, the half-conscious want of the early masters in their search was this: they were dissatisfied with mere lyric burst, mere singing of the tune; *they must talk about it; they must get somewhere.* They quickly felt that melody was, after all, mere theme or text; there was no progress until you discussed it.

This element of discussion, of progress, which, in a sense, had been lost in the fugue, now achieved in a novel way, was the crowning virtue of the new form for sonata and symphony. So here is the problem: to express the definiteness which had been lost with the words; to go beyond mere striking of the melody; to start the pace for a genuine art, which, beyond creating pretty phrases, will find a language for ever deepening and ever differentiating shades of feeling, approaching the clearness of verbal thought. Finally, in the structure of the whole work will lie the art-form, which will build and co-ordinate in supplementary moods one homogeneous expression of a great emotional idea.

How this special purpose of discussion was carried out, the need being clear, will be easily seen; further, too, how each element—of tonality, of duality, of discussion—reinforced the other.

The final achievement was this:

A melody begins with clear intonation of the key, by harmonic sounding of the main chord. It is succeeded presently by a second, which is contrasted in every way—in character, in movement, and in key. Now see how duality helps tonality. Black is black, after all, only in contrast with white. So the original tonic key is not really clear, until a departure into the complementary dominant, with the second melody. Thus the contrast, with well-marked cadence, sharpens the effect of each.

When the two melodies have been stated, there is, of course, a sojourn, a cadence, in the complementary key, the dominant. This in itself invites a return homeward to the original, or tonic. At the same time, the clearness of stated melodies is assured by a repetition from the beginning. And now the story really begins: the characters are described; now they act and talk; the several musical ideas are discussed, singly or together, to new surprises of climax and beauty; they take on the guise often of new melodies, or melodies of kindred beauty are suggested. Thus (not to bind ourselves beyond the hint of analogy) the themes pass from the mere phase of lyric utterance to that of epic narrative, not without strong dramatic power. Now must come the close; and see once more the interrelation of key and theme, of tonality and duality. The melodies reappear in the original order, but with change in key; for the second must close in the tonic. And, again, the balance is maintained; for, while the earlier melody had the advantage of first appearance, the second has the last word in this, the principal tonal territory.

And thus a symphony (which, etymologically, means a sounding together, using, as it did, all the resources of instrumental sound, and in Beethoven's Ninth even pressing voices into service) had, from the time of Mozart, the ambitious purpose of expressing a sort of modulation through three or four moods of one dominant feeling. I use the word "feeling" for lack of a better. In its highest phase, this purpose sometimes is a kind of poetic view of life, colored by what is at the time the individuality of the composer.

QUESTIONS

1. Do you believe that music played by instruments can express more, or less than can be expressed by voices? Why?
2. Listen to the first and second themes of an opening symphonic movement. How do these themes contrast? Do they have the same tempo? texture? melodic flow? rhythmic vitality?
3. Check the number of movements in various symphonies. Why do you suppose some symphonies have three movements, while others have four movements? If you knew there were symphonies that had only one movement, or five movements, how would you justify the number of movements?
4. In the preceding essay, what is meant by "humor" in music? Can music actually make one laugh, be "funny?" Look up the word "scherzo" and discuss its meaning.
5. Listen to a piece by Scarlatti, and another by J. S. Bach. How do they compare? Can you mistake one for the other? Why?

THE OPERA *Nineteenth-Century operas hold
an unrivaled position in the repertory of present-day
opera houses. Whereas most of the operas from the
eighteenth century and before have been forgotten
(those of Mozart and Gluck being the principal
exceptions), the operas of von Weber, Rossini,
Donizetti, Bellini, Verdi, and Wagner have kept their
popularity down to the present time. In the following
essay Lionel Salter presents, with felicity and good
humor, a survey of the work of these and other
composers. Salter is an English harpsichordist and a
conductor for the British Broadcasting Company.
He is also critic for the* Gramophone *and Director of
Music Productions for the B.B.C.'s Television Service.*

The Heyday
of Opera

LIONEL SALTER

By THE TIME OF MOZART THE OVERTURE HAD come to be of some importance in the dramatic scheme. The earliest operatic overtures had been mere flourishes to engage the audience's attention and get it to stop talking: Lully set the fashion (followed for nearly a century) for a highly organised formal orchestral prelude consisting of a slow introduction leading to a fugal *allegro* (and then sometimes a minuet). But Gluck, in his reforms of the opera, felt that the overture should have a more direct reference to the drama which followed, and set the atmosphere for it. This theory he put into practice in his own works, where we find for almost the first time a consistent relationship of mood between the overture and the opera: in *Alceste* and *Iphigenia in Tauris* the music actually flows straight on between the two. This scheme was adopted by Mozart in *Idomeneo* (as well as in *The Abduction from the Harem* and, later, *Don Giovanni*), but an innovation of Mozart's was to introduce in the overture themes from the drama itself. In *Don Giovanni*, for example, the very first music we hear is the fateful theme of the stone guest who is to bring about the Don's downfall; and *The Magic Flute* overture is interrupted by the thrice-repeated call of the trumpets which the priests of Sarastro are later to blow in their solemn ceremonies.

An even closer alliance was forged by Beethoven in his sole opera, *Fidelio* (which was never really successful although the first version of 1805 was twice radically changed for later productions). Indeed, in a sense the overture and the opera were too closely identified in his case. For, seeking constantly for perfection, he wrote altogether four different overtures: the first three were called after the heroine, Leonora, but the third in particular (using themes from the opera) sums up the action so profoundly and with such dramatic force that to play the opera after it is like going over the ground twice over. Besides which, it proved impossible to step from the tension, dramatic climax and final rejoicing of the overture back to the simple atmosphere in which the action opens; so that eventually Beethoven was forced to write a shorter and less weighty fourth overture—which is thematically independent of the opera.

opera in france. Fidelio was based on a true incident during the French Revolution, though in the story the scene is changed to Spain. The heroine has disguised herself as a boy and taken service as a jailer's

---

Opera and Ballet / Salter

assistant in order to rescue her husband, who has been imprisoned (without any trial) by the governor, his political enemy: her attempts to save him from being secretly murdered look like failing, when a trumpet is heard off-stage announcing the arrival, in the nick of time, of a Minister of State on a visit of inspection. (The off-stage trumpet provides a thrilling moment during two of the *Leonora* overtures also.) The work is what has been termed a 'rescue opera,' such as had already been made familiar in France by Méhul and, above all, by Cherubini, who though of Italian birth contributed largely to musical life in Paris, and whom Beethoven greatly admired. Another foreign composer who did much to raise the prestige of French grand opera (as opposed to *opéra comique*, a lighter, more romantic style with spoken dialogue instead of recitative, successfully practised by composers like Boieldieu) was Spontini. His grandiose heroic operas, which to please French taste made good use of the ballet, were taken up enthusiastically in Germany and held the stage there until ousted by the new German opera style established by Weber's *Der Freischütz*. It is worth noting, incidentally, that at the start of the century the tenor finally replaced for good the earlier male-soprano hero; and this pattern of casting has remained to the present day. The emphasis, however, was at first entirely on vocal display, the tenor's position being hotly contested by the leading soprano, who expected the composer to provide her with plentiful oportunities for showing off her virtuosity.

THE ITALIAN SCENE. The singers in Italian opera still ruled the roost, and, like favoured film stars of today, had the power to approve or reject what was offered them. They often insisted on new solos being written for them, sometimes had very definite ideas about how they would 'make their entrance,' and even on occasion dictated the choice of words if they had some particular 'mascot' word they liked to have in their big solos. The composer had to stomach the facts that his music would be regarded as a basis which the star performers would embroider at their pleasure, and that he would probably have to re-write a good deal of it during rehearsals: after all, he was usually hired for the season by a theatre manager and had to write an agreed number of works specifically for that particular company. He would be lucky if any opera ran for more than a couple of dozen performances, and always had to have the next one ready up his sleeve in case of sudden failure. In any case, the public would pay little attention to much of the performance. Opera was very much an occasion for social intercourse, and besides holding constant polite conversations in each other's private boxes, it was quite common for the audience to eat or gamble while the music was going on: in fact, less important arias were sometimes known as *arie di sorbetto* (refreshment arias). The grand opera (*opera seria*) of the time consisted largely of solo arias and duets, with few larger ensembles, and the story was carried forward in long recitatives. In contrast, the comic opera (*opera buffa*) had more ensembles, and unlike the *opera seria* usually had a bass as one of the principal singers (often a 'heavy father' or crusty old bachelor).

ROSSINI AND HIS FOLLOWERS. A composer who raised *opera buffa* to new heights, and who became the idol of all Europe, was Rossini, whose rhythmic zest and gift for writing sparkling melodies, as well as his brilliant handling of the orchestra, conquered Italy, London, Vienna, and Paris alike. His particular specialty was to end his overtures (which, out of sheer laziness, he sometimes used over again for other operas) with a long exciting orchestral build-up which earned him the nickname of 'Signor Crescendo.' Yet only one of his works firmly holds the stage today, the sparkling *Barber of Seville* (to whose story *The Marriage of Figaro* is the sequel); though occasionally his *Cenerentola* (the Cinderella story without the magic) is performed. Rossini did not write comic operas: he did much for *opera seria* also, introducing bass soloists and ensemble work as a normal thing; and he made some attempt to control his singers' accustomed privileges. His most important serious opera was *William Tell*, written (in French) for Paris in 1829. When, after its triumphant first night and acclamation by all the music critics, Rossini found that a change of government meant the cancellation of the rest of his contract with the Paris Opéra, he suddenly gave way to the exhaustion which the composition of forty operas in less than twenty years had cost him, and thereafter, though he lived nearly forty years more, wrote next to nothing.

Two more Italian composers may be mentioned here who inherited Rossini's skill in writing for the voice. The refinement and grace of Bellini's music has frequently been likened to that of Chopin, who admired him greatly, and whose delicately ornamented melodic line owes much to the example of Bellini. His works are rarely heard today in England, though *La Sonnambula* (*The Sleepwalker*) is still played in Italy, and *Norma* (about a Druidic priestess in ancient Gaul) was revived not long ago at Covent Garden; but on the whole his melodic gifts have not compensated for the lack of dramatic power and the shallowness of his orchestration. Donizetti was a most prolific writer, with sixty-five works to his credit, and like Rossini excelled in both the serious and comic styles. Of the former, his chief work is *Lucy of Lammermoor,* based on Walter Scott (it set the fashion for florid 'mad scenes' for operatic heroines); of the latter *The Daughter of the Regiment* and the popular *Don Pasquale* are outstanding.

SUPERNATURAL AND HISTORICAL SUBJECTS. In Germany, as we have seen, the influence of Cherubini and Spontini had made itself felt, but

Opera and Ballet / Salter

in the ensuing years some native composers came to the fore and headed German opera in a new direction—that of what is known as Romanticism, with the emphasis on folk-lore, legends, and the supernatural. Spohr's *Faust* pointed the way, but the first work of genius in this field was Weber's *Der Freischütz*, a German forest legend about a hunter who, in order to win a competition, accepts a pact with the devil and is provided with magic bullets. This opera, produced in 1821, created a furore and has retained much of its popularity. It is a *Singspiel*, that is to say with the music interspersed with spoken dialogue (not until Spohr's *Jessonda* and Weber's own *Euryanthe* two years later were attempts made at continuous music in German opera); but the famous scene of the casting of the bullets in the Wolf's Glen utilised the speaking voice over music (known technically as *melodrama*) most effectively. *Der Freischütz* is also noteworthy as one of the earliest operas in which the overture is compounded of material from the opera itself. Hundreds of German romantic operas by lesser composers followed, but they have become of purely local interest, and we must now follow another German who worked mainly in Paris—Meyerbeer.

France at this time was the operatic hub of Europe, but apart from Boieldieu the only native French composer of reputation was Cherubini's pupil Auber, who wrote several *opéras-comiques*, including *Fra Diavolo*, sometimes heard today. He also wrote some serious operas, of which one, *Masaniello* (whose story dealt with a revolution against oppression), fired the Belgians to revolt against their Dutch rulers: it was also one of the first operas to have a tragic ending. Rossini's supremacy over the French operatic stage, stemming from his *William Tell* (1829), faded before the bright light of the newcomer Meyerbeer (who was fully aware of his debt to Auber, Rossini, and Weber). His works, planned on the vastest scale, demanded sumptuous stage settings and very large orchestras (for which he wrote elaborate parts), but despite the head-shaking of the management they made the fortunes of the Paris Opéra. The supernatural element which was so conspicuous a feature of *Der Freischütz* was exploited by Meyerbeer in *Robert the Devil* (1831), which was largely responsible for the fashion for 'church scenes.' Then, taking his cue from Auber, he produced two historical operas, *The Huguenots* and *The Prophet*, which by their sheer size and length, besides their tense subjects, made a deep impression. His manner was imitated by his contemporary Halévy, who scored a triumph with *The Jewess*; but none of these ambitious blood-and-thunder works are produced nowadays, and the likelihood is that we should find them intolerably dated.

THE BRIGHTEST STAR OF ITALIAN OPERA. At almost the same time as Donizetti was writing his last operas, a new star was rising and beginning a career which sums up by itself the whole development of Italian opera during the next forty-five years. Verdi's beginnings were humble: he came of a poor peasant family, and the music in his blood was the vigorous but often crude music of the people. Faced with his earliest works, it is only with an effort that one remembers that opera was originally an aristocratic entertainment: the vocal parts here are intended not for the elegant interpreters whom Bellini had in mind but for the lusty voices beloved by the uncultivated public, and the orchestration has more than a hint of the brass band style in which Verdi was brought up. But his melodic vitality and sense of stage effect are undeniable; and in addition to these virtues he showed an increasing interest in characterisation. His personages are not just stock figures but are real people, with all the complications of character one meets in real life. It was also Verdi's fortune to become associated, in the Italian public's mind, with the movement against Austrian rule; and his constant clashes with censorship served to endear him to his audiences.

His first operas made particularly effective use of the chorus. Then followed *Ernani* (based on Victor Hugo, the dramatist most in vogue with the Romantics) and *Macbeth* (which Verdi later revised—it is the latter version which we hear nowadays); but the earliest of his stage works to have remained firmly rooted in the repertoire of today's opera-houses is *Rigoletto* (1851). Some of its immediate success was due to the play (again by Hugo) having been banned; and even as an opera —a particularly sensational one—it was necessary to change a real-life King of France into a fictitious Duke of Mantua. What is of special interest is that Verdi had the daring to make the principal character not merely a baritone, but an ugly hunchback into the bargain. Two years later Verdi brought out two more operas—the involved, passionately romantic *Il Trovatore* (*The Troubadour*), which was a success, and the much more original *La Traviata* (based on Dumas's *The Lady with the Camellias*), which was the reverse. Its failure had been attributed to the absurdity of having a very stout actress take the part of the heroine (who is supposed to die of consumption) and to the generally low standard of singing; but the audience was also considerably taken aback at an opera having for its plot a middle-class, everyday subject of its own time.

VERDI'S LATER OPERAS. Invited to write an opera for Paris, Verdi followed Meyerbeer's lead (in *The Huguenots*) by choosing a massacre for the subject—*The Sicilian Vespers;* but as the Austrian censorship refused to allow the representation of any revolt against authority, the libretto had to be changed before it could be presented in Italy. Similarly *A Masked Ball*, which marked a new high level in ensemble writing and orchestral colour, and which mingled tragic and comic elements, had

Opera and Ballet / Salter

to suffer an absurd transplantation of its plot from Sweden (where its story of a royal assassination belonged) to Boston, U.S.A.! Yet Verdi's fame had by now made him the leading Italian composer of his time, and his work was in great demand throughout the world. Of his next three operas, *The Force of Destiny* was written for St. Petersburg, *Don Carlos* for Paris and *Aïda* (1871) for a new opera-house in Cairo (to celebrate the opening of the Suez Canal). This last work, designed as a spectacle on the grandest scale, represents one of the highest peaks in Verdi's output: it combines theatrical magnificence with a great warmth of human emotion, and technically, besides the grandeur of the writing for orchestra and chorus (which reaches its climax in the Triumph Scene of the second act) and the originality of the final scene, which shows two simultaneous lots of action, it is remarkable for its dramatic continuity. Verdi had come a long way from his early days, when it was enough to provide a series of immediately effective melodies for his singers: in *Aïda* the thought is far more distinguished, and the breaks between musical numbers are reduced to a minimum.

Some years previously Verdi had made the acquaintance of the poet and musician Boito (whose own *Mephistopheles* has, despite its great length, kept the stage in Italy, if not elsewhere). Together they worked on a Shakespearian opera, *Othello*, which was produced in 1887, when Verdi was 73 years old. It was a triumph, although some of the critics could not at first appreciate the great developments which had taken place in the composer's style. His music was now truly continuous, the dramatic recitative being fused with the lyric sections, and the orchestra being given a new importance (though it never steals the limelight from the singers). Then, to everyone's astonishment, Verdi proceeded to write with Boito yet another opera, and, for the first time in his career, a comic opera at that—and this at the age of nearly 80! *Falstaff* is an amazing achievement, for the brilliance and grace of its invention, its lightness of touch, and the warmth of its characterisation: musicians agree in thinking it his masterpiece, though with the general public it has never had the easy popularity of his early operas such as *Rigoletto* and *La Traviata*.

THE RISE OF THE NEW GERMAN STYLE. In the same way that Verdi monopolises Italian opera for so long, so, by one of those curious parallels, German opera in the second half of the nineteenth century is summed up in the work of Wagner, whose influence was without question the most far-reaching in the whole history of the art. He first came into prominence in 1842 (the same year as Verdi's early *Nabucco*) with *Rienzi*, a Meyerbeer-ish piece written to his own libretto—as was always his practice—with orchestration which audiences of the day found intolerably noisy. (The same fault had been found with Meyerbeer's operas.) The following year saw the production of *The Flying Dutchman*, in which among other styles Wagner carried on the romantic, supernatural tradition established by Weber, though giving the orchestra a more important role. His interest turning towards old German legends, he produced *Tannhäuser* (1845) and *Lohengrin* (1850), whose idiom was at first regarded as quite beyond understanding, though now they are regarded as the most easily approachable of all Wagner's operas. Of *Lohengrin*, whose orchestral writing revealed a most original imagination at work, Liszt said that 'with it the old operatic world came to an end'; but in fact it consisted in essence of the old series of set numbers—arias, ensembles, and choruses. One thing which was new was the orchestral prelude to each act, setting the mood for the following scene. There was no overture built on various themes from the opera or summarising the development of its action: indeed, only once more, in *The Mastersingers*, was Wagner to write a formal overture made up of elements from the work itself—and even that was to run straight on into the opening scene.

The unsettled circumstances of Wagner's life at this time—he was a political exile for twelve years—created serious obstacles to the production of his works; but they gave him time to clarify his mind about his operatic ideals. Thinking along the lines laid down by Gluck, he envisaged opera as something quite different from the forms then current: he was working towards an 'art of the future,' a *music-drama* to which each of the elements of the theatre—libretto, music, staging, scenery, costumes, lighting—would contribute its part. In such a fusion of the arts, all at the service of the drama, the personality of the singers could not be allowed to intrude. It would be impossible to continue breaking up each act into separate numbers and recitatives: the music would have to be continuous, flexible enough in character to be more declamatory or more lyrical as the situation demanded, but planned *as a whole*. To unify his music-drama Wagner evolved a system of developing 'leading motives' (themes attached to persons, ideas or emotions, which recur as the characters return or are mentioned or the ideas and emotions come to the fore). This was not entirely new, as is sometimes supposed: Spohr had used the device for structural purposes in his *Faust* (1816), and others had pointed the way before that. (Incidentally, it was Spohr, too, who had first cast scenes as continuous wholes without breaks.) The ebb and flow of these leading motives created a kind of running commentary on the action and thus gave a major role in the unfolding of the drama to the orchestra. The musical emphasis, in short, had moved from the stage to the orchestra pit, and in his later works Wagner's vocal parts actually grow out of the orchestral texture. The orchestral forces themselves had to be of unprecedented size to keep pace with his imaginative demands—whoever before would have dared to ask for eight horns or six harps, for example? Nor did Wagner allow himself to be restrained in any particular by the limitations of existing instruments: special instruments, such as a bass trumpet and a whole family of tubas, had to be built to satisfy his requirements. Even the musical language employed had to be expanded to express the depths of emotions which Wagner brought into play; and his greatest contribution to the art of music (as distinct from that of opera alone) lies precisely in the enormous development of chromatic harmony (and hence melody) for which he was responsible. Similarly with every facet of the theatre: he bubbled over with ideas about production, scenery, and costumes.

WAGNER'S MATURE MUSIC-DRAMAS. All these innovations—which were to set the musical world ablaze—were brought into play with his next creation, a drama on a vast scale based on the old German legend of *The Nibelung's Ring*. Wagner wrote this as a tetralogy, that is, a sequence of four operas, each occupying a whole evening; and the *Ring* cycle is now recognised as one of the greatest landmarks in the history of opera. Actually, his original intention had been to write one drama called *Siegfried's Death*, but the plot was so difficult to make clear that he found himself obliged to add a preliminary drama to introduce it, then another to explain *that*, and finally yet another to get back to the fundamentals of the story. That is why we get one of the tiresome features of *The Ring*—the way various characters enter and relate the whole plot (so far as it concerns themselves) up to the point at which they have arrived—a kind of 'new readers start here.' The resources required by *The Ring* were so enormous (they are still a strain on any opera-house) that, not surprisingly, Wagner had to wait a long time for its production, even in separate parts; but by a stroke of good fortune, the eccentric young King Ludwig II of Bavaria became a fervent admirer of the composer, and enabled him to build a theatre—to his own plans, of course—exclusively devoted to performances of his works. Bayreuth is still the centre of the Wagner cult: if it did nothing else it persuaded audiences that opera (or music-drama, rather) was something to be taken seriously.

Among the innumerable points of interest in *The Ring* are the orchestral preludes (not overtures) to the operas. *Rhinegold* begins, with breath-taking boldness, with 136 bars of nothing but the chord of E flat, rolling upwards from the orchestral depths, to represent the bed of the great river from which the action springs; and the music flows imperceptibly into the start of the opera. Similarly, before the curtain goes up on *The Valkyrie* there is a 120-bar representation of a storm, out of which Siegmund staggers on to the stage; while to start Act 3 the orchestra depicts the Valkyries flying through the air on their battle-steeds. In each case, in fact, the orchestral prelude serves a specifically dramatic purpose.

In *Tristan and Isolde* (which Wagner wrote during the long period spent on *The Ring* but which was produced first, in 1865) the prelude expresses the almost unbearable intensity of the classic love-story which is the basis of the opera, and Wagner pushed his chromatic harmony to new limits which many of his contemporaries found quite intolerable; but it served as a major stepping-stone to twentieth-century music. Three years later came another masterpiece, this time a romantic comedy called *The Mastersingers of Nuremberg.* In its mediaeval subject of a young knight-musician winning over the conservative Guild of Mastersingers by the beauty of his unorthodox songs can easily be seen Wagner's allegory of himself in his own musical world. His last opera, *Parsifal,* is a large-scale religious drama which, in this country at least, is more likely to be heard in concert performance than in the theatre, to which many people still think its subject is ill-suited.

QUESTIONS

1. Opera has been called the "silliest of the arts." Can you suggest why this is? How does an opera differ from a musical comedy? an oratorio? Are these forms "silly?"

2. For many people the taste for opera is controversial. List whatever appeals to you in opera, and whatever does not appeal to you. Compare and discuss these items.

3. In most operas the hero is usually a tenor, and the villain a bass or baritone. The heroine is usually a high soprano and the villainess (if there is one) is a low soprano or contralto. Discuss the choice of these voices for their special roles. What, for example, makes a tenor more "heroic" than a bass?

4. Look up *aria* and *recitative.* What are their functions in opera?

5. What, exactly, are the differences between *opera seria, opéra comique, opera buffa,* and *music-drama?* Can you give examples of each?

THE CHURCH   *Albert Schweitzer is known*
throughout the world as a selfless physician,
philosopher, and humanitarian. In the musical world,
Schweitzer is known as an organist of uncommon
feeling and power and an authority on Johann
Sebastian Bach. More than fifty years ago Schweitzer
wrote a book on Bach that has since influenced all who
perform Bach's music. As a first-rate organist,
Schweitzer is able to discuss Bach's music
authoritatively, and, as a historian, he is able to place
Bach in his proper historical context. To deepen
further his already profound grasp of church music,
Schweitzer went on to study organ building and in
1909 presided over a conference that set up world-wide
regulations for organ construction. In this essay
Schweitzer traces the early development of the organ
and congregational singing in the Protestant service.

The Chorale in
the Church Service

ALBERT SCHWEITZER

$\mathfrak{H}$OW WAS THE CONGREGATIONAL SONG INTRO-duced into the church service at the time of the Reformation? It is usual to look upon the question as very simple and to suppose that the people had little by little come to sing the melody while the organ played it. Did the sacred instrument really teach the congregation in this way?

We may read through all Luther's writings without finding a single place where he speaks of the organ as the instrument accompanying the congregational singing. Moreover he, the admirer of true church music of every kind, gives no directions as to how the organ is to coöperate in the service. It is really incredible, however, that in the few places where he mentions the organ at all, he speaks of it not enthusiastically but almost scornfully! He does not look upon it as necessary or even desirable in the evangelical service, but at most tolerates it where he finds it already.

His contemporaries shared his view. We need not be astonished that the Reformed Church dealt drastically with the organs and banished them from the churches. In the Lutheran and even in the Catholic churches at that time it fared almost the same. It had always had, indeed, its adversaries. No less a person than St. Thomas Aquinas had declared war on it, not regarding organ music, or indeed instrumental music in general, as calculated to stimulate devotion. In the sixteenth century, however, complaints against it arose on all sides, and the Council of Trent (1545-1563), which dealt with all the doubtful questions relating to the church and its service, was compelled to enact severe regulations against the erroneous and too prevalent employment of the organ in worship. Catholics and Protestants alike at that time imposed on it a term of penance, in order that it might alter its ungodly nature, in default of which the Church would excommunicate it.

It had fully merited this disgrace. The character of the tasks allotted to it may be seen from the *Caeremoniale Episcoporum* issued by Pope Clement VIII in the year 1600. The organ preludised in order to give the tone to the priest or the choir. It further gave out the liturgical songs and hymns in alternation with the choir, one verse being sung and the next played on the organ. It was never used, however, to accompany the choir. The primitive structure of the organs of that time quite forbade this; their heavy keys did not permit of polyphonic play-

THE CHORALE IN THE CHURCH SERVICE from *J. S. Bach*, Volume 1, by Albert Schweitzer (translated by Ernest Newman); The Macmillan Company. Reprinted by permission.

ing, while their crude, untempered tuning made it as a rule impossible to play on them in more than one or two keys. Since therefore they could not coöperate, the choir and the organ functioned in turns. When the organ had completed its verse, the text, in accordance with the above-mentioned regulations of the Pope, was either recited loudly by a chorister, or else sung, which latter was recommended as the better course.

With the organ employed in this independent way, abuses could not fail to creep in. As the organist was unable to play polyphonically on his instrument, he was tempted to amuse himself with quick running passages in his preambles to the verses or during the course of these. Still worse was it when he indulged in well-known secular songs, which seems to have been a wide-spread practice. In 1548 an organist in Strassburg was dismissed from his post for having played French and Italian songs during the offertory.

At a later date the organ unwarrantably deprived the choir of many of the hymns, taking almost everything upon itself. The extent to which this had become prevalent appears from an incident that happened to Luther, which he tells in his best style in the *Table Talk*: "When I was a young monk in Erfurt," he says, "and had to make the rounds of the villages, I came to a certain village and celebrated Mass there. When I had dressed myself and stepped before the altar in my fine attire, the clerk began to strike the *Kyrie eleison* and the *Patrem* on the lute. I could with difficulty keep from laughing, for I was not used to such an organ; I had to make my *Gloria in excelsis* conform to his *Kyrie*."

It seemed so much a matter of course at that time to substitute the organ for the choir in the liturgy that this clerk, in default of an organ, simply had recourse to the lute!

In the Evangelical church the rôle of the organ had for a long time now been the same as in the Catholic church. It preambled to the hymns of the priest and the choir and alternated with the latter; only now the congregational song is merely an addendum, to which the organ preambles and wherewith it alternates. In Wittenberg it preambled to almost all the vocal pieces, whether of priest, choir, or people, and shared with the choir in the rendering of the *Kyrie*, the *Gloria*, and the *Agnus Dei*. We learn this from Wolfgang Musculus, who in 1536 attended the Concordia conferences at Wittenberg, and described the singing at the service in the Wittenberg parish church on the fifth Sunday after Easter.

This explains the curious injunction which we find in the church ordinances of the fifteenth and sixteenth centuries, namely that the organ "shall *strike* into the song in the churches." It means that certain verses are to be played by the organist alone, the congregation being silent. At the same time the caution is given that this must not happen too often, but at the most two or three times in the one hymn. It is so laid down in the "Strassburg Church-ordinance" of 1598, and, in exactly the same way, in the "Nuremberg Congregation ordinance" of 1606. At first, and for another three generations at least, there was no question of the organ *accompanying* the congregational singing.

How did the choir stand with regard to the congregational chorale? Did it take the place of the organ, guiding and supporting the song of the people? A glance at the earliest hymn books appointed for the service shows us that this solution did not occur to Luther.

The *Erfurt Enchiridion* of Justus Jonas was a hymn-book not for the church but for the home, as, indeed, its title expressly indicates. The melody alone was noted over the poem, so that the father of the household could give it out to the children and the servants. The Strassburg reformer Catharina Zell hoped that "a poor mother should go to sleep, and, if at midnight the crying child had to be rocked, sing it a song of heavenly things"; this would be the right kind of lullaby, and would please God more than all the lullabies played on the organ in the Catholic church.

The *Church chorale book* published at Wittenberg in 1524 by Luther and Walther, while the *Enchiridion* was being printed at Erfurt, makes no reference whatever to congregational singing. It merely consists, in fact, of the vocal parts of chorales written in four and five parts, and the coöperation of the faithful is barred at the outset by the fact that the chorale melody lies in the tenor, not in the soprano. These vocal parts—which were probably engraved by Luther's friend, the painter and wood engraver Lucas Cranach—are those of chorale motets sung by the choir, and therefore having a cantus firmus, as was customary in the religious and secular music of that time.

Luther was not only a reformer but an artist. The logical outcome of his reforming ideas would have been a remodeling of the church service on the lines of the simple home service, in which case the congregational chorale would have been the only music used in the church. This, indeed, is the line we find him pursuing in his first drastic treatise on the service. But, as in most men of genius, there was a fatal side to his greatness that prevented him from thinking out his ideas to their logical conclusion, and made him endow a thing and its antithesis with equal life. He was an admirer of the contrapuntal music of the Netherlands school. He regarded artistic music as one of the most perfect manifestations of the Deity. "When natural music is heightened and polished by art," he said once, "there man first beholds and can with great wonder examine to a certain extent (for it cannot be wholly seized or understood), the great and perfect wisdom of God in His marvellous work of music, in which this is most singular and indeed astonishing, that one man sings a simple tune or tenor (as musicians call it), together with which three, four, or five voices also sing, which as it were play and skip delightedly round this simple tune or tenor, and wonderfully grace and adorn the said tune with manifold devices and sounds, performing as it were a heavenly dance, so that those who at all understand it and are moved by it must be greatly amazed, and believe that there is nothing more extraordinary in the world than such a song adorned with many voices." The wonders of contrapuntal polyphony have never been so admirably described before or since.

His favorite composers were Josquin des Près (1450-1521), the court musician to Louis XII of France, and Heinrich Isaak's pupil Ludwig Senfl (died 1550), who was successively in the service of the courts of Vienna and Munich. His remark upon Josquin is well-known: "He is the master of the notes; they have to do as he wills; other composers have to do as the notes will." On one occasion, when a motet of Senfl's was being performed in his house, he called out: "I could not write such a motet if I were to tear myself to pieces, just as he, for his part, could not preach a sermon like me."

The musician in Luther could not tolerate the banishment of choir and art-song from the church, as many people desired, or the restriction of the choir to leading the congregational singing. "And I am not of the opinion" he says in the preface to Walther's chorale parts of 1524, "that on account of the Gospel all the arts should be crushed out of existence, as some over-religious people pretend, but I would willingly see all the arts, especially music, in the service of Him who has given and created them."

A licence was thus granted to the art in the Lutheran service; it took its place in the ritual as a free and independent power. All the phases of the development of music in general are to be clearly seen in the Lutheran service. Finally, when the motet, under the influence of Italian art, was transformed into the cantata, bringing not only instrumental music but an undisguised opera-style into the church, the service actually came to be interrupted by a sacred concert, which was looked upon as its culminating point. It was at this juncture that Bach came on the scene. On the covers of his scores he writes, not "cantata," but "concerto."

Thus had Luther not been an artist, Bach would never have been able to write his sacred concert-music for church purposes and as part of the church service. Would he nevertheless have written it in any case? What would he have done had he been born in Zürich or in Geneva?

At first, then, the congregational chorale was not supported either by the organ or by the choir, but sung *unisono* without accompaniment, precisely as in the Catholic church at the end of the Middle Ages.

We must not overestimate the number of the congregational chorales that were sung during a service. Where a choir existed, the congregation took little part in the singing, being restricted to the *Credo,* sung between the reading of the Gospel and the sermon, and perhaps a communion hymn. In Wittenberg—so it appears from the account given by Musculus—the congregation as a rule did not sing, but left even the chorales to the choir. In other places—Erfurt, for example—it was customary for the people to sing alternately with the choir between the Epistle and the Gospel, in such a way that the choir sang the sequence and the people joined in with a German chorale appropriate to the time of the year. Five or six chorales in the year sufficed for this, since the same chorale was used on each Sunday during that particular period.

In the churches that had no choir, more importance attached to the congregational singing, since in that case the *Kyrie,* the *Gloria,* and the *Agnus Dei* were sung in the corresponding German chorales. But here again, as a rule, fifteen or at most twenty chorales, which had been laid down, once for all, for their particular Sundays, sufficed for the whole year.

On closer inspection we get the impression that the congregational singing, instead of gaining ground, was in the course of the sixteenth century driven back by the art-singing and by the organ, the pretensions of the latter increasing everywhere, in spite of all ordinances.

There was thus good cause for the attempt that was made, at the end of the first century of the Reformation—not indeed by a musician but by a priest—to improve the position of the chorale. In 1586 the Würtemberg court preacher Lucas Osiander published his *Fünffzig geistliche Lieder und Psalmen, mit vier Stimmen auf kontrapunktweise, für die Kirchen und Schulen im löblichen Fürstentumb Würtemberg, also gesetzet, dass eine gantze christliche Gemein durchaus mitsingen kann* (Fifty sacred songs and psalms, for the churches and schools in the worshipful principality of Würtemberg, set contrapuntally in four parts in such a way that the whole Christian congregation can always join in them). This was the first real chorale book in our sense, except that it was written for the choir instead of for the organ. The fact that Osiander relies only on the choir, not on the organ, for the leading of the congregational singing, proves that the instrument in his time had no concern whatever with the latter.

In his preface he expresses his confidence that he has made things easier by removing the melody from the tenor to the soprano, and thinks that when the laity recognize the tune they will joyfully take part in it.

Was not his confidence misplaced? It was indeed only a half-measure, a false compromise between polyphony and melody. If he wanted polyphony, he should have allowed the whole congregation to sing in chorus in four parts, as was the custom later in Switzerland; on the other hand, if he wished to do without polyphony, he should have let the choir sing in unison, acting, as it were, as precentor, somewhat in the way the village cantors in his day led the chorale without choir or organ, simply by the unison singing of the school children. His desire, however, was to reconcile artistic singing and popular singing, and instead of a solution he achieved only an unstable compromise. For what support could the harmonies of a choir—and the choirs at that time were very weak in numbers—give to a *cantus firmus* sung by a mass of people?

Hans Leo Hassler also tried to make a forward step in this direction, and published, besides his splendid *Cantiones sacrae* and *Sacri concertus* (for performance by the choir only), his *Kirchengesäng, Psalmen und geistliche Lieder auf die gemeinen Melodien mit vier Stimmen simpliciter gesetzet*, which, according to the preface, were so constructed that the ordinary man could sing them in the Christian assembly to figurate music.

It would be wrong, however, to suppose that all the masters of church music who, in the sixteenth and seventeeth centuries, removed the melody to the soprano part, were imitators of Osiander, and that it was for purely practical reasons that they abandoned the earlier system. The real reason is quite different and must be sought in the fact that in the meantime German church music had shaken off the influence of the purely contrapuntal music of the Netherlands school and had fallen under that of the Italians, in which the melodic style began to dominate the contrapuntal. Melchior Vulpius, Seth Calvisius, Michael Praetorius, and Johann Eccard thus follow in their admirable music not so much the lead of the Würtemberg Court preacher as the trend of the art itself.

It was a pure accident that through this change in polyphonic art the possibility was opened to the congregation to join in the *cantus firmus* with the choir. How far it availed itself of it we do not know, for in the history of art, as a rule, we never get to know the things that would be of practical interest to us, for these, being looked upon as matters of daily custom, are not recorded. The fact that at this epoch the term "chorale" begins to be applied to the melodies sung by the congregation throws no light on the question, unless we regard it as proving that by this time the melodies of the church song had ceased to be congregational property and had become the property of the choir.

In any case the composers themselves, in spite of the fine practical suggestions as to congregational singing that they put forward in their prefaces, thought only of the choir when composing, as is shown by their counterpoint, which, with all its simplicity, becomes richer and more and more in the style of the motet. For us these chorale pieces, with their singularly beautiful blending of Italian and German art, are choral works pure and simple, and the idea of trying again the experiment of letting the congregation join in them would not occur to us. But if only we could hear them even as choral works! When will the time come when these treasures are exhibited each Sunday in our church services?

The attempts to have the singing of the congregation led by the choir were made about the end of the sixteenth century and in the first decade of the seventeenth. By the middle of the seventeenth century the question is settled by the organ assuming this rôle. In 1650 appears the *Tablature-book* of Samuel Scheidt, with a hundred chorale harmonizations intended for the accompaniment of the congregational singing.

This was no thought-out experiment, but a solution arising out of the facts, i.e. the progress of organ-building. The sacred instrument had in the meantime been made more practically fitted for polyphonic playing, and endowed with such fulness of tone that it overwhelmed the small and weak choirs of that time. Whereas hitherto it had accompanied the choir, which supported the singing of the congregation, its powerful tone now made it possible for it to assume the lead. But again we cannot be sure of the date at which the organ began to support the choir in the chorale, or when it began to coöperate with the choir in general. This was certainly not the case before the beginning of the seventeenth century. Vulpius, Praetorius, Eccard, and the others appear to know nothing of it. But as early as 1627 Johann Hermann Schein, Cantor of St. Thomas's church in Leipzig, adds a figured bass—intended for "organists, instrumentalists, and lutenists"—to the four, five, and six-part chorale pieces for the choir in his *Cantionale* of that year; and this most probably points to a joint performance by choir and organ.

We must not, however, conceive the organ accompaniment to the chorale, as it was practiced in the second half of the seventeenth century, as a supplanting of the choir by the organ in the chorale. The choir, even in Bach's time, coöperated in the chorale as in earlier times —polyphonically, indeed—although the organ took the lead, as it were, a kind of second and stronger choir without words.

This transference of vocal polyphony to the organ by means of chorale accompaniment was of cardinal significance to the art of organ music. The chorale was the teacher of the organists, leading them from the false and fruitless virtuosity of the keyboard to the true, simple organ style. From this moment German organ music severs itself from that of

Music for the Church / Schweitzer

Italy, France, and the Netherlands, and, always under the control of the chorale, pursues the path along which, in the course of two generations, it was to arrive at perfection. Scheidt, already in possession of the true organ style derived from the chorale, sees that his life-work consists in combating the "colored" organ style of the school of the Dutchman Sweelinck. It is an illustration of how an idea is, in the end, always stronger than circumstances. Organ music did not come to perfection in Paris or in Venice, where everything seemed to be in its favor, but among the poor cantors and schoolmasters of an impoverished country, as the Germany of the two generations after the Thirty Years' War was. How small Frescobaldi, the organist of St. Peter's in Rome, whose fame among his contemporaries was so great, seems beside a Samuel Scheidt, whose name was unknown on the other side of the Alps!

From the moment when organ, choir, and congregation together gave out the chorale, it was inevitable that the antiphonal method, under which the organ alone performed certain of the verses, should sooner or later fall into disuse. But of the perfection of these independent organ renderings at that time we may judge from Scheidt's *Tablatura nova,* published in 1624. It consists for the most part of a species of variations upon the chorales most generally used—the number of variations corresponding to the number of verses of the song—and upon the hymns of the various seasons of the church year, which at that time were still sung in Halle in Latin, and not, as in other places, in German. In addition there are liturgical pieces, such as the *Kyrie, Gloria, Magnificat,* and the *Psalmus sub communione* "Jesus Christus unser Heiland," which are all treated in the same way.

The Celli Tablature that appeared twenty-three years earlier is on the same lines, except that it also contains the complete "catechism songs."

How long the custom, testified to in all contemporary tablatures, of rendering vocal pieces on the organ alone, still lasted after the process of decay had once set in, can no longer be ascertained. When we consider the extremely numerous arrangements by Bach of the chorale "Allein Gott in der Höh sei Ehr," we are inclined to think that even down to his day there persisted, under certain circumstances, the practice testified to by Scheidt, of the organ responding to the *Gloria* intoned by the priest at the altar.

As to the position of the congregational singing in Bach's time, we have only conjecture to go upon. One thing at any rate had been achieved—the number of the hymns affiliated to the service had considerably increased. Each Gospel had one or more of these allotted to it, so that the same ones were always sung on a particular Sunday. They were called the *Cantica de tempore;* in the hymn-books they formed the first class and were arranged according to the Sundays of the ecclesiastical year. The cantor selected them himself without consulting anyone else. In our day, on the contrary, the hymns are always selected by the clergyman, to tally with the spirit of his sermon.

This use of the *Cantica de tempore* helps us to understand how the organists of the time of Pachelbel and Bach came to write cycles of chorale preludes for each Sunday of the ecclesiastical year.

Whether the congregation took possession of all these hymns and took an active and hearty part in the singing of them is, however, another question. It is well known that Mattheson and the famous Hamburg musicians thought nothing at all of the congregational chorale, and in general refused to recognize singing of this kind as music. From this we may conclude that it did not occupy a prominent place in their churches, and that they, for their part, did nothing to encourage it. It must have been the same in other towns that had celebrated choirs. The cantata—that sacred concert intercalated in the service—absorbed all the interest, and the art-song, as at the beginning of the Reformation, had once more triumphed.

We do not know whether things were better in this respect in Leipzig than in other towns. The truth is that no remark of Bach's has come down to us to show that, in contradistinction to his contemporaries, he felt any particular interest in congregational singing. In his Passions, at any rate, he does not desire its co-operation, in spite of the splendid rôle that he assigns to the chorale in those works. It is highly probable that in Bach's time the singing of the Leipzig congregations was not so good as is commonly supposed.

Not until the concert style of music was banished from the service, in the generation after Bach, and the town choirs that had been allotted to the churches ceased to exist, did congregational singing become the characteristic and sole service-music of the Protestant church. In the epoch of rationalism and pietism the ideal was realized which the Reformation had indeed perceived, but, for conservative and artistic reasons, had not pursued. However barbarously rationalism behaved towards the old hymn, it did good work for congregational singing. Its ultimate aim, of course, was to substitute a new kind of hymn for the old, the diction and the ideas of which had by then become so antiquated as to unfit it for use as a real congregational hymn.

Whether the problem has been really solved by allowing the organ to support the congregational singing is doubtful. The method has established itself, because it is practical. But the ideal is not congregational singing of this kind, directed by, and dependent on, the organ; the true ideal is free and confident unaccompanied singing, as in the congregational singing of the Middle Ages and of the first Reformation period. Perhaps that complete and unfettered coöperation of organ, choir, and worshippers was, in its way, an ideal, towards which we shall some day aspire more than we do now.

QUESTIONS

1. Why has the organ come to be regarded as a "sacred" musical instrument? When did this phenomenon develop? Who was responsible?
2. What does Schweitzer mean when he says, concerning Renaissance organs, "their heavy keys did not permit of polyphonic playing?" What is the meaning of polyphonic?
3. Besides the organ, what other musical instruments have you heard used in church? For what purpose were they used? Do you believe that some instruments can be classed as "religious," and some as "secular?" Which ones? Why?
4. What was Martin Luther's purpose in having the congregation participate in the singing of the church service? Did this affect the musicality of the service? In what ways?
5. Do you think professionally-trained choirs are an asset in the singing of the church service? Discuss the singing in your own church. Is the choir a professional one? Are they paid for their services? Do you think it is ethical to be paid for singing in church?

COMPOSERS IN THEIR TIMES / 1

Middle Ages   *The* troubadours *and the*
trouvères, two French minstrel groups, were active
from the end of the eleventh century through the
thirteenth century. These two groups have provided
us with the most important collections of secular
monody. Along with the troubadours and the
trouvères were the minstrel entertainers and performers
known as jongleurs. *Similar musical groups*
developed in Germany, where the Minnesingers
took over from their French counterparts. Wilhelm
Langhans (1832-1892), author, composer, and violinist,
received his Ph.D. from the University of Heidelberg,
where he later taught. He is especially known for his
two-volume continuation of Ambros' History of Music.

ROUBADOURS,

ROUVÈRES,

and MINNESINGERS

WILHELM LANGHANS

HROUGH THE LABORS OF A HUCBALD, A GUIDO, and a Franco, the soil in which a genuine art-music could grow-up was, indeed, prepared; yet it was a considerable time before the first buds of such a thing ventured to show themselves. The European nations were still too deeply sunken in lethargy and barbarity to allow to art free space for its development; when all at once an event happened which powerfully transformed not only the religious and political situation, but also the collective intellectual life of Europe. And that was the Crusades, beginning in 1096.

It was not only to the members of the religious and knightly orders that the summons of a Peter of Amiens, a Bernard of Clairvaux, for the rescue of the holy sepulchre from the hands of the infidels was addressed; to all who should join the expedition eternal salvation was promised. And in consequence of this, multitudes belonging to the most diverse conditions of life, who were eager for the adventure, took part in the march to Jerusalem, as in a general pilgrimage. For the great majority of the Crusaders, however, the impressions and experiences gained in the East must have had a lasting effect, since . . . the civilization of that country was, even from the reign of the Abassides, especially of the caliph Haroun al Raschid (800 A.D.), who belonged to that dynasty, in every respect superior to that of the West.

Similarly, the singers and instrumental musicians in the retinue of the Crusaders found in the East rich inspiration and nutriment for their art. For, although the Oriental music—like that of the Arabs in Spain—was of its very nature ill-adapted to the solution of ideal art-problems, yet the singing-method of the Orientals, with its characteristic richness of ornamentation, as also their musical instruments (the lute and the guitar), which had been unknown to the Crusaders; moreover the noisy instruments used in the Saracen military music (the drum and the kettle-drum), all these elements, after they had been introduced into the western music, necessarily gave the latter an altered character.

Still more important appears to be the enrichment experienced by the poetry of the West in consequence of the Crusades. The separation—often for years—from home and family brought about a deepening of the emotional life till then unknown; a new species of poetry arises in which the feeling for chivalry and love-service (*Minnedienst*) finds its expression, the so-called "gay science" (*gaya ciencia*), indigenous es-

TROUBADOURS, TROUVÈRES, AND MINNESINGERS from *The History of Music in Twelve Lectures* by Wilhelm Langhans; G. Schirmer, Inc.; 1886.

pecially to the soil of Provence, favored as it is by a happy climate and the lively disposition of its inhabitants.

Here the grandees of the land devoted themselves to this science, the first being Count William of Poitiers (1087-1127), afterwards King Thibaut of Navarre (1201-1254), these however, always only as *originators* of songs, whence they were also called *Trouvères* (from the French *trouver*), a word which has become in our English tongue (more identical with the Italian synonym *trovatore*) *Troubadours*. The *execution* of the songs composed by them, as also the instrumental accompaniment of them they handed over to the so-called Minstrels (derived from *ministerialis*, from the Latin *minister*, a "helper"), also called *Jongleurs* (from the Latin *joculator*, "merry-maker"), who belonged to a lower class of society and were often ranked with buffoons, as is seen in a contemporaneous sculpture of the church of St. George at Bocherville near Rouen, representing among a group of instrumental musicians a human figure walking on his hands. [Later studies show that certain troubadours not only composed songs but performed them as well.]

An exceptional position among the troubadours is occupied by Adam de la Hale, called after his deformity and his native place, "the hunchback of Arras," inasmuch as he unites in his person the composer of songs and the executive musician. He was moreover well-versed in the strict art-forms also, so far as they had then been developed, and ranks among the first musicians who undertook to compose four-voiced vocal pieces. His *Robin and Marian* (a dramatic pastoral), the subject of which is the naïve description of a rustic love affair, was performed in 1282 at the court of Robert the second, of Artois, at Naples; it is therefore the oldest example of dramatic art in France, for which reason Adam de la Hale is rightfully indicated in the history of French literature as the founder of comic opera.

The same intellectual current that in the case of the Roman peoples had called into existence the art of the troubadours, expressed itself among the ancient Germans who had remained unmixed in Germany, in the form of erotic poetry called, in their tongue, *Minnegesang*. The "minnesinger" differed, however, from the troubadour in that he himself sang his songs and accompanied them on an instrument, usually a small three-cornered harp. Such an instrument is often seen depicted in ancient manuscripts, among others in that of Godfrey of Strassberg's *Tristan and Isolde*, belonging to the first half of the 13th century, and found in the court library at Munich.

Moreover the minnesingers did not belong, as the troubadours did, exclusively to the knightly order. Of the singers participating in the *Sängerkrieg auf der Wartburg* (contest of singers on the Wartburg), in 1207, under landgrave Herrmann of Thuringia, Wolfram of Eschenbach, Walter of the Vogelweide, Heinrich Schreiber, and Heinrich of Zwetzschin were, as the chronicler puts it, "knightly men"; on the other hand, Biterolf was "one of the landgrave's household servants," and Heinrich of Ofterdingen, a burgess of Eisenach. The musical difference of the German minnegesang, or love song, from the song of the troubadours consisted in this: that the latter made the text subservient to the melody, whereas with the former the poetry becomes the principal thing, and the characteristic song-melody is supplanted by the recitative style of the ecclesiastical chant.

This predominance of the poetical over the musical element is exhibited also in the songs of the mastersingers, who undertook the care of art after it had passed over from the knightly singers to the burghers and respectable artisans. According to F. H. von der Hagen (*The Minnesingers and Song-poets of the 13th, 14th and 15th Centuries*, Leipzig, 1838), by the so-called "tones" of the mastersingers are meant not only the song-melodies themselves, but also the metrical schemes; hence they have special reference to the poetry.

Concerning the interior economy of these singing societies organized after the manner of a guild, we find copious information in Wagenseil's book, *Von der Meistersinger holdseligen Kunst* ("Of the delightful art of the Mastersingers"), published in Nuremberg, 1697. In our own time Richard Wagner has renewed the memory of the mastersingers in his poem bearing that title. In these works we are made acquainted, in the first place, with the Tablature, by which is meant the whole body of laws for the government of the guild. The members are divided into three classes: Whoever has learned the various tones is a "singer"; a higher degree, the rank of "poet," is attained by him who composes a new and suitable text to one of the tones; but to acquire the dignity of "master," the union of both faculties, the poetical and the musical, is requisite.

> The poet who, with brain so witty,
> To words and rhymes, by himself prepared,
> Can shape from the tones a new strain or ditty,
> He is a Mastersinger declared.

The conscientiousness and the zeal shown by the members of the guild, in the observance of their laws, can serve as a gratifying testimony to the feeling for art entertained by the German burgherdom, even though the artistic results of those efforts have only extremely little value. The melodies of the mastersingers were like the church psalmody: monotonous and lacking in expression, although they were embellished at the cadencing sections with all kinds of ornamentation. The relation of their music to poetry was as good as none at all; as a rule the tune was not determined by the text, but vice-versa, the text by the tune;

frequently the tune was composed first, and after it was found to be free of faults the author was required to make a suitable text to it, upon a determined biblical or spiritual subject. With this homely manner of art-education, which moreover is manifested in the strange names given to the tunes—there was, for instance, "an Over-short evening-red tune," a "Black ink tune," a "Short monkey tune," a "Gormandizer-in-secret tune," etc.—neither poetry nor music could especially thrive. Yet the mastersinger schools had unquestionably a good effect on the morality of their members, and much as we may feel repelled by the pedantry inherent in their artistic efforts, yet on the other hand the tendency of these simple natures, aiming at the ideal in the midst of all the worry of common-place life, deserves the warmest recognition. This view is taken by Richard Wagner also when he makes his mastersinger Hans Sachs (1495-1576) answer as follows the question as to the rules of the Guild: "By what man were they first devised?"

> By certain sorely troubled masters,
> Their hearts oppressed by life's disasters;
> By suffering overweighted,
> A model they created,
> That they might take it,
> And ever make it
> A memory of youthful love,
> In which the soul of Spring should move.

The schools of the mastersingers fell, after the Thirty Years' War, more and more into decay; only those of Nuremberg and Strasburg maintained, up to the close of the preceding century, a certain importance. The German mastersong did not actually come to an end before 1839, when the last surviving members of the School at Ulm handed over their corporation badges to the Liederkranz of that city, and thereby dissolved their guild. The mastersingers were, moreover, of advantage to the music of their time because, taking their example, the instrumental musicians also united in corporations organized like guilds, gave up the wandering life which they had previously led, and took up a permanent abode in the cities.

Thus arose, as early as 1288, in Vienna, a society under the name of the *Nicolai-Bruderschaft,* and in 1330 in Paris the *Confrérie de St. Julien des Ménestriers* (Minstrels), these latter under a director with the title *Roi des violons* ("King of the violins"), whose rule continued till the 17th century when it was terminated by Louis XIV, after the last director, Dumanoir II, had arrogated the jurisdiction over all the musicians of Paris, including the organists, and thus brought on himself his downfall.

Side by side with the minnesong and the mastersong (but independent of each other) the folk-song had, in the last centuries of the Middle Ages, been developed. The so-called Limburg Chronicle, edited by the scribe Johannes (1317-1402), gives the earliest details concerning the nature of the folk-songs, and of the contemporaneous instrumental music ("pipe-playing," as it calls it). But unfortunately there are no musical specimens; these, however, are found in great number in a manuscript of the 15th century, called, after the place where it originated, the *Lochheim Songbook*. The melodies therein given are remarkable not only for the significant voice-leading and the skilfully organized rhythms, but also for the fidelity with which they reproduce the subject-matter of the poetry and give expression to that which language is unable of itself, alone, to utter.

QUESTIONS

1. Look up the names of Hucbald, Guido, and Franco. What were their contributions to music?
2. Who are the present-day counterparts of the troubadours and jongleurs? Can you name any of them? Discuss your selections.
3. What, exactly, is the difference between a troubadour and a jongleur?
4. Look up the story of the Wagner opera that deals with the Mastersingers. How would you "modernize" the plot? Can it be done? Give your reasons.
5. In what Gilbert and Sullivan operetta do we find a "wandering minstrel?" In what period is this operetta laid? Does this minstrel have any relation to the minstrels mentioned in the essay? In what ways?

COMPOSERS IN THEIR TIMES / 2

Renaissance *Orlande de Lassus* (1532?-1594)
*was one of the greatest and most important of the
Renaissance composers. Apparently equally at home
with sacred and with secular music, he is generally
regarded as a master of polyphonic composition. His
fame during his lifetime was so widespread and his
musical talent so well established that he was variously
known as "The Belgian Orpheus" and "The Prince
of Music." He was among the most prolific composers of the Renaissance, creating a staggering total of
some two thousand compositions. In her especially
lucid essay on a difficult subject, Edna Richolson Sollitt
manages to show us a portrait of one Renaissance man.*

Orlande de Lassus

EDNA RICHOLSON SOLLITT

*O*RLANDE DE LASSUS WAS BORN AT MONS, HAInault, in 1532; this date is established by an inscription on the portrait by Johan Sadeler painted in 1593, "at the age of sixtyone," and by his epitaph, which shows the agreement of his heirs with this date. This must be considered decisive, although Samuel Quickelberg, who was acquainted with Lassus in Munich in 1565, and who wrote the oldest biographical notice concerning him, places the date at 1530.

Many musical historians have made Lassus the object of special study and research; among these may be mentioned Delmotte, Bäumker, Declève, Destouches, Mathieu, Mantovani, Sandberger, Van der Straeten, and Van den Borren; the last named has published the most recent as well as the fullest and most exact study of the master and his work. [But see Gustave Reese's *Music in the Renaissance*, 1954.]

In common with other biographers of Lassus, Van den Borren attacks the ancient piece of misinformation which makes the renowned artist the son of a counterfeiter; his paragraphs on this matter are conclusive: they do not merely attack the libel; they demolish it. Orlande de Lassus is generally known in Belgium as Roland de Lattre, and the form Lassus is considered as a Latinization. This is an error, based on the statement of the Hainault annalist, Vinchant, according to which statement the master changed his original name of de Lattre to escape the shame of the family disgrace. It is true that a Jehan de Lassus was condemned at Mons for counterfeiting in 1550; but there is no remotest particle of evidence connecting this man with the great musician; the name is very common in that part of the country. This would seem enough, but Van den Borren goes on to mention an argument which has escaped others. The name of the criminal was de Lassus, not de Lattre; there would be no object in changing from the latter to the former, from a name with no odium attached to it to one so burdened! The two names are, besides, utterly without connection: de Lassus derives from de-là-dessus; de Lattre from de l'Atre. Thus is this piece of mediaeval gossip effectively countered.

Vinchant tells us that Lassus was born in the "rue dicte Gerlande" (de la guirlande), and that he was a choirboy in the Church of St. Nicolas in the Rue Havré. Quickelberg relates that the young Orlande

---

ORLANDE DE LASSUS from *Dufay to Sweelinck* by Edna Richolson Sollitt; Ives, Washburn; 1933.

commenced his studies at seven years of age, and was taught the first principles of music at eight and a half years.

His voice was so beautiful that he was three times stolen from the school where he lived with the other choir-boys. We may recall in this connection the "frantic search," mentioned by Van der Straeten, which was made in the Netherlands for high voices of good quality by agents of the various princes throughout Europe. On the first two occasions the boy Orlande was recovered by his parents; on the third he consented to follow his abductor into the service of Fernand de Gonzaga, Viceroy of Sicily, who was at that time commanding the forces of Charles V at the siege of St. Dizier. This siege took place between the 8th of July and the 7th of August, 1544, when Orlande was about twelve years old.

After the peace of Crespy in September of that year, which peace cut short a march on Paris, Gonzaga set out to return to his estates in Sicily, taking the boy with him. They arrived in Sicily in November of the following year, being delayed for some reason not known to us.

The transfer of Gonzaga to Milan occurred the next May, and again Orlande went with him. In Milan the boy enjoyed the first quiet existence which he had known since his abduction. The maestro di capella at Milan was at that time a Netherlander, Verecore, and Orlande was placed in his choir. When his voice changed he was taken to Naples, where he lived for three years with the Marquis de la Terza. This nobleman was himself a poet, a man of distinguished taste and real accomplishment in the arts. Naples had already enjoyed the musical influence of Tinctoris and Diego Ortiz, and the environment was an excellent one for the young musician.

From Naples Lassus went to Rome; after six months as guest of the Archbishop Altoviti, as Quickelberg relates, he was named director of the choir at San Giovanni Laterano. No documents have come to light relative to this activity. What a contrast was the environment at Rome to that of Naples! From princely luxury and worldly gaiety to the quietude of a sanctuary; from villanelles to masses. The young Palestrina was becoming known in Rome for his work as master of the boys at the Julian Chapel, and his devout and genial efforts, emphasized by his success, made a deep impression on Lassus. Palestrina was about twenty-eight years old and Lassus twenty-one when the latter arrived in Rome.

After two years in Rome, Lassus was recalled to the Netherlands by the grave illness of his parents. The journey was long; he arrived to find them already dead. Some writers state that the composer then went upon a journey to England in the company of a noble Italian amateur, Cesare Brancaccio, whose acquaintance he probably made at Naples; Brancaccio had a diplomatic mission to fulfill in England; there are records concerning its failure and his deportation to France. It is far from certain that Lassus made this trip to England or accompanied Brancaccio to France. What is certain concerning this period is that Lassus was settled in Antwerp late in 1554 or early in 1555. This is fixed by a dedication of his first book of madrigals, villanelles, etc., dated May 13, 1555, when he had been already some months in Antwerp.

The Antwerp of that period was a delightful place of residence for a talented young musician. The musical and artistic life was highly developed, and the city was able to sustain this life, being a center of world commerce. The great firms of every country had offices and representatives there. One of the most important of these was that of Fugger, the banking family of Germany, the richest family of that age. The name of Fugger is encountered in every sort of commercial and cultural history of northern Europe for many years.

Such commercial princes as these have at various times had a strong influence on art development. When they are enlightened and cultivated, and their influence is active in behalf of worthy artists, they are benefactors indeed; when, as sometimes happens, they are merely eager for prominence, desirous of being considered lovers of art yet unable to place their patronage with discrimination, such families can hinder or destroy much that is of value, by the negative process of aiding what is mediocre or worse. For it is as impossible for artistic excellence to thrive surrounded by an encouraged mediocrity as it is impossible for delicate flowers to flourish in a bed where weeds are given careful tendance.

Very fortunately the Fuggers were a family of cultivated artistic amateurs; and there were other families of wealthy and discriminating art-lovers in the Netherlands at that time, several of them in Antwerp. These were happy to welcome with enthusiasm an artist so eminently gifted as Lassus. He remained two years in Antwerp, and they must have been two of the pleasantest years of his life.

The reputation of the young musician was made in these years, and his first published works appeared here and in Venice simultaneously. We have already mentioned the book of madrigals and villanelles; this was published by Tielman Susato in 1555. The same year Gardano placed on sale in Venice the first book of Lassus' five-part madrigals. In the next year appeared the first book of the composer's motets, which were issued by Jean de Laet, afterwards the partner of Waelrant.

Established thus in the midst of powerful friends and admirers, and already known as the composer of varied and interesting works published in far separated countries, it is certain that Lassus had a reputation commensurate with his abilities. Albert V, Duke of Bavaria, learned that Antwerp possessed a musician of this distinction, and was desirous of acquiring his services for the ducal chapel. Orlande was invited to Munich in 1556.

The Bavarian Court Chapel had been established since the fourteenth century; the eminent Swiss musician, Senfl, had been active in its service for a number of years previous to the arrival of Lassus, and the reigning duke had increased the personnel of the chapel. From the autumn of 1556 we have constant mention of Lassus in the chapel records and those of the Bavarian court. These records make plain the importance of the eminent musician in his new environment. Not that he was given a high office at once; on the contrary, he entered as a simple singer, modestly taking his place without comment. But his genius made itself felt from the beginning.

In 1560 the Duke sent him on an important musical mission to the Netherlands; he was to engage singers and choirboys for the chapel. This we learn from a letter of Margaret of Parma, Regent of the Netherlands. She calls Lassus "maître de chapelle du Duc de Bavière." The Bavarian records make no mention at this time of a change in the status of Lassus; Sandberger believes that the advancement came to him in 1563. Whatever his title, however, it is plain that Lassus had in 1560 the confidence and respect of his patron and was invested with a very real power in the chapel.

The first work of the composer to be published in Germany was issued in Nuremberg in 1562 and was dedicated to the Duke. In October of that year Lassus accompanied the Duke on his journey to the coronation of Maximilian II at Frankfort; they visited Prague, Bamberg, and Wurzburg, also.

Van den Borren mentions the preparation in 1563 of a codex which contains the Penitential Psalms of Lassus; the two volumes have each a portrait of Lassus "by the court painter, Hans Muelich." We have already been told by Van Aerde that a codex containing works by de Rore had been prepared for Albert by "Johan Mielich, the court painter"; also Ambros, in the third volume of his history, uses this version of the name. The portrait of Lassus shows, says Van den Borren, "a large forehead, somewhat receding, the hair close-cut, the arch of the eyebrow well defined. The eyes are large, and have a rather vague expression, traducing the strength and finesse of Lassus' intelligence. The nose, 'd'aspect flaireur' (an untranslatable description, this) seems to prolong the receding line of the forehead. The mouth is sensual; the beard is short and cut in a round. The whole appearance of the artist is unusual rather than attractive."

In 1564 and 1565 occurred the first French publication of an entire volume of Lassus' work, by the firm of LeRoy and Ballard; previously these editors had included single pieces in their collections. In 1562 and

1567 Lassus visited Italy to engage singers and players of instruments. During the latter journey occurred the regrettable incident concerning the Duke of Ferrara; to a courteous dedication of a work by Lassus the Duke responded with so niggardly a recognition that "a diplomatic question was avoided only by his supplementing this in an indirect manner." Lassus remained but a short time in Ferrara and returned to Munich.

In the "Discorsi" of Troiano are found descriptions of the many festivities organized and conducted by Lassus in 1568 on the occasion of the wedding of the young Duke William with Renée of Lorraine; in these descriptions Orlande is praised for his polished and modest manners. The festivities, remarks Van den Borren dryly, were of a variety and were given under conditions calculated to astonish those who still labor under the delusion that the sixteenth century was devoted entirely to a cappella polyphony. Many works were performed entirely by instruments, many by instruments and voices, in addition to those for voices alone.

We learn that in these festivities Lassus took part also in a comedy improvised for the occasion; his rôle was that of Lorenzo Magnifico, and "he appeared on the stage wearing a mask which at first sight raised a shout of laughter."

In 1570 Lassus was given a patent of nobility, valid for his descendants as well as for himself; this was bestowed by Maximilian II. In 1571 he made a long-desired journey to Paris. He was received with honor and acclaim; Charles IX showed him every attention, and the publisher, LeRoy, arranged the introduction of everyone of note in Paris at the time. Orlande "returned to Munich loaded with honors and money."

Many letters of Lassus to the young Duke William about this period show us the humor, gaiety, and wit of the composer. These letters are written in "a mosaic of French, Latin, and German, following and interlarding each other with burlesque vivacity, giving them a flavor of frolicsome roguery worthy of a college youth in delirium." This gaiety was but one side of the nature of Lassus, however; it was a surface covering a character deeply religious and most sensitive. He was at times melancholy, and always introspective. The Penitential Psalms were composed in a sincere outpouring of belief and feeling.

In 1574 Lassus went again to Italy. Interesting letters tell us of his experiences in the Tyrol, experiences which the traveller of today finds unchanged to a startling degree. Arrived in Rome, Lassus was received in audience by Pope Gregory XII, who greatly enjoyed meeting the composer, we are told, and who conferred upon him the honorary title of Chevalier de St. Pierre. This Italian voyage of Lassus was not highly successful; only four singers were engaged, with "a viol-player and some dancers." The Duke was not pleased; the journey had been costly; it was not until some months later that serenity was restored between Lassus and his patron.

Magnificent offers were made to Lassus in 1574 by the King of France. Large sums of money and honorable titles were promised him in an invitation sent through his publisher, LeRoy, who doubtless would have been happy to see the great musician established in Paris. As Lassus had already planned his journey to Italy before receiving this invitation, we know that his voyage was not "a start toward Paris, interrupted by news of the death of the French King." This piece of misinformation has been incorporated as fact into some musical histories; but the full correspondence of Lassus, available now, shows clearly that he returned to Munich before May 5th, and the king did not die until May 30th. Another myth concerning Charles IX is that Lassus composed the Penitential Psalms to assuage the King's remorse for the events of St. Bartholomew's Eve; as we know, these Psalms were written thirteen years before that date and were for the private use of the Duke of Bavaria.

The letters of Lassus to Duke William are particularly frequent and intimate in the years from 1574 to 1578. These missives speak of little dinners, of gardening, of musical jests, and a thousand other trifles in the lives of friends. In 1579 the composer signed an agreement to remain throughout his life at the Bavarian court. Shortly after this Duke Albert died, leaving gigantic state debts to be immediately faced by his son and successor, the genial, light-hearted William.

The first things to be sacrificed to the pressing necessity of the ducal position were the artistic luxuries of Albert; the chapel was reduced at one blow from 44 members to 22; two years later it was further reduced. The payment of wages to Lassus was faithfully carried out, but the musician found himself hampered in all his plans by the small number of performers; he had long been accustomed to having at his command a body of singers and players without parallel in Europe.

Lassus remained faithfully attached to the Bavarian house. He offered to release his claims to funds which he had received from Albert and re-loaned at interest; William, however, would not hear of his sacrificing this part of his earnings. The entire episode is greatly to the credit of both William and Lassus. The Duke, now weighted with cares of State and overwhelmed with debt, changed from the gay young man who had exchanged sprightly letters with Lassus to a careworn, serious ruler. He became deeply religious, and Munich grew to be a stronghold of Catholicism. This was well suited to the true nature and feelings of Lassus, as we know; he was the loyal friend of the Jesuits at Munich; their Seminary there has a portrait of him. This is a contrast to the former portrait; here the composer is graver, more dignified, and somewhat melancholy.

Lassus went to Italy for the last time in 1585. He made a pilgrimage to Loreto, and afterward visited Ferrara. This time he was received there with the greatest honor. The court of the art-loving Alfonso II enjoyed one of the earliest and most complete orchestras of Europe; remembering the delight of Lassus in using the instrumental facilities at his disposal in Munich, we may imagine his deep pleasure in the performances at Ferrara.

Returning to Munich Lassus became more and more subject to melancholia. His physician was one of his best friends; the relations with the ducal family were all that could be wished, and Lassus was given every honor and privilege which the Duke was able to bestow; there was no true cause for the gloom which clouded the days of the master. It was disease and not reality which tormented him. He passed from his suffering to death in 1594. His heirs erected a monument the following year; it is now in the Bavarian National Museum. But no monument is needed to Orlande de Lassus. His own work is the most glorious of monuments.

The compositions of Orlande de Lassus may be divided into eight groups: motets; Masses; Magnificats; Passions; madrigals; villanelles, moresques, and miscellaneous pieces; French songs; German lieder.

The motets form the most important group of his works, both from the point of view of musical value and that of numerical preponderance. The sons of Lassus, Ferdinand and Rodolphe, issued in 1604 a collection as complete as possible, calling it "Magnum opus musicum." This collection contains one hundred motets for four voices, 24 for two voices, 24 for three, 167 for five, 159 for six, 11 for seven, 24 for eight, two for nine, three for ten, and two for twelve voices.

Among the motets must be included the Penitential Psalms, which were composed for Duke Albert and not published until 1584, five years after the Duke's death. These Psalms are for five voices, but various sections of single numbers are for two, three, or four voices. Also among the motets are: the "Lectiones," in two parts, one with text from Job, and one concerning the Nativity; Offices, five in number; the Stabat Mater; and Lamentations (five voices).

The Magnificats were published complete by Rodolphe de Lassus in 1619. This edition included the Nuremberg collection, those of the Patrocinium of 1576 and of 1587, and sixteen posthumous works.

The Passions are four in number; one was included in the Patrocinium of 1575.

The madrigals of Lassus comprise the second, fourth, sixth, eighth, and tenth volumes of the magnificent Breitkopf and Härtel edition of the complete works, which edition was begun in 1894 to commemorate the 300th anniversary of his death. The eighty-nine madrigals for five voices appeared in a half-dozen volumes published between 1555 and 1587, and in a series of collections issued at different dates. There are forty-one four-voice madrigals; thirteen of these were published prior to 1560, the rest between that date and 1587. The six-voice pieces were all published after 1578. There are two madrigals for seven voices, and three for ten.

The villanelles, songs concerning the loves of peasants and shepherds, are souvenirs of the Neapolitan period of Lassus; they are written principally to texts in the Neapolitan dialect and are eighteen in number. The moresques are dialogues, serenades, etc., concerning Giorgia, Lucia, Cathalina, Zanni, and other figures; the patois of the Moorish-Italian lower classes is used for the texts of most of these pieces. They show an aspect of the composer which reflects his observations of the tumultuous and teeming life of Naples' streets. They are, on occasion, far from edifying.

The French songs number 146; they form the twelfth, fourteenth, and sixteenth volumes of the complete works. There are 67 for four voices, 58 for five, one for three, four for six, and five for eight.

The German lieder are 93 in number; 25 for three voices, 17 for four, 41 for five, nine for six, and one for eight.

QUESTIONS

1. Why is Lassus considered an important composer? What were his particular contributions to music?
2. Can you suggest reasons why the general public is unfamiliar with the work of Lassus? Can you name some other Renaissance composers?
3. Name some contemporaries of Lassus living in other countries. Are they generally familiar names? Why? Is Shakespeare a contemporary? What accounts for his fame?
4. Look up the name of Fugger. Compare the contribution of the Fugger family to music with that of the Esterhazys, the family discussed in the essay on Haydn.
5. Look up the words, "madrigal," "villanelle," and "motet." What do they have in common? Do you know whether composers still compose pieces with similar titles? Can you find some examples?

COMPOSERS IN THEIR TIMES / 3

Baroque   *Musicians, music critics, historians may
disagree about the significance of one composer
or another. But about Johann Sebastian Bach
(1685-1750) there is no question. Along with
Mozart and Beethoven, Bach is justly considered one
of the undeniably great composers of the past
three hundred years. Born into the most important
musical family in history, Bach was known in his
lifetime as an extraordinary organist, but a composer of
church music whose skill was spent on archaic and
academic forms; his star was pale beside that of
a Handel, a Telemann, or even a K.P.E. Bach.
Richard Anthony Leonard, author and music
historian, shows us in an exceptionally well-constructed
essay the middle and late period's of Bach's life.*

RICHARD ANTHONY LEONARD

$\mathcal{S}$HORTLY AFTER HIS SECOND MARRIAGE A RIFT began to appear in the placid relations of Bach and his patron. The prince also married and his bride caused a decided change in the order of things at Cöthen. She was a light-minded and flighty young person, described as caring only for "balls and fireworks." Her appreciation of music was adolescent. In the playing of her husband's Kapelle, and particularly in the weighty music of its director, she had no interest whatever. Bach termed her an *"amusa"* and, realizing that the prince's interests were diverted from his music, he began to look about for another post. For a long time the urge seems to have been strong in him to get back into church music, to a post which would put a choir and an organ once again at his disposal. In 1723 he got what he wanted.

In Leipzig there was a famous school for boys, St. Thomas's, a venerable institution that had been founded in the thirteenth century. Bach heard that the cantorship was vacant, so he applied for the post. The duties of the cantor included teaching singing and Latin to some fifty boys between the ages of fourteen and twenty-one, and acting as music director of the two churches with which the school was connected —St. Thomas's and St. Nicholas's. It was the latter phase of the cantor's duties which attracted Bach, for it meant that he had to provide an elaborate program of music in one of the two churches every Sunday and on certain feast days.

Early in 1723, Bach underwent the trials for the appointment, and on Good Friday of that year he conducted his hastily composed *St. John Passion* in St. Thomas's Church, as proof of his ability. A few months later he was formally appointed. The leave-taking from Cöthen was under unforeseen and tragic circumstances. Nine days before Bach and his family departed the *amusa* died. Two years later the prince married again; but in 1728, five years after Bach left his service, he too was dead. Bach's affection for the young nobleman who had treated him so kindly is shown by his journey to Cöthen to attend the prince's funeral and to provide music for the memorial service.

The Leipzig post was Bach's last. He remained there for twenty-seven years until his death in 1750. He went to Leipzig in his thirty-eighth year, an artist with almost two decades of very great accomplishment behind him. All this, however, was in reality only the prelude to what was to come. The music of the Leipzig period is difficult to

BACH from *The Stream of Music* by Richard Anthony Leonard; copyright 1943 by Doubleday and Company, Inc. Reprinted by permission.

Composers in Their Times: Baroque / Leonard

appraise, because in physical bulk alone it is gigantic. Bach was a busy man much of the time, occupied with the routine tasks of his cantorship; yet during these years he composed the *St. Matthew Passion* and the colossal Mass in B minor, which are his greatest works; the *Magnificat*, six motets, a series of organ pieces that crown his entire accomplishment for that instrument, more superlative works for the clavier, and a vast series of church cantatas. Not only is this music enormous in physical bulk, but some of it is on a scale of architectonic design that is mountainous, and inspired beyond any music composed before its time or since.

Viewing these accomplishments, it is hard to believe that the cantorship of St. Thomas's was a sorry disappointment to the composer. The existing record of his office is a long recital of misunderstanding and petty bickering, quarrels with associates who tried to cheat him out of his perquisites, with church authorities who treated him like a hack, and with narrow-minded rectors who had no sympathy with his music and no realization of his stature as an artist. When Bach went there in 1723 he found that the school was badly run down, in the hands of an old rector who was tottering and senile. The boys were an undisciplined gang of young ruffians, morally weakened by having to beg in the streets of Leipzig for donations to the school, and often ill and miserable from undernourishment and neglect. Their musical education was poor and their voices were wretched. Moreover, the older singers and instrumentalists who were hired from the town to fill out the choir and the orchestra were also inadequate. When Bach complained about these conditions he only got himself on bad terms with the rector and the town council.

With the death of the old rector in 1729 a new one named Gesner was appointed, and for the next five years improvement and order reigned at St. Thomas's. Gesner was young, a good organizer, and a scholar, and his regard for Bach's music and attainments was marked. But Gesner was followed in 1734 by one Johann August Ernesti, a hardheaded bigot who became one of Bach's worst persecutors. He hated music, disparaged its importance even in front of the boys, and did his best to humiliate the cantor. Bach was something of a match for him. Always proud when his dignity was affronted, and pugnacious when the rights of his office were at stake, the composer stood by his guns to the bitter end. One of his worst encounters with Ernesti would be essentially comic if it did not involve the personal feelings of one of the world's greatest geniuses. It began when the boys of the choir, unruly because Bach was a poor disciplinarian, behaved in a scandalous manner during a wedding. This led to a quarrel between Bach and Ernesti over the right to appoint a prefect. The battle lasted for two years, during which time both cantor and rector bombarded the council with petitions, charges, and countercharges. It did not end until Bach at last petitioned the King of Saxony. His majesty resolved the matter by a compromise, with Bach on the long end of the stick.

Bach and his family lived in one of the wings of the school building itself. When they first came to St. Thomas's the ancient structure was overcrowded and badly in need of repair. It housed the family of the rector, the schoolrooms and dormitories of the boys, and the family of the cantor. The crowded and unsanitary conditions are blamed by Professor Terry for the depressing record of mortality among Bach's children during his early years in Leipzig. Of the first eight children born to Anna Magdalena only two survived, one of whom was an imbecile. The other six children died at ages ranging from one day to five years. After Bach had been there eight years the building was enlarged and renovated. Of the five Bach children born thereafter four were healthy and survived their father many years. Among them was Johann Christian (1735-1782), one of the most illustrious of the sons. Through his successes as a composer in London he became known as the "English" Bach.

In the gloomy, congested quarters of the cantor one room was reserved for his study. It was small and narrow, lighted by a single window. A thin whitewashed partition separated it from one of the classrooms, and from it could be heard the sound of a near-by mill wheel. This was Bach's workroom for many years.

The composer's regular salary at St. Thomas's was small, but it was increased by special fees which he earned at funerals and weddings, so that his income amounted to about five hundred dollars a year. To this were added allowances for corn, firewood, and wine. Bach once remarked that in certain years his income from funerals was a disappointment, because the air of the town of Leipzig was good and therefore deaths were fewer.

The most important of Bach's duties as cantor was the composition of music for the church services. Anyone wishing to trace reasons for the slow decline of Protestantism since the eighteenth century might do well to examine the regular Sunday service which took place in St. Thomas's and St. Nicholas's during Bach's tenure. It was a mixture of worship, preaching, and music of appalling length. It began at seven in the morning and lasted until nearly noon. The discomforts to the congregation resulting from such a stupefying ritual can only be imagined. Some slight relief was afforded the boys in the choir: if the church got so cold that they could no longer endure it, they were marched back to the school to listen to a sermon. The only respite for adult worshipers occurred about midway in the eighteen-part service, when (on alternate Sundays) the choir would perform a cantata, accompanied by organ and orchestra. The cantata was an elaborate collection of solos, recitatives, duets, and choruses, with occasional orchestral interludes. It lasted about half an hour.

The cantata as a musical form occupied Bach's attention over a space of forty years. He wrote his first in 1704 when he was the boy organist at Arnstadt, and his last in Leipzig in 1744. The sum total is two hundred and ninety-five cantatas, but the great majority belong to the Leipzig period. There, in the space of about twenty years, he composed about two hundred and sixty-five cantatas, an average of one a month. About two-thirds of these are extant. It is true that there were other cantors of his time who were even more prolific than Bach in the production of these works, but his achievement remains monumental. What in other hands was simply a routine and hack production, he maintained at the level of great art.

The cantata was in reality a sacred concert which had gradually grown up in the Lutheran service. It was customary for the cantata to be linked with the particular Gospel of the day; in fact it was a kind of musical exposition of the Gospel text. For the words of some of his early cantatas at Weimar Bach went directly to the Bible, piecing together various verses to suit his purpose. Thereafter he began using librettos which had been prepared by various religious writers and which were in common use throughout Germany. These librettos provided the composer with a ready-made framework for his music. There were rhymed stanzas, portions of blank verse, excerpts taken directly from the Bible text, and generally as a conclusion a stanza from one of the old Lutheran hymns—all bearing directly on the day's Gospel.

Bach's treatment of the words of his cantatas was identical with his procedure in his organ chorale preludes. He sought always to make his music express as vividly as possible the ideas conveyed by the words. He painted pictures, imitated sounds, portrayed emotions, often with complete realism. The musical symbols that he used were the same as those he evolved for the chorale preludes, a tonal language that anticipated the speech of many of the nineteenth-century song composers.

In a number of his last cantatas Bach dispensed with librettos entirely and evolved the so-called "chorale cantatas." Just as the organ chorale preludes are a polyphonic expansion of the simple old hymns, so the chorale cantatas are an even more elaborate and extended glorification of these same sacred songs. Using both the words and music of some chorale as his basic thematic idea, Bach constructed recitatives, ariosos, duets, choruses—weaving a spreading polyphonic fabric out of a single slender thread. Only at the end of the cantata was the basic hymn tune heard in its original form, when the choir, proclaiming it simply but with Bach's incomparable harmonization, was probably joined by the congregation.

Even though his immense collection of cantatas comprises by far the greater bulk of Bach's entire output, it remains the least known of all his work. The reason lies partly in the fact that the cantata as part of church worship is long since obsolete. It had passed from the liturgy of many churches even during Bach's lifetime. In modern times few countries have had musical organizations with the training and the traditional background necessary for adequate performances of Bach's cantatas. These works require soloists of exceptional talent and intelligence, first-rate instrumentalists, and choruses equipped to sing in a musical style of great difficulty—in short, a group as perfectly trained and organized as a modern symphony orchestra. In America, where virtuoso orchestras are common, choruses of the same caliber are comparatively non-existent. Public interest in choral music is as low as that in symphonic music is high and widespread. Until some revival of interest takes place in the field of choral music, that vital part of Bach's art represented by his cantatas must remain virtually unknown in this country —like a gallery of great paintings locked from the public gaze.

On the afternoon of Good Friday, 1729, the congregation of St. Thomas's assembled according to an ancient custom to hear a presentation of the Passion of our Lord in musical form. In this particular year the biblical account was to be that contained in the Gospel according to St. Matthew. Bach was ready with a newly composed work, and around him in the organ loft he had assembled an exceptionally large group of singers and instrumentalists. In addition to his regular chorus there was a second chorus made up of singers who did not usually perform at the church; organists were ready at both organs; and there were two orchestras, the usual group being augmented by players from the town, the school, and a local university. This impressive band of performers must have indicated to the congregation that the cantor had prepared something of an exceptional order.

One of Bach's pupils who was present at this first performance of the *St. Matthew Passion* recorded that the congregation was confused by what it heard and left unappreciative. "Some high officials and well-born ladies in one of the galleries began to sing the first chorale with great devotion from their books. But as the theatrical music proceeded, they were thrown into the greatest wonderment, saying to each other, 'What does it all mean?' while one old lady, a widow, exclaimed, 'God help us! 'Tis surely an opera-comedy!' " It is doubtful if the cantor himself, retiring to his home in the Lenten twilight after his strenuous labors, had any realization of the magnitude of his accomplishment.

Representations of the Passion of Jesus Christ, both musical and dramatic, are as old as the Church itself. Medieval mystery plays, oratorios, and musical Passions all stemmed from the same impulse—a desire to illustrate and act out the stories of the Bible, so that they could be made clear and vivid to the masses who no longer understood the Latin tongue of the Catholic service. The Passion as a musical form had begun in the early centuries of the Church as a simple dramatic recitation. Through the Middle Ages it had been joined to music, with the parts of the Evangelist, the Saviour, and the Disciples intoned in plainsong instead of merely recited. With the gradual enrichment of the art of music the Passion evolved into an elaborate and extended form, employing soloists, chorus, and instrumentalists.

The exact number of Passions which Bach wrote is in doubt, despite exhaustive research by Bach experts. Only two are extant—the *St. John Passion*, which he composed hurriedly for his examination as cantor, and the *St. Matthew*. It is known that he composed a *St. Mark Passion*, which is lost. There is a strong possibility that he composed a fourth, also lost. However, it is certain that of all these works it was the *St. Matthew* which received his most mature inspiration, that it was the most elaborately conceived and the most carefully wrought. Thus we are fortunate in having Bach's masterpiece in the Passion form, and the greatest work of its kind in existence.

The literary framework of the *St. Matthew Passion* indicates the process of evolution that must have gone on through the centuries which preceded it. Composers obviously had grown tired of repetitions of the same words from the Gospels describing the Passion; they sought to vary and to enrich the scenario itself. Bach's work indicates how this was done. The main burden of the story is taken directly from the Bible— from Chapters XXVI and XXVII of St. Matthew. These biblical verses are set to music by Bach in the form of recitatives, with the words of the Evangelist sung by a tenor and those of Jesus by a bass. Interspersed between these verses are short poems, not from the Bible but from the pen of Picander, a religious writer of the period. Bach set these in the form of arias and choruses with orchestral accompaniment; and in essence they are a sympathetic commentary, like that of the chorus in the Greek drama, upon the biblical story as it unfolds. Finally, several of the old Lutheran chorales are also set between the recitatives and arias. These were sung by the chorus, joined probably by the congregation.

The framework of a Passion was thus a piece of literary joining which required considerable skill. The man who made Bach's libretto was one Christian Friedrich Henrici, who wrote under the pen name of Picander. He was a post-office official and tax collector. On the side he amused himself by writing satirical verse, some of it scandalously vulgar. Quite incongruously he turned to religious poetry, writing one of the most popular sets of cantata texts. Bach knew Picander well, and most of his Leipzig cantatas are to this writer's words. Like the church cantata, the Passion was a dying form when Bach produced his masterpiece. It did not disappear from the liturgy of the churches as rapidly as the cantata, but it was definitely on the way out. In reality Bach said the last word, for in the whole history of religious music there is nothing to compare with his portrayal of the Passion of Jesus Christ. This work stands at the end of a long evolution of devotional music; it is modern in complexity and scope, but its mystical fervor, its emotional ecstasy, its passionate absorption in the divine epic of the Christian faith—all this is medieval in spirit. That spirit was soon to vanish from music, just as a century before Bach's time it had begun to disappear from the art of painting.

For Bach the Passion of Jesus Christ was no mere religious allegory; it was a drama of reality, and its poignancy touched the deepest chords of his nature and his lifelong faith. In the *St. Matthew Passion* he is first of all a tonal dramatist, striving to bring to life with all the power and vividness at his command the personal portrait as well as the epic tragedy of the Man of Sorrows. He took full advantage of the tragic and dramatic side of the story; in fact it is astonishing how nearly operatic in the modern sense many of his devices are. But the focal point of the entire work remains always the portrait of the Saviour. Through the long and complex score—the swirling masses of choral polyphony; the arias with their incredible richness of texture, and their adorning obbligatos of violin, oboe, and flute; the devotional chorales, strewn through the score (in Terry's phrase) "like jewels of price"—through all this gorgeousness it is nevertheless the music accompanying the words of Jesus which achieves the inspirational apex of the entire score. By the simplest means Bach attains his ends. When the Evangelist relates his story it is fairly simple recitative, accompanied by sparse chords from the orchestra. When the voice of Jesus is heard it is always to the accompaniment of soft string passages. No more moving music has ever been written for the human voice. The brooding sadness, the infinite compassion of the Saviour are limned in these vocal lines; while around Him, in the superb harmonies of the strings, glows the nimbus of divinity. In this portrait Bach is like a Rembrandt of the tonal art. He had seen in his own heart the piercing vision of the man he was portraying; he had enveloped his subject with his own boundless sympathy.

The *St. Matthew Passion* had a few performances in the Leipzig churches while Bach was still alive, but it seems to have made no special impression. After the composer's death it lay silent and forgotten for more than three quarters of a century. On Good Friday, 1829, exactly a century after its premiere, Mendelssohn revived it with a performance in Berlin. With that event began the resurrection of Bach's music for the modern world.

Great as it is, the *St. Matthew Passion* does not stand alone in Bach's catalogue. One other work, the Mass in B minor, must be ranked with it as a summation of the composer's art.

In July 1733, Bach's oldest son, Wilhelm Friedemann, was installed as organist in a church in Dresden, and his father went along as his sponsor. While there Bach took the opportunity to ask a favor of his sovereign, Augustus III of Saxony. He wanted an appointment as court composer, an honor which was finally conferred three years later. To pay homage he sent Augustus the manuscript of the *Kyrie* and *Gloria* of a Mass in B minor, together with a letter in which the composer referred to the work as a "trifling example of my skill in Musique."

Sometime during the next few years (no one knows exactly how or when) the composer added to the Mass by constructing a *Credo*, *Sanctus*, and *Agnus Dei*. Much controversial ink has been shed on the question of how Bach, a stanch Lutheran, came to write a Roman Catholic Mass. Terry's explanation seems to be the most logical. The original *Kyrie* and *Gloria*, he points out, were in reality part of the Lutheran church service. When Bach expanded the work with a *Credo*, *Sanctus*, and *Agnus Dei* he did not create a purely Roman Catholic Mass. For one thing the work is far too long for a church service, and it departs in a number of instances from the strict letter and order of the Roman liturgy. Terry believes that "the Mass is neither Roman nor Lutheran in intention and outlook, but the expression of a catholic Christianity. . . . Bach's genius was Teutonic in its inclination to complete a design" . . . and "in the compulsion to express himself in an art form which he had studied deeply."

The final Mass is gigantic in size. It consists of twenty-four movements, for chorus, orchestra, and five solo voices. Fifteen of the movements are for chorus, with six solos and three duets. A complete performance requires almost three hours. The work was not entirely original; the composer borrowed and adapted about one third of the movements from his other works—chiefly from his church cantatas. Bach appears to have worked at the Mass over a period of five years, and the adaptations of the old sections as well as the composition of the new were done with extreme care, so that the vast architectural scheme could be satisfying in every detail.

The Mass in B minor contrasts strongly with the *St. Matthew Passion*. The latter work is far more personal, both in style and approach. It relates a biblical story, first translated into the German language and then into illuminating and deeply expressive music. The Mass in B minor has, of course, no story to tell. It expounds in music the tenets of a great faith. Its text is in general the Ordinary of the Roman Mass. Bach takes those Latin words, phrase by phrase, and builds them into lengthy movements. The result is a series of stupendous murals, each affirming a phase of the beliefs which are the foundation stones of Christianity. In his *St. Matthew Passion* Bach had worked with the deeply human perceptions of a Rembrandt, and at times the mystical insight of a Leonardo; in the Mass in B minor he is a Michelangelo, the painter of colossal frescoes. His vision sweeps across vast distances, spanning heaven and earth.

The main burden of this structure is carried by the choruses. The arias and duets between them, though bearing the thread of literary continuity, are in reality moments of respite from the weight and impact of the choral masses. It is true that some of them fall below the inspirational level of the greatest arias in the *St. Matthew Passion,* perhaps because the words of the liturgy are often dogmatic abstractions which almost defy musical setting. The best of them is the pathetic *Agnus Dei* for contralto.

The choruses dwarf everything else by comparison. All but one are in five vocal parts, with the orchestra adding a contrapuntal web of its own. The dimensions of the Mass, its exalted mood, the majesty of its subject, are all set in the first four measures of the *Kyrie eleison* which open the work. There follows a long and stunning exposition, developed fugally, the vocal lines interweaving and overlapping in a bewildering pattern of sound as they proclaim again and again a powerful basic theme. The inspirational level is high, but Bach maintains and even surpasses it in the fourteen choral movements that follow. Some are exultations of the most brilliant sort, like the *Gloria in excelsis Deo,* or the dazzling fugue *Cum sancto spiritu.* Others are solid, broadly developed affirmations of dogmatic faith; for example, the *Credo,* which is based on a theme intoned in the church for more than fifteen hundred years. Still others are poignant and sorrowful—like the second *Kyrie eleison,* the *Qui tollis,* and the *Et incarnatus*—movements which are saturated with pathos and tenderness.

The *Crucifixus* stands alone in the entire range of musical expression. Bach's portrayal of the tragedy of Calvary exemplifies the enigma in which his art remains eternally wrapped, defying analysis and dissection. For this supreme moment in the history of mankind the composer had first to decide upon a musical form commensurate with the idea. He chose a passacaglia. A desolate falling theme in the bass, four measures long, is repeated, note for note, thirteen times, while above it the chorus intones its grief-stricken vision of the dying Saviour. Thus the basic structure of this music, which is unplumbed in emotional depth, is found to be a problem in pure musical mathematics.

In the nineteenth movement, the *Confiteor*, there is an adagio of twenty-six measures, to the words "*Et expecto resurrectionem mortuorum.*" Here Bach paints the prophecy of the great Resurrection. All contrapuntal movement suddenly slows down; the music evolves through a long series of harmonic progressions which are a hundred years ahead of the composer's time in their daring modernity. The dead rise from their tombs for the Last Judgment.

The climax of the entire Mass (and of the composer's whole creative effort) is reached with the *Sanctus*. In a six-part chorus the scene of paradise and the Almighty unfolds. "Holy, holy, holy, Lord God of Hosts. Heaven and earth are full of Thy glory." We behold the adoration of the heavenly hosts, with the higher voices of the chorus simulating the antiphony of the seraphim and the quiring angels, while the basses intone a vast theme that strides in octaves—gigantic pillars of tone upon which the nave of heaven rests. The movement is one great rolling thunder of music that seems to echo to the last boundaries of a limitless creation.

When Bach finished the Mass in B minor he was close to fifty years old and entering the last phase of his life. He never again attempted anything of such dimensions, and the swift current of his production began to abate somewhat. However, there was not the slightest sign of a flagging inspiration. He maintained his standard to the last days of his life.

After years of not composing for the organ he returned to that instrument, making several collections of his chorale preludes for publication. A number of these were based on the Lutheran Catechism hymns. They contain some of his weightiest music and are massive specimens of his mature organ style. Two works especially tower above the rest— *Aus tiefer Noth* [In Deepest Need], a gloomy and ascetic monument in six-part harmony with double pedal; and the incredible *Kyrie, Gott heiliger Geist* [Kyrie, Thou Spirit Divine]. Bach himself never surpassed the latter work, either in the development of a mountainous structure of tone from a few notes, or in the building of dramatic climax.

In this last period of his life the composer also returned to the clavier. His most notable work was Part II of *The Well-Tempered Clavier,* which appeared in 1744. This second set of twenty-four preludes and fugues is one of those rare species of the arts—a sequel which actually surpasses the original.

The so-called *Goldberg Variations,* published in 1743, were written to order. The Russian envoy to the Dresden court was a certain Count Kayserling, who was tortured by chronic insomnia. He hired a clavicenist named Goldberg, a young pupil of Bach's, to play for him at night when he could not sleep. He also commissioned Bach to compose something that would soothe his nerves during the long wakeful hours. The fee was a generous one—a snuffbox containing one hundred louis d'or. Bach responded with a set of thirty variations, a work of such amplitude and quality that the count certainly got his money's worth.

Goldberg must have been a performer of unusual ability, for these variations bristle with technical difficulties. Until recently they were seldom performed in public, because they were originally written for harpsichord with two keyboards, which permitted the hands to cross each other in a manner impossible on the modern piano keyboard. Modern editors have found ways to surmount these difficulties and today the *Variations* are frequently played, despite their great length.

The main theme which Bach used for his thirty-room structure is a charming Aria in G major, ornate with grace notes. The variations grow out of this central stem in a bewildering variety of melodic and rhythmic ideas. However, they are far from being simply variations. Digging under the surface of this luxuriantly blooming plant, one finds the real roots of the composer's ideas. The piece is actually a kind of passacaglia. A bass line of thirty-two notes governs the entire piece. It is not strictly adhered to, but nevertheless it forms the basis of all growth. Even that is not the end of the technical design. At every third variation a canon is introduced, that is, a strict imitation of the particular theme of the movement in another voice. There are nine of these canonic movements in all, each at a different interval, beginning with the unison and ending with the ninth. Moreover, there are movements in the form of a fughetta, a French overture, and a quodlibet, the last being an ancient form in which the theme is combined contrapuntally with folk tunes. In this case Bach used two popular German songs.

From this elaborate structural framework it would be easy to infer that in the *Goldberg Variations* the old cantor was chiefly bent on showing off his technical wizardry, like a pedagogue compiling a dry textbook of mathematical problems and their solutions. The *Variations* could in fact be used as an instructional work for the use of ornamentation, variation, passacaglia, and canon. If that were their main virtue they would be dead these many years, instead of holding their place among the most beautiful works in keyboard literature. They prove again the paradoxical fact of Bach's creative processes—that mathematical problems were far from shackling his imagination; that actually they stimulated the flow of his ideas, with the result that many of his works which are most rigidly bound in technical fetters are the most poetic, emotional, and humanly expressive of all.

Sometime during the last decade of his life Bach rounded off his organ works in the prelude-and-fugue style with four famous specimens. They are the preludes and fugues in Eb major, C major, E minor (the "Wedge" Fugue), and B minor. All are big works, representing the accumulated thought and the technical mastery of the composer's lifetime at his favorite instrument. The B minor Prelude and Fugue is probably the ripest of all. Its key, it is worth noting, was obviously a favorite of Bach's; he used it for many of his finest works. The Eb Fugue, popularly known as the "St. Anne" Fugue, is most frequently played. Speaking of this piece, and of the final entry of the main theme in the pedals—a thrilling, roaring declamation—Harvey Grace quotes an old English musician who said that it sounded "as if it ought to be fired off with cannon!"

In the spring of 1747, when Bach had reached the age of sixty-two he enjoyed a unique personal triumph, on the occasion of his visit to the young King of Prussia, later to be known as Frederick the Great. This is one of the few episodes in the composer's life which is documented in some detail.

Bach went to Potsdam to see his son, Karl Philipp Emanuel, who was harpsichordist in Frederick's court orchestra. The King, who later became the arch-Prussian war lord, was passionately fond of music. He had studied the flute from childhood (to the disgust of his tyrannical father, Frederick William I), and he tried seriously to become a composer. The story is told that one evening Frederick stood, flute in hand, before his orchestra, ready to play a concerto. The list of visitors to the court was handed to him. Suddenly he exclaimed, "Gentlemen, old Bach is here!" The composer was quickly summoned from his son's house. He had no time to change from his traveling clothes, a detail which embarrassed him in the presence of the King.

Frederick gave over the flute concerto and took the old man through his palace, showing him the new Silberman claviers with hammer actions—forerunners of the modern piano. Bach asked the King for a fugue subject upon which he might extemporize, and Frederick wrote one out for him. Bach's improvisation astonished the King, but the composer still held something in reserve. The next day he returned to the palace, and this time on a subject of his own he imrovised a six-part fugue. Several times Frederick cried out in amazement, "There is only one Bach!"

A few months later the composer repaid the King with a graceful tribute. He sent Frederick *The Musical Offering*, in which he used the

King's theme as a subject of two fugues and a number of canons, adding for good measure a trio for flute, violin, and clavier.

The journey to Potsdam was Bach's last. He was an old man now, and the body that had borne such a heavy burden of labor for so many years began at last to fail. Even so, he was not ready to stop. He set to work upon *Die Kunst der Fuge* [The Art of Fugue], a study which would demonstrate with finality his mastery of the old form. The resulting work is one of the most unusual in music; it is a puzzle which remains unsolved because the composer died before its completion, leaving doubt about certain of his purposes.

One phase of the work is perfectly clear. By taking a single theme and treating it in a great variety of ways, developing it through all the devices known to fugal and canonic procedure, from the simplest to the most astonishingly intricate, Bach intended to expose, as it were, the mechanism of his art as a writer of fugue. However, when the work was published there was nothing to indicate for what instrument or instruments it might be intended. It was long believed, therefore, that *The Art of Fugue* was not intended to be played at all, but was instead a tremendous abstraction, aimed chiefly to instruct and to inform. Even Schweitzer found no aesthetic purpose in the work. He wrote, "It introduces us to a still and serious world, deserted and rigid, without color, without light, without motion; it does not gladden, does not distract; yet we cannot break away from it."

Various modern editors have sought to prove that the piece is much more than cold theory. Some of them have scored it for instruments, and worked out completions of the final fugue left unfinished by Bach. The best proof that *The Art of Fugue* is suited to actual performance and is music in its fullest sense was an arrangement for chamber orchestra made in 1927 by Wolfgang Gräser, a young Swiss genius of music (and of mathematics, physics, and oriental languages), who killed himself in 1928 at the age of twenty-two. Convincing as his arrangement is, Gräser's is clearly not the last word on the subject, and *The Art of Fugue* is likely to fascinate and mystify students of music and Bach arrangers in particular for generations to come.

Bach did not complete *The Art of Fugue* because his eyesight began to fail. He was finally persuaded to consult an English oculist, Chevalier John Taylor, who was then visiting and practicing in Germany. Early in 1750, Taylor performed an operation of some kind on Bach's eyes. The operation failed and Bach emerged totally blind. The excruciating pain of the ordeal and the long confinement that followed broke down the composer's physical strength. This same Taylor, a few years later, performed a similar operation on Handel. The results led Edward

MacDowell to remark that Bach and Handel were in every way different, "except that they were born in the same year, and killed by the same doctor."

For weeks Bach lay in his bed, a broken man. During the year preceding the operation he had turned for the last time to his beloved chorale preludes, and in moments when his eyes would permit was copying and revising eighteen of them for the engraver. Contained in this collection are some of his finest examples in the form, among them the exquisite *Schmücke dich* [Deck Thyself, My Soul, with Gladness]. Almost a century later Robert Schumann heard this work performed by Mendelssohn, to whom he afterwards wrote, saying that around the old chorale hymn "hung winding wreaths of golden leaves, and such blissfulness was breathed from within it, that you yourself avowed that if life was bereft of all hope and faith, this one chorale would renew them for you. I was silent and went away dazed into God's acre, feeling acutely pained that I could lay no flower on his urn."

The last of the collection, *Wenn wir in höchsten Nöthen sein* [When We are in Deepest Need]," remained unfinished during the last days when the blind composer lay waiting for death. Making his last effort, he dictated to his son-in-law the completion of this work, changing its title to that of another hymn on the same tune, *Vor deinen Thron tret' ich allhier* [Before Thy Throne I Come].

Ten days later, on the twenty-eighth day of July 1750, Bach died. He was buried in the ancient graveyard of St. John's Church in Leipzig.

Neglect of Bach's music began almost with the instant of his death. Public interest in it was so small that when Karl Philipp Emanuel published *The Art of Fugue* only a handful of copies were purchased, and he finally sold the plates for the value of the metal. The oldest son, Wilhelm Friedemann (who later became an alcoholic), cared so little for his father's work that he lost a number of the manuscripts of the cantatas which had been willed to him. The sons did not even care for their stepmother. Anna Magdalena died ten years later in poverty. Gradually the manuscripts and published works of the father dropped from sight; soon the place of his grave was forgotten. During the next seventy-five years the name "Bach" meant not Johann Sebastian but Karl Philipp Emanuel.

It would be wrong to assume that the age which neglected Bach's music must be accused of a lack of aesthetic perception. Bach belonged to the baroque era, and he arrived on the scene in time to sum up that style in music. Long before he had finished, the baroque had begun to fade. The younger composers found they could no longer express themselves in the formulas which a century of usage had worked dry. They wanted no more of fugues and chorale preludes, of toccatas, passacaglias, and chaconnes. They were as sick of them as churchgoers were tired of cantatas and Passions.

In France the baroque age had passed into the rococo, impelled by the enormous personal force of Louis XIV. Art, music, and architecture all reflected the spirit of a new age that was to rule Europe. The baroque had been ornamental and florid, with its lush, decorative exterior covering a platform of massive strength. It had aimed to impress, to glorify, to move deeply. The rococo was also decorative; but it was delicate, refined, poetic, with an elegant charm that was essentially shallow. Its purpose was to entertain, to beguile.

The German composers could not help but be impressed by these changes, but their own version of the rococo was a much more sober product than the French. Theirs was chiefly a rationalizing process, and part of it took the form of simplification. New ideas and procedures had to be sought and explored. Polyphony, which had ruled musical thought for a thousand years, began to crumble. Bach himself had exhausted the possibilities of contrapuntal science; no one could follow his purely mathematical skill. The New Music with which his sons were experimenting would be based instead on homophony, a musical pattern built upon a single line of melody instead of several. The great new form which arose was the sonata; soon the symphonic orchestra would appear, and the string quartet. For the next century the best creative minds would be engaged in the development and exploitation of these new concepts of musical form and medium. The opera would flourish as never before, while music for the church would rapidly decline.

In this evolution Bach's music had nothing to offer. It belonged to a vanished past whose ideas and methods the newer composers were trying to avoid and to forget. Moreover, only a small portion of it had been published in the composer's lifetime, so that it could influence little even those whose predilections might be toward the music of the past.

Almost a century had to pass before the wheel would turn full circle. When composers like Chopin, Mendelssohn, Schumann, and Liszt, all romantic emotionalists, discovered Bach and the emotion that lay under his technique, they regarded him with amazement and adoration. Schumann declared that music owed him a debt as great as religion owed to its founder; for Wagner he was "the most stupendous miracle in all music." With Mendelssohn's revival of the St. Matthew Passion in 1829 the Bach resurrection began, and all through the rest of the nineteenth century the work of discovery and compilation and editing went on. It was not until 1894, after long search, that the composer's bones were found and identified in St. John's graveyard. By that time he needed no epitaph but his name.

The history of mankind has recorded no greater achievement than his, in that entire realm of human endeavor which is called art.

QUESTIONS

1. Leonard points out that church authorities treated Bach "like a hack," and rectors "had no sympathy with his music." Can you suggest reasons for this apparent unconcern with Bach's music?
2. What sort of composition is Bach's *Well-Tempered Clavier?* In a music dictionary look up "clavier." What is its meaning? How does it differ from "clavichord?"
3. Bach has been considered by many as one of the greatest composers of religious music for the Protestant church. Yet today, in most churches, his music is relatively infrequently performed. Can you suggest reasons for this?
4. How many cantatas did Bach compose? What is a cantata? How many "Passions" did Bach compose? What is a "Passion?"
5. Explain how Bach, a Lutheran composer, was able to compose his *Mass in B minor,* when the Mass belongs to the Catholic liturgy. What do you believe was Bach's intention in composing this work?

COMPOSERS IN THEIR TIMES / 4

Classical   *Wolfgang Amadeus Mozart was born in Salzburg in 1756 and died in Vienna in 1791. His life has been the subject for countless biographers and his music the subject for countless analysists. The most exhaustive and definitive biography has been the four-volume work of Otto Jahn, originally published in Germany between 1856 and 1859. For the past one hundred years Jahn's work has been a standard Mozart reference book. In the following essay Nicolas Slonimsky, composer, musicologist, giant among twentieth century lexicographers, and editor of the newly revised* Baker's Biographical Dictionary of Musicians, *shows how it is possible for error to creep into the work of some of the world's great scholars.*

The Weather at Mozart's Funeral

NICOLAS SLONIMSKY

THE STORY OF MOZARTS EARLY DEATH AND HIS burial in a mass grave fills some of the most poignant pages of history. The last chapter of virtually every biography of Mozart contains a melancholy description of the funeral itself during a raging December storm. In his basic biography of Mozart, Otto Jahn writes:

At 3 o'clock in the afternoon of December 6, Mozart's body received the benediction at St. Stephen's Church . . . A heavy storm of snow and rain was raging, and the few friends who had assembled for the funeral procession stood with umbrellas around the bier, which was then carried through the Schulerstrasse to the Cemetery of St. Mark. As the storm grew still worse, the mourners decided to turn back at the gate, so that not a friend stood by when the body was lowered into the grave.

Subsequent biographies and entries in musical dictionaries reproduced Jahn's description of the funeral with only slight variations. Here are some quotations:

On the day of the burial the weather was so bad that even the few friends who followed the coffin turned back at the gate.
(Eitner, *Quellen-Lexikon*)

His few friends accompanied the coffin only halfway owing to bad weather.
(Riemann, *Musiklexikon*, 11th ed.)

On the 6th December the plain coffin was carried through the streets on the shoulders of two men, followed by the faithful Süssmayr. At St. Stephen's Church a few others joined the procession, including, it is thought, Albrechtsberger, Lange, Schikaneder, Van Swieten, and Salieri; but the appalling weather —it was a day of storm and heavy snow—soon drove them all home.
(Ernest Newman, *Stories of the Great Operas*, N. Y., 1928, p. 315)

Mozart's burial took place on the afternoon of December 6. It was a third-class funeral at the cost of 8 gulden and 36 kreuzer plus 3 gulden for the hearse. The plain pinewood coffin was consecrated in the Church of St. Stephen. A few friends . . . followed the bier with umbrellas to the gate. Then the mournful procession was scattered. Stormy December weather drove even the last of the faithful back to town. Not a single friend reached the cemetery of St. Mark to throw a handful of earth on the grave of the dead master.
(Bernhard Paumgartner, *Mozart*, Vienna, 4th ed., 1945, p. 466)

At 3 o'clock in the afternoon of the 6th his body was removed to St. Stephen's; the service was held in the open air, as was the custom with the poorest class of funeral, and Van Swieten, Süssmayr, Salieri, Deiner, Roser and Orsler stood

THE WEATHER AT MOZART'S FUNERAL by Nicolas Slonimsky from *The Musical Quarterly*, January 1960; copyright 1960 by G. Schirmer, Inc. Reprinted by permission.

round the bier. They followed as far as the city gates and then turned back, as a violent storm was raging, and the hearse went its way, unaccompanied, to the church-yard of St. Marx [*sic*].

(*Grove*, 5th ed., 1954; essentially identical with the first edition, 1880)

A small group joined the funeral procession; of the family there were the brothers-in-law Hofer and Lange, while the ailing Constanze was absent; further, the friends Van Swieten, Salieri, Albrechtsberger, Roser von Reiter, Orsler, Süssmayr, and Deiner. Schikaneder had excused himself. Inclement weather, with driving snow and rain, forced these few to disperse at the gate.

(Erich Schenk, *W. A. Mozart*, Vienna, 1955, p. 784)

In his semi-fictional biography, *Mozart, Genius und Mensch* (Hamburg, 1955), Adolf Goldschmitt gives this vivid description of Mozart's burial (p. 346):

The storm roars and howls through the Stubentor in the faces of the mourners. They struggle through up to the gate. Then opens a vast expanse, filled with dancing, galloping snowflakes . . . "How long still to go?" howls the storm. The snow mutters, "How long still to go?" as it crunches under the feet of the marchers. Then from its nests in the hats, in the furs, and in the crape, the snow begins to melt and drip, and to ask: "Does it make any sense?" . . . In this dreadful storm, in this whirling, crackling snow, in which their feet keep slipping, which makes all thought uncertain and questionable, is not this effort, this struggle senseless? The first who begins to understand is the Baron van Swieten. He speaks to Salieri, who marches next to him, but in the storm his words are blown away . . . One after another, the others follow him with mourning hearts.

An "entr'acte" contributed by Sir George Grove to the program book of the 6th concert of the Glasgow Choral Union, of December 8, 1874, gives a definitive summation of facts and fancies regarding Mozart's funeral, to which little was added later:

Van Swieten undertook to arrange for the hearse and coffin—it would have been more to the purpose if he had also volunteered to pay for them. The undertaker's charge was 8 florins 36 kreuzers, and the hearse 3 florins, in all but some 25 shillings—the mere price of an opera box at one of the performances of *Don Juan* at Vienna, but a heavy charge on a widow's purse. And these two were the only visitors. Schikaneder, the Manager, for whom Mozart had written his *Zauberflöte*, and who had made money enough by that and Mozart's other pieces to rebuild the largest theatre in the city—he, irredeemable snob as he must have been, never came near the house, but contented himself with running about the town in tears, saying that Mozart's ghost was pursuing him, and leaving the poor widowed Constance in her penniless misery and trouble . . . For that they were very poor, there can be no doubt . . . No wonder, therefore, that it was late in the day before the arrangements for the funeral of such a pauper could be made. It was three in the afternoon of the 6th before the coffin was deposited in one of the chapels on the north side of St. Stephen's. Van Swieten, Salieri, Süssmayr, and two other musicians named Roser and Orsler, appear to have been the only persons present, besides the officiating priest and the bearers of the coffin. It was a terribly inclement day; rain and sleet coming down fast; and an eye-witness describes how the little band of mourners stood shivering round the hearse with their umbrellas up as it left the door of the church. It was then far on in the dark cold December afternoon, and the evening was fast closing in before the solitary hearse had passed the Stubenthor, and reached the distant graveyard of St. Mark, in which, amongst the "third class," the great composer of the "Jupiter" Symphony and the Requiem found his resting place. By this time the weather had proved too much for all the mourners; they had dropped off one by one, and Mozart's body was accompanied only by the driver of the carriage.

In all these accounts there is complete unanimity as to the stormy weather raging on the day of Mozart's funeral. Yet the early biographers of Mozart make no mention of the storm. There is nothing about it in Schlichtegroll's *Nekrolog* for the year 1791, nothing in Niemtschek's biography (Prague, 1798), and, significantly enough, nothing in Nissen's account of Mozart's life and death, first published at Leipzig in 1828. Nissen, who married Mozart's widow, was most anxious to explain her position at Mozart's death. He writes:

> Baron van Swieten came immediately after his death, so as to weep with the widow, who had lain in the bed of her dead husband in order to catch his disease and die with him. In order to prevent her from surrendering herself to her despair, she was taken to Herr Bauernfeld, an associate of Schikaneder, and later to Herr Goldhahn. [p. 572]

> Stricken by Mozart's death, the widow herself fell severely ill, so that Baron van Swieten had to take care of the burial of Mozart's body. Since he had to observe the greatest possible economy for the family, the coffin was put in a common grave and all other expenditures were also avoided. [p. 576]

Mozart's widow and his sister-in-law Sophie Haibl contributed to the posthumous publication of Nissen's book, and it is inconceivable that they should have omitted from their account of Mozart's death and funeral the dramatic phenomenon of a heavy storm. Besides, stormy weather at the funeral would have offered an extenuating circumstance for the widow's absence. And of course it is most unlikely that Mozart's closest intimates should have simply forgotten the weather.

No mention of the storm is found in the *Nouvelle Biographie de Mozart* by Oulibicheff (Moscow, 1843) or in the *Life of Mozart* by Edward Holmes (London, 1845). In fact, no biography before Otto Jahn's has any reference to the subject.

Where did Jahn find his information? The answer is provided in an inconspicuous footnote in Vol. 4, p. 688, of Jahn's biography of Mozart, published at Leipzig in 1859. The footnote cites No. 28 of the *Wiener Morgen-Post* of the centennial year 1856, but vouchsafes no direct quotation from that journal. Subsequent biographers have dropped this bibliographical reference, relying entirely on the authority of Jahn for the authenticity of the report.

This all-important article, the source of the information about the storm, was published anonymously in the *Wiener Morgen-Post* on

January 28, 1856, as a contribution by "one of the people," and the implication is plain that this supposed eye-witness account was being published for the first time. Here are the essential parts:

Mozart's body received benediction at St. Stephen's on December 7, [An error, corrected in all Mozart biographies. That the funeral took place on December 6 is established by the parish entry at St. Stephen's.] at 3 o'clock in the afternoon . . . The burial was of the third class, costing 8 florins, 36 kreuzer. Besides, the hearse cost 3 florins. The night of Mozart's death was dark and stormy. Also at the benediction it began to blow and storm. Rain and snow fell together, as though nature wished to show its anger with the great musician's contemporaries who came to his funeral in such small numbers. Only a few friends and three women followed the body. Mozart's wife was not present. These few people stood with umbrellas around the bier, which was afterwards conducted through the Schulerstrasse to the cemetery of St. Mark's. As the storm grew still heavier, even those few friends decided to turn back at the gates, and betook themselves to the tavern of the Silver Serpent.

Thus we find that the legend of Mozart's sad funeral in a forbidding blizzard rests on the account of the only one of the participants to record the event. Unfortunately, this witness, who remains anonymous, tells his story sixty-four years after the event took place. Since it is quite unlikely that a child would have attended the funeral of a musician, we are in addition dealing with a very old man—or perhaps with a Romantic steeped in Jean Paul and E. T. A. Hoffmann. Can the deposition of such a witness—and as we have seen, there are no others—be accepted? Furthermore, the opportune publication of this story in January 1856, exactly a hundred years after Mozart's birth, and never previously, raises the suspicion that it was composed *ad hoc*. We had better rely on the testimony of science itself, for science, too, keeps a diary. Moreover, this diary is impersonal, factual, and not subject to the vagaries of *Empfindsamkeit*.

Such testimony is offered by the records of the Vienna meteorological bureau, which go back into the 18th century. I sent an inquiry to the Zentralanstalt für Meteoroligie und Geodynamik of Vienna, and to my amazement and delight received a prompt answer from Professor F. Steinhauser, dated July 9, 1959. He reports the following entry in the records of the Vienna Observatory under the date of December 6, 1791:

	8 a.m.	3 p.m.	10 p.m.
Barometric pressure	27″ 7½‴ ′	27″ 7″ ′	27″ 8″ ′
Temperature	+2.6° R	+3.0° R	+3.0° R
Wind	weak east wind at all these times of the day.		

The barometric pressure is given here in Vienna inches and Vienna lines (12 Vienna lines equal one Vienna inch; one Vienna line equals 2.195 mm.). In English measure, the average barometric pressure of 27″ 7½‴ ′ equals about 28.5 inches. The temperature, here given in the

Réaumur thermometric scale, varied from 37.9 to 38.8 degrees Fahrenheit.

Professor Steinhauser adds to his report another precious document: an entry in the diaries of Count Karl Zinzendorf, kept in the Austrian State Archives, in which the weather conditions of the period are punctiliously noted. In Vol. 36 (year 1791), p. 287, of the diary, under the date of December 6, is found the following observation: "Temps doux et brouillard fréquent."

Mild weather and frequent drizzle or mist! Zinzendorf's observation corresponds well with the weather report, the virtual absence of wind, and temperature above the freezing point at all times of the day, ruling out the possibility of snow.

Certainly an intermittent drizzle could not be regarded as deterring Mozart's friends from following the coffin to the grave. And, as we have found, Mozart's family never claimed that the weather was inclement. Professor Steinhauser advances the explanation that in the 18th century it was customary to accompany the body to the grave only when the cemetery was situated in the immediate vicinity of the church. St. Mark's, where Mozart was buried, was about half an hour's march from St. Stephen's Cathedral. Women rarely, if ever, attended funerals at the time and this may well account for Constanze's absence. It should be observed, also, that Nissen does not seek to excuse her absence in the funeral procession, but only her inability to make arrangements for the burial.

Who were the mourners? Nissen and other early biographers are silent on the subject. Otto Jahn lists the following: Baron van Swieten, Salieri, Süssmayr, Joseph Deiner (who was summoned from the Silver Serpent to dress Mozart's body), the 'cellist Orsler, and the Kapellmeister Roser. Whether Emanuel Schikaneder, Mozart's librettist and intimate friend, was present, will never be known. Some biographers add to this list the names of Mozart's brothers-in-law, Lange and Hofer, and also Albrechtsberger.

Most interesting is the inclusion of Salieri among the mourners, in view of the rumor that spread soon after Mozart's death accusing Salieri of poisoning him. It was Anselm Hüttenbrenner, a pupil of Salieri, who was the first to claim that Salieri attended Mozart's funeral. In his obituary article on his teacher, in the *Allgemeine musikalische Zeitung* of November 1825, he wrote: "Salieri spoke of Mozart always with exceptional respect. . . . He visited Mozart two days before Mozart died, and was one of the few who accompanied the body." Hüttenbrenner was not yet born when Mozart died, and his testimony may be accepted at best as a remembrance of what Salieri himself told him;

but Hüttenbrenner does not make even that claim. The assertion that Salieri was present at the funeral therefore rests on a very flimsy foundation.

No one has yet suggested that Salieri attended Mozart's funeral to look at the result of his "dreadful deed" and to make sure that Mozart, whom he was supposed to have poisoned, was indeed dead.

The rumor of poisoning found literary expression in Pushkin's play *Mozart and Salieri*, written in 1830—that is, only five years after Salieri's death. Among Pushkin's papers was found a note relating to this play:

"During the first performance of *Don Giovanni*, while the entire audience, which included great connoisseurs, silently admired Mozart's harmony, a hiss was heard. Everyone turned to its source in amazement and indignation, and the celebrated Salieri left the theater in a rage, consumed by envy. Some German periodicals report that on his deathbed he admitted a dreadful deed, the poisoning of great Mozart. An envious rival who could hiss *Don Giovanni* was capable of poisoning its creator."

Even the most vicious detractors of Salieri never claimed that he had ever demonstrated in public his hostility to Mozart and his lack of appreciation of Mozart's music. On the other hand, we know that Salieri attended a performance of *Die Zauberflöte* on October 13, 1791, that Mozart himself took Salieri in a carriage to the theater, and that Salieri was so entranced with the music that "from the overture to the last chorus there was not a single number that did not call forth from him a bravo! or bello!"

Among fantastic tales regarding Salieri's guilt was this: In 1822 Rossini asked Salieri to introduce him to Beethoven. Salieri obliged, and took Rossini to Beethoven's house in Vienna. When Beethoven caught sight of Salieri, he turned to Rossini and cried out: "How dare you come to my house with Mozart's poisoner?" Salieri hastily retreated, and was so shaken by the encounter that he suffered a mental collapse leading to complete insanity. The tale is hardly worth refuting, for Beethoven proudly acknowledged that Salieri was his teacher and dedicated to him several works, all this, of course, many years after Mozart's death.

That Salieri died nearly insane is true. His friend Rochlitz wrote in the June 1825 number of the *Allgemeine musikalische Zeitung*: "Salieri lost himself in dark delusions . . . He imagined that his reputation was ruined, and sometimes accused himself of dreadful crimes."

Edward Holmes, in his *Life of Mozart* (New York, 1845, p. 360, note), makes Salieri's self-accusation specific:

Mozart's notion that he had been poisoned was always treated by those about him as a fantastic idea . . . The tale of poisoning, however, having transpired, Salieri, the known inveterate foe of Mozart, was fixed upon as the imaginary criminal. It is a singular fact that Salieri, who died in the public hospital of Vienna, thought fit on his deathbed to make a solemn deposition of his innocence before witnesses, and that the document thus duly signed and attested was made public.

No such document has ever come to light, or has been mentioned in the literature on Salieri. But the Soviet musicologist Igor Boelza, in his book *Mozart and Salieri*, published in Russian in 1953, asserts that Guido Adler discovered in the Vienna archives a communication from Salieri's father confessor to the Archbishop of Vienna reporting that on his deathbed Salieri not only admitted poisoning Mozart but also explained in detail how he administered the slowly working venom. According to Boelza, Adler had no time to publish the document, but spoke about his findings to the Soviet music scholar Boris Asafiev. However, Asafiev never referred to the story in any of his published writings. Since both Adler and Asafiev are dead, the *onus probandi* of the existence of Salieri's confession rests with Boelza, who has so far not corroborated his original report.

The calumny grew as rapidly and as luxuriantly as the one in the famous aria of Don Basilio in *The Barber of Seville*. Voices for the defense were barely audible in the noise. One of the most determined among Salieri's defenders was the Austrian composer Sigismund Neukomm, whose communication on the subject appeared in an English translation in the *Quarterly Musical Magazine* of London, 1826, pp. 336-38:

The public papers persist in repeating that Salieri has confessed himself the cause of Mozart's untimely end, but none of them have mentioned the source of this horrible report, which defames the memory of one, who for fifty-eight years has engaged the universal attention of Vienna.

It is the duty of every honourable man, when an unfounded report is current, by which the memory of a celebrated artist will be dishonoured, to relate all that he knows . . . Mozart and Salieri entertained for each other a mutual esteem, without any intimate friendship, for they were accustomed at Vienna, each to acknowledge the other's distinguished merit. No one could impute to Salieri any jealousy of Mozart's talents, and whoever was acquainted with him (as I was) will agree with me, that this man led, for eight and fifty years, an unblemished life, employing himself simply in his art, and taking every opportunity of doing good to his neighbours. Such an one, I think, could be no murderer—a man who, during the four and thirty years that have passed since Mozart's death, has preserved that delightful flow of spirits which has rendered his society so attractive.

Even if it were proved that Salieri declared himself when dying the perpetrator of this dreadful crime, one ought surely not so easily to receive as truth, and promulgate as such, the words which escape from an unhappy dying old man of seventy-four, worn out by ceaseless pain, when it is known how much his intellects had decayed for months before his decease.

The tale of Salieri's murderous crime was revived in Nazi Germany by Mathilde Ludendorff, M.D., in a book entitled *Mozarts Leben und gewaltsamer Tod*, published by a Ludendorff family printing press (Ludendorffs Verlag) at Munich in 1936. She develops the thesis that Mozart was murdered by the Freemasons, among whom were Salieri, van Swieten, and the mysterious messenger who commissioned the Requiem. Taking advantage of their proximity to Mozart and his trust in them, they slowly poisoned him. Nissen, also a Mason, covered up the crime in his biography of Mozart. Constanze was innocent, and knew nothing about the plot. Mozart's crime, in the view of the murderers, was the revelation of secret Masonic rites that he made in *Die Zauberflöte*. True, Mathilde Ludendorff admits, Mozart himself was a Mason, but he was drawn into the Masonic Order through his racial and personal simplicity. At first, he failed to understand the sinister nature of the Order. When his eyes were finally opened, he decided to expose the misdeeds of the Freemasons, thus sealing his death warrant, immediately upon the production of *Die Zauberflöte*.

Mathilde Ludendorff dismisses the fact that all these people were Catholics in good standing by claiming that the official religion was for them nothing but a cloak to cover their true intentions and beliefs. She also offers a brilliant solution to the psychological puzzle presented by the actions of Baron van Swieten, a rich man who let Mozart be buried in a pauper's grave. It seems that according to the Masonic laws, the body of the transgressor must be cursed, that its skull should be removed so as to prevent decent burial, and that his grave should be unmarked. The thesis thus accepts the long discredited story, possibly based on the known fate of Haydn's cranium, that Mozart's skull was detached from the body and hidden, and it also advances the notion that Constanze was kept away from the cemetery by van Swieten under the pretext of safeguarding her health. In all fairness, it should be noted that Mathilde Ludendorff herself concedes that some people might regard her as mad. Her book certainly justifies that supposition.

To sum up: Mozart's pusillanimous friends, colleagues, patrons, competitors—even his alleged murderer—who stayed away from his funeral could not blame the atmospheric conditions. The tale of Mozart's funeral was a product of the Romantic age. Melodramatically inclined biographers could not very well have Mozart dying, racked with fever, surrounded by friends while exhaling his last immortal melody (as pictured in a well-known 19th-century painting), and so had to be content with a storm-tossed funeral. The Victorians could not stomach the heartless unconcern of the rich Baron van Swieten, who carefully reduced the costs of the funeral to fit the family's depleted purse, but such a realistic attitude was quite in keeping with the unromantic spirit of the time. Even Nissen speaks of the necessity of "holding down expenditures," which explains the third-class funeral. But meteorological records, with relentless objectivity, demolish the Romantic picture, for they inform us that though the funeral took place in the dead of winter, it happened that December 6, 1791, was a relatively mild day that could have prevented no one from marching all the way to St. Mark's Cemetery and throwing a handful of earth on Mozart's grave—if he so wished.

Some thirty-five years later another great Viennese musician, Ludwig van Beethoven, was laid to rest, but he was accorded a grand funeral worthy of his fame, and his grave was well identified. *Mirabile dictu,* the famous thunderstorm at the time of Beethoven's death, reported by all Beethoven biographers, actually did occur! Dr. Steinhauser not only supplied the report on the Vienna weather during Mozart's funeral but also was kind enough to communicate to me a complete account of the meteorological conditions on the day of Beethoven's death, March 26, 1827. At three 'clock in the afternoon stormy weather began, and at four o'clock lightning and thunder struck, with strong winds.

As for Beethoven's defiant gesture with a clenched fist at the "powers of evil," as the peals of thunder filled the air, this story owes its origin to the selfsame Anselm Hüttenbrenner who was responsible for the highly dubious details of Salieri's presence at Mozart's funeral, and must be regarded as another example of musico-biographical folklore.

QUESTIONS

1. How is it possible for a false or misleading biographical item to appear in the work of one authority after another? Discuss the meanings of "primary" and "secondary" sources.

2. Do you think Slonimsky's research on the weather has any special value? In what way? How does it contribute to music?

3. Go to the library and select a Mozart biography. Find the account of Mozart's funeral and compare the information given with the information in Slonimsky's essay.

4. Look up the name of Salieri. How important was he in his time? Can you suggest why today Mozart's name is known the world over while Salieri's name is relatively unknown?

5. What does Slonimsky mean when, concerning the 18th century, he speaks of "the unromantic spirit of the time." And that "the tale of Mozart's funeral was a product of the Romantic age." Discuss what is meant by "the spirit" of a given time.

COMPOSERS IN THEIR TIMES / 5

Romantic *As we move away from a man's life, it becomes increasingly difficult to discover the truth about him, his life and work. Thus, the biographer turns, whenever he can, to letters, documents, sketches, and other writings by writers who knew the man personally. This is not to say that these writings are more factual than later writings; often contemporaries are moved by personal feelings. Nonetheless, their writings are valuable and interesting because they are based on first-hand experience, if not knowledge. Of the four contemporaries included here, W. C. Müller was a tutor and teacher in the city of Bremen; Wenzel Tomaschek was a composer; Karl von Bursy a physician at the Salzburg Johannis Hospital; the last was a journalist for the Stuttgart Morning Blade in 1823.*

BEETHOVEN
and His Contemporaries

LUDWIG NOHL, Editor

OUR FIRST SKETCH IS BY THE PHILOLOGIST, DR.
W. C. Müller, of Bremen, to whose meeting with Beethoven we shall
presently refer, and who immediately after the master's death wrote
"Something about Ludwig van Beethoven" in the Leipsig *Allegemeine
Musikalische Zeitung*. Although neither exhaustive nor thoroughly accurate, this account gives a clear idea of the unhappiness of his boy-
hood, and is, therefore, worth preserving.

Beethoven's Boyhood
W. C. Müller

WITHIN the last few weeks the newspapers have contained much that
is interesting about this celebrated composer, details about his illness,
the assistance sent from England, his death and funeral. To the lovers
of art, and even to the world in general, the fullest particulars concerning this extraordinary genius are valuable. The following brief
sketch may, therefore, not be out of place. It is a faithful one, for we
have, for several years, corresponded with Beethoven and his most
intimate friends, and in 1820 we made his personal acquaintance.

We learn from the church register that Beethoven was born at Bonn,
December 17, 1770, not 1772 as has been generally stated. On this
point he was himself mistaken: time passed unheeded by him; in the
tone-world in which he lived, periods flowed on without divisions of
days and years. His father was tenor singer in the chapel of the Elector
of Cologne, Maximilian Franz, one of the brothers of the Emperor
Joseph II. Like all the children of the Empress Maria Theresa, the
Elector was a warm lover of music and had one of the most perfect
bands of the time. Some relatives of the celebrated Romberg were members of it; two of them are still living—Ries the elder, father of the
famous pianist, and Beethoven's best pupil, and Simrock, music publisher at Bonn. These are our chief authorities for particulars about
Beethoven's youth.

He received from his father, in early childhood, his first lessons on
the piano and violin; and not being compelled to attend to anything
else, both wrote and spelt badly. When a boy he had an ungainly figure;
as a youth his appearance was not more graceful, nor in his fiftieth year

---

BEETHOVEN AND HIS CONTEMPORARIES, from *Beethoven and His Contemporaries*,
Ludwig Nohl, editor, W. Reeves; 1880.

Composers in Their Times: Romantic / Nohl

do we in this respect find any change in him. What a striking contrast to Mozart! Ludwig led a very retired life and was under strict orders from his father to remain constantly in his room practicing; he did not, therefore, feel the loss of society. He was shy, and in what little intercourse he had with others would answer in monosyllables; but he thought and observed a great deal, abandoning himself to the emotions and brooding fancies awakened first by music and afterwards by the poets. Mozart, on the contrary, was taken into society when only seven years of age; whence his pliant, affable, sympathetic, and kindly disposition, his early skill in composition, and the perfect regularity and universally pleasing character of his cosmopolitan music. Beethoven when a boy did not think of preserving his fancies for himself or for others, by committing them to paper; he early began to indulge his imagination on the piano, and more especially on the violin, and was so absorbed and absent-minded that he had many a scolding from his mother for not heeding the dinner-hour.

After giving up the violin, he pursued his beloved art on the piano. It is highly probable that in his twelfth year, he was acquainted with all the forms used by the contemporary composers, Haydn, Mozart, Sterkel, for they appear in his three sonatas which the father published in Ludwig's eleventh (thirteenth) year, and dedicated to the Elector of Cologne. They clearly indicate the young beginner, and how much of them is original cannot be determined, for they are not distinguishable from the style of the day; the figures are borrowed from the above-named masters, and the phrases are deficient in roundness and rhythm. Very opposite is the character of the pianoforte trios, known as his first works. Not only is the form very different, but each trio contains a tone-picture capable of being conceived in the imagination and plastically represented. In his fourteenth year, he was cembalist in the orchestra, that is he accompanied with the double bass in the symphonies; in his sixteenth year, he became organist to the Elector.

While in this position he once incurred the displeasure of his kind patron. To humiliate a confident and boastful Italian singer, who despised all German music, Beethoven was persuaded by his colleagues to put him out in the tune and time of a certain aria. The attempt succeeded to the satisfaction of the band; but as the disturbance occurred during mass, Beethoven received a sharp reprimand; he did not, however, betray the instigators of the trick.

Hitherto his style of playing had been powerful, but rough, although very rich in new forms of fancy. He was universally admired, but being simple, modest, and unpretending, was not envied. In his eighteenth year, some of his companions took him with them to Mayence, that he might appear there as a virtuoso. They were fortunate enough to receive an invitation from the Abbé Sterkel, intendant of the band, a well-known pianist, whom Beethoven much wished to hear. The Abbé played one of his sonatas with great delicacy of execution. Beethoven stood in a corner listening intently; such refined playing he had never heard. Then he was asked to play. Persistently refusing, his companions led him to the piano by force; he began timidly, but soon forgot his surroundings, and launched forth into an improvisation which the Abbé could not sufficiently praise. He was asked to perform his published variations on "Vieni Amore"; but as he did not know them all by heart, he played seven new ones which were still finer. His friends were amazed at the refinement of his playing, which had become as delicate as the Abbé's. We cannot attribute this to a desire of annoying his patron, as has been suggested.

A Pianoforte Competition
Wenzel Tomaschek

OPINIONS differ as to their relative superiority, but the majority incline towards Wölffl. I will endeavour to describe the peculiarities of both, without showing preference to either artist. Beethoven's playing is more brilliant, but less delicate, and fails sometimes in clearness. He appears to most advantage in improvisation, and it is indeed marvellous to see how easily and logically he will extemporise on any given theme, not merely by varying the figures (as many virtuosi do with much success—and bluster), but by a real development of the idea. Since the death of Mozart, who was to my mind the *non plus ultra* of players, no one has given me so much pleasure as Beethoven. Wölffl is, in this respect, inferior; his claim to superiority is that in addition to his thorough musical knowledge and excellence in composition, he performs passages which really appear impossible of execution, with astonishing ease, clearness, and precision. Of course, the size of his hand is a great help to him. He always plays with taste, and in the *Adagii* especially is so pleasing, so equally removed from coldness and exaggeration, that he not only excites admiration, but gives pleasure. Wölffl's unassuming and amiable behaviour naturally contrasts favourably with the somewhat haughty manners of Beethoven.

Beethoven had already attracted public notice by various compositions, and passed in Vienna for a pianist of the first rank, when in the latter years in the last century, a rival arose in the person of Wölffl. Then was in a manner repeated the Parisian feud of the Gluckists and Piccinists; and the numerous lovers of art in the Imperial city divided themselves into two parties. At the head of Beethoven's admirers was the amiable Prince von Lichnowsky; among the most zealous defenders of Wölffl was Freiherr Raymund von Wetzlar. This highly cultured gentleman, with true British hospitality, used to keep open house during the summer, at his pleasant villa at Grünberg, near the Imperial castle of Schönbrunn, for foreign and native artists, to whom it was a resort as agreeable as it was desirable. The interesting competition between the two *virtuosi* was a source of endless enjoyment to the select party assembled there; each artist produced his latest work, or gave free play to the momentary inspirations of his fancy, or they would improvise at two pianos alternately, on each other's themes; and the duet *capriccii* which they thus composed would doubtless have been well worthy of preservation.

For mechanical dexterity it would have been difficult, perhaps impossible, to have awarded the palm to either of the combatants; kind nature had been more liberal towards Wölffl in providing him with a gigantic hand, which made tenths as easy to him as octaves were to others, and enabled him to play successive passages of these intervals with the speed of lightning. In improvisation, Beethoven already displayed his inclination towards the dismal and gloomy; while luxuriating in the boundless tone-world, he was emancipated from everything earthly, the spirit broke its fetters, shook off the yoke of bondage, and soared triumphantly into aetherial realms; now his playing would be like a wild foaming cataract, and the enchanter would force from the instrument astounding effects, almost beyond its possibilities; then sink exhausted, murmuring soft complainings, dissolving in melancholy; then the soul rose again, triumphant over earthly sorrows, turning heavenward with devotional strains, and finding soothing consolation in the innocent bosom of holy nature. But who can fathom the depths of the sea? Beethoven's improvisation was like the sacred Sanscrit language, whose hieroglyphics the initiated alone can decipher. Wölffl, on the other hand, trained in the school of Mozart, was always equal, never dull, and being invariably clear, was more accessible to the majority; art served him merely as a means to an end; he never made it a pompous show-piece of dry learning; and he never failed to excite and sustain interest by a well-arranged succession of ideas. Any one who has heard Hummel will understand what this means.

An unprejudiced and impartial observer derived a great deal of pleasure from watching the two Macenates, seeing with what anxious attention and approving looks they followed the performances of their *protegés*, and then with true chivalrous courtesy how each yielded the palm to his rival.

But of this the *protegés* themselves took little account; they were best able to appreciate each other's merits, and accordingly entertained a mutual esteem. As upright, honest Germans, they proceeded on the praiseworthy principle that the path of art was broad enough for all. Wölffl showed his respect for Beethoven's genius by dedicating to him his Pianoforte Sonata, Op. 7, which appeared about this time. He soon disappeared from public life, for he died early. He was wanting in that strong, enduring, intellectual energy and ideality which sustained our master in the most troubled circumstances, causing him ever to rise with renewed strength from every sorrow and misfortune. This competition increased his fame as it added to his knowledge.

A Visit in the Year 1816
Karl von Bursy

Must I not note and commemorate the day on which I made the acquaintance of Beethoven? I went to see him yesterday, but could not find him, as Herr Riedl (music publisher) had given me a wrong address. He lives at No. 1056 in the Seilerstadt, and not as Madame Nanette Streicher wrote to me, No. 1055. I always had the idea that Beethoven must live in a princely palace, and under the protection of a Maecenas of his noble art. How great, then, was my astonishment when a herring-seller directed me to the next-door house, saying, "I think Herr van Beethoven lives there, for I have often seen him go in." I inquired on the ground-floor, and learned that Beethoven lived on the third story, up three flights of stairs. What a contrast to my expectations! A wretched house, and the third floor! A narrow stone staircase led to the room where a Beethoven creates and works. I confess I felt overpowered, as if going into the presence of the sublime. It was, indeed, no everyday sight I was to see, no everyday man with whom I *hoped* to speak; for I could not be sure that I actually should. A small door at which I rang led me into a little vestibule, opening into the kitchen and children's room. I was received by a servant who, with his family, seems to belong to Beethoven's household. He wanted to admit me at once, but I gave him my letter from Amenda and waited anxiously for an answer. The servant at last returned, saying, "Have the kindness to walk in"; and I stepped behind a thick woollen curtain into the study. Beethoven entered from an adjoining room. It seemed hard and unnatural only to pay a ceremonious compliment to the master of my art. I should like to have seized his hand and imprinted on it a kiss of deepest reverence.

If Jean Paul was altogether unlike my previous conception, Beethoven fairly corresponded to what I had imagined. He is short, but sturdy looking, with grey hair, which he wears thrown back, rather a red face, and fiery eyes small, but deeply set, and full of intense life. He is very much like Amenda, especially when he laughs. Beethoven inquired after him first thing, and spoke of him with much friendliness. "He is a very good fellow," he said. "I unfortunately live at a distance from my friends, and am left alone in odious Vienna." He asked me to speak loudly, as his hearing was very bad just then. He wished in the summer to go into the country and to Baden for the sake of his health. He has not been well for some time, and has composed nothing new. I asked him about Berg's opera text, and he said it was very good, and with a few alterations should do very well for composition. Hitherto, his illness had prevented him from undertaking such a work, and he wished to write Amenda himself about it. I shouted into his ear that for such a work one must have plenty of time and leisure. "No," he said, "I do not go on continuously. I always work at several things at once, and take up first one, then the other." He often misunderstood me and had to pay the greatest attention to catch what I said. This of course much disconcerted me, and sharing my embarrassment he spoke the more himself and very loudly.

He told me much about Vienna and his life there. He is full of wormwood and gall, dissatisfied and defiant, pouring out cursings against Austria and especially Vienna. He speaks quickly and with great vivacity. He often strikes the piano with his fist so violently that the room resounds again. He is not reserved, for he soon adverted to his personal affairs and told me a great deal about himself and his circumstances. This is exactly the *Signum diagnosticum* of hypochondraism. To me this hypochondraism was very welcome, for I thus heard from his own lips a great deal about his life. He complains of the times, and for many reasons. Art, being no longer so far above the multitude, is not so much esteemed, nor nearly so well paid. Is it creditable that a Beethoven can have cause for a pecuniary complaint? O ye rich! How poor must you be, if you have nothing to spare for Beethoven! He would have abundance, and you would want nothing. Give him a portion of the treasure you squander, and your life will be rich in good deeds. Generations to come will thank you for every care and grief from which you have released Beethoven; for he must be free from earthly anxiety, if he is to give the world its due. His power is so stupendous that he would unceasingly be laying up a rich store for present and future art-honouring people. "Why do you stay in Vienna, when any other court would gladly offer you an appointment?" "Circumstances keep me here, but it is very miserable and wretched," said he, "things could not be worse. One can trust nobody. No one fulfils anything that is not down in black and white. You have to work for a miserly payment, and then do not get what was promised." Beethoven composed an occasional cantata for the congress, but it was never performed. After many cabals he gave a concert at the Redouten Saal. The Emperor of Russia paid 200 ducats for his ticket. Beethoven was particularly pleased that the General Intendant of the Imperial Stage, Count Palfy, received a severe reprimand. He is not at all partial to him.

Beethoven seems very anxious about money; and I must confess this makes him more human, and brings him closer to us. It shows that he is only a dweller in the dust and gives him a kinship with us, for as an artist he does not belong to earth. I felt nearer to him when he thus talked about the chief need of life. Sad enough, but true. I freely admit that the less ideal side of the ideal artist drew me nearer to him. So commonplace is the ordinary man! I did not speak much about music to one so immeasurably my superior. From vanity? No! That the consummate artist might not look into my lowly sphere, that his eye might be spared the mean prospect—such was the cause of my silence.

He was pleased to hear that *Fidelio* had been so frequently well received in Berlin. He lamented the loss of Milder Hauptmann. "Her place is vacant," he said, "none of the singers here can sing as she did. We could not pay her, so she did well to go to Berlin. Music is very much on the decline in Vienna and is quite neglected, and the public will put up with anything."

His brother having died recently, Beethoven has undertaken the education of the orphan son. He talked much about it, and took this opportunity of finding fault with the schools here, to which he had sent the little fellow, but soon removed him. "The boy must be an artist or a *savant*, that he may lead a noble life." He expressed some grand views on life. When he is silent his brow contracts, and his gloomy appearance might inspire fear, did we not know that such a lofty artistic soul must have noble springs. Confidence growing up between us, he allowed me to visit him frequently, for he only went backwards and forwards to Baden; I was to go to him whenever he could be helpful to me. He wrote down my address and parted from me with the friendly words, "I shall fetch you some day."

Thus I saw him whom I have so long esteemed, loved, and honoured. If Beethoven were not so deaf, I should certainly gain his affection and confidence. In spite of his apparent hardness and coldness, he is rendered warm and gentle by the devotion of a spirit not seeking support from his mind. His house, which looks on to the Green Bastion, is cheerful and kept tolerably clean and tidy. On one side of the vestibule is his sleeping apartment, on the other his music room, in which stands a locked piano. I saw but little music; some pieces of music paper lay on the writing table. Two good oil portraits of a man and a woman hung on the wall.

Beethoven was not, like Jean Paul, dressed in rags, but quite in gala costume, confirming what I had already heard about his being vain, which of course renders his deafness still more annoying to him, and accounts for his excuses that he generally heard better than just then. I find, after inquiry, no grounds for the assertion that he is sometimes mad. Herr Riedl assured me that he was not so at all, and only had what is called artist's spleen. On that point everyone thinks differently. Riedl, for example, as a dealer in works of art and publisher of several of Beethoven's works, probably considers the high price which he puts upon his manuscripts as evidence of such spleen; for, indeed, he said to me that Beethoven charged monstrously for his compositions. My ideas of artistic spleen are something like these commercial ones. To a consummate artist like Beethoven, having a high estimate of himself, esteeming people only for what they are, not for their title or appearance, proud towards the proud, and haughty towards the haughty, so infinitely below him—to such a man would I grant that artistic spleen, which indeed raises him in my estimation. If Beethoven did not feel his worth he would not be Beethoven, nor the great artist whom I had hitherto revered.

On the 25th July, I have recorded a visit to Beethoven, at one o'clock. Availing myself of his promise, I went to him with my copy of *Fidelio*, that it might be consecrated by his handwriting as a sacred memorial of the master-singer. He was not at home. The servant showed me into his room, and I wrote my request on a little sheet of paper. I felt quite strange dipping his pen into his ink. The air around seemed like a breath from Parnassus, and the quill as if it had been plucked from the golden wings of Pegasus. While the servant was gone for a minute into the next room, I was seized by a demoniacal desire. For a moment my better sense prevailed, and I withstood the temptation. But the evil spirit triumphed. I was left a little longer alone, and the temptation acquired irresistible force. My weak will was powerless against it, and the deed was done. Like Faust, who could not conceal his compact with the evil one, but was branded by a scar on the left hand, so a black spot on my light coat exactly over the heart testified to the triumph of the demon. Beethoven's much worn pen, corresponding in its form to his characteristic writing, was the enticing fruit with which the serpent allured me. I quickly seized it, and the sin was committed, the theft accomplished. The *corpus delicti* now lies in my desk, and is a constant memorial of a moment of weakness.

I went to Beethoven on July 27th, at seven o'clock in the morning; I found him at home and had a good half-hour's pleasant chat. He said a great deal against Vienna and spoke with much rancour. He wished himself out of the city, but felt obliged to remain on account of his nephew, a boy of ten, whom he would gladly train as a musician, if there be any chance of his becoming eminent. He already plays the piano exceedingly well. Beethoven has now taken him into his house and means to get him a teacher. He was very kind, and the pressure of his hand at parting made me feel of more value in my own eyes, and raised me from the commonplace sphere of everyday life.

I found Beethoven at his writing table, with a sheet of music before him, and a glass machine in which he was making his coffee. Neither of his two pianos were yet open. I asked him about Berg's opera text. "It does not answer to be an opera composer here, for the managers of the theatres do not pay us." He inveighs against the music publishers for making such confusion in his works by their new editions. They give the numbers according to their fancy. Thus, Mollo has recently re-published the Trio Variations in E flat major as Op. 82; but this number properly belongs to four songs and a much earlier one to the variations. It is indeed low roguery. Everything relating to bookselling is marked by the greatest meanness. There is no sincerity shown in this kind of business.

Beethoven's Character
Stuttgart *Morgenblatt*

LUDWIG VAN BEETHOVEN is one of those who are honoured, not only by Vienna and Germany, but by Europe and the whole civilized world. Beethoven, Mozart, and Haydn form an unapproached triumvirate in modern musical art. In spite of Italian "kling-klang," and modern charlatanism, the intellectual depth, unfailing originality, and the ideality of a great spirit command the homage of every true worshipper of the divine Polyhymnia. Let us, however, speak not of his works, but of himself.

Beethoven's life has, as he says, been chiefly a life of thought. The events of the outward world concern him but little; he is quite given up to art. Midnight finds him at his desk, and sunrise calls him to it again; his activity is unceasing. But he dislikes being asked to compose, for he wishes only to give forth the spontaneous fruits of his genius. Art is to him a divine gift, not a means for obtaining fame or money. Despising all that is false, he strives after truth and character in art and in life. The first time *Fidelio* was performed, the overture belonging to it could not be given, and another overture of Beethoven's was substituted. "They clapped," he said, "but I was ashamed; it did not belong to the whole."

He is incapable of deception. If he vouchsafes any opinion on a composition, it is sure to be a true one; and he immediately dissolves connections which he finds inimical to his upright manliness and lofty ideas of honour. He has a strong, decisive will, but he only desires what is right; and, what is rare in our times, he not only commits no in-justice, but will suffer none. He shows a delicate respect for women, and his feelings towards them are of virgin purity. He is gentle towards his friends, all of whom have, in some way or other, experienced the kindliness of his disposition.

He possesses a rich fund of humor, and he castigates anything he despises with pungent sarcasm. Verbal communication is, unfortunately, only possible on his side; but art, science, and nature compensate him for the loss of society. He is a great admirer of Goethe, and recalls with pleasure the time he spent with him at Carlsbad (Teplitz). "I heard better then," he said in that gentle tone which, in his happy moments, is so impressive.

He is particularly fond of out-of-door life; even in the worst winter weather, he is not easily kept at home a whole day; and when spending the summer in the country, he is generally out before sunrise in Nature's blooming garden. No wonder, then, that his works are glorious like herself, and that, in the contemplation of them, we are drawn nearer to the spiritual world. He receives daily proofs from all parts of Europe, and even of America, of the recognition of his genius. He has been much troubled by the loss of all his letters during his removal from the country to town, and which was occasioned either through the carelessness or faithlessness of the person entrusted with the transport of his goods. Being so absorbed in his art, he is frequently imposed upon.

One evening when he was taking supper in a restaurant, an English naval captain, hearing the waiter mention his name, came up to him, and expressed the immense gratification which it gave him to see the man whose glorious symphonies he had listened to with pleasure even in the East Indies. The Englishman's simple, unaffected tribute of respect gave him genuine pleasure; but he dislikes merely curious visitors, for his time is very precious. His whole soul is bound up in his art, and in his nephew, Karl, to whom he is a father in the truest sense.

Beethoven's physique indicates intense strength, and his head recalls Ossian's grey-haired bards of Ullin. The portrait of him in the shops is very good. He is quick in his movements and hates slowness. His table is simply but well appointed, and he is particularly fond of game, which he considers most wholesome food. He takes wine with moderation, drinking generally only the red Austrian, as the Hungarian does not agree with him. In the winter, when he is in Vienna, he likes to look through the newspapers over a small cup of coffee in a coffee-house, to smoke a pipe, or to converse with his friends before taking his after-dinner walk. As he works far into the night, and rises very early, it often happens that he takes an hour's nap after his walk. He finds it injurious to live in a house with a northerly aspect, or exposed to strong winds, for he is very subject to rheumatism, to which he attributes his deafness. This last wet summer, which he spent at Hetzendorf, was therefore very bad for his health, and for two months he suffered intense pain in his eyes.

It is remarkable that, although deprived of the sense through means of which he works so powerfully on other minds, he can produce the softest *piano* when he sits down to his instrument, and abandon himself to his fancy. He receives a pension from the Austrian court, and although this by no means covers his expenses, he declined a tempting offer made to him at the time when the French made their ruler an emperor.

He has just finished a Mass, which he is publishing by subscription. His Imperial Highness and Eminence the Archduke Rudolph and Louis XVIII are among the subscribers. A symphony, some quartets, a Biblical oratorio, translated for him into English by the American consul from the United States, and an opera, the libretto written by Grillparzer, may be expected.

QUESTIONS

1. We know that Beethoven, as a boy, was forced by his father to "remain constantly in his room practicing." Do you know of any present-day counterpart to this circumstance? Look up some articles on Van Cliburn in the *Reader's Guide*. What were his practicing habits? What can you discover about the pianist Ruth Slenczynska?

2. Would you say Beethoven had a happy childhood? Why? How did childhood events contribute to his greatness as a composer? Could his greatness have been achieved under other circumstances? How, for example?

3. In previous centuries there seemed to be no clear-cut distinction between composers and performers; that is, one man encompassed both roles. Today these are considered separate roles. Can you name any famous contemporary performers who are also famous composers? Can you suggest what accounts for this situation?

4. Some of Beethoven's great works were composed while he was deaf. Can you suggest how it is possible for a composer to compose music when he is deaf?

COMPOSERS IN THEIR TIMES / 6

Impressionist *Impressionism is a style inspired in part by poets and painters. Taking hold as it did in the latter part of the nineteenth century, it has been variously considered: (1) the last gasps of the Romantic period; (2) a separate period that acted as a transition between the Romantic period and the Modern period; (3) the small birth-cries of the Modern period. In any case, impressionism has had many advocates who, in turn, have had many disciples. The characteristics of the style, having been embraced by many present-day composers of popular music, is still with us. Kurt Pahlen, a graduate of the University of Vienna, teacher, and writer, in the following essay, surveys the principal works of the foremost impressionist composers.*

THE IMPRESSIONISTS

KURT PAHLEN

I T WAS CLAUDE DEBUSSY WHO REPRESENTED MUSICAL impressionism in its purest form. He was born in St. Germain-en-Laye, in France, in the year 1862, and, when he was but twenty-two, won the coveted *Prix de Rome* of the Paris Conservatory. For a moment, public attention was focused on this new and officially proclaimed musical hope of France and accompanied him on his journey to the Eternal City. But the overture which he wrote there and which he submitted to the Paris jury, as was the custom, startled the learned men by its highly individual musical language. Debussy was trying to find a way beyond Wagner by the use of new sound combinations which in their boldness outdid even those of *Tristan*. And that at a time when the work of Wagner had not as yet fully penetrated French understanding! Contrary to every usage, Debussy's overture was not performed, and the young musician's name was shunted aside. Debussy removed himself more and more from the world. For a long time, this picturesque and exceptionally interesting artist lived the life of a recluse, listening to his inward voices and building up a world of tones which was his exclusively. He spent the years from 1892 to 1902 on a single creation, the greatest of his life, the musical drama *Pelléas et Mélisande,* inspired by the lyrics of Maurice Maeterlinck. This work cannot be compared with any other opera. It occupies a unique place in musico-dramatic literature. Perhaps it is the only entirely successful attempt to unite two conflicting worlds: impressionism and the theater. Not even Debussy himself made another such attempt. The other work he wrote for the stage was a sort of medieval mystery play, *The Martyrdom of St. Sebastian,* based on a text by Gabriele d'Annunzio, in which all dramatic action is supplanted by intoxicating and never-before-heard harmonies.

There is a striking similarity between Debussy's art and the ideological world of his impressionistic colleagues of the brush. Their subjects are frequently the same: delicate landscapes—lost as in a fog, clouds, and above all, and over and over again, the water to which Debussy felt mystically attracted. It returns in hundreds of forms in his music, from the spring representing the eternal leitmotif in *Pelléas et Mélisande,* the *Reflets dans l'eau,* and the *Jardins sous la pluie,* to the *Nuages,* the *Sirènes,* the age-old Breton legend of the *Cathédrale engloutie,* and finally to the superb symphonic poem *La Mer.* Again and again, Debussy

THE IMPRESSIONISTS from *Music of the World* by Kurt Pahlen; copyright 1949 by Crown Publishers, Inc. Reprinted by permission.

finds his way back to the water, inventing new tones and shadings for the mysterious element, which once had so powerfully stirred Schubert.

Symphonic art, with the constantly expanding sound possibilities of the modern orchestra, offered to Debussy's impressionism an inexhaustible field of activity. In every one of the following works, a definite picture rises before our eyes: *L'après-midi d'un faune*, written for the famous Russian dancer Nijinsky; the three Nocturnes—*Nuages, Fêtes, Sirènes*—in the last of which the composer added the mysterious effect of an inarticulate humming female chorus; *Ibéria*, full of genuine Spanish life, although the composer had never set foot on that country's soil—neither had Bizet when he wrote *Carmen*, nor the highly gifted Alexis Chabrier (1841-1894) when he composed the fiery tone poem *España*—and finally *La Mer*, the culminating point of Debussy's orchestral art, with its subdivisions: *The Sea from Sunrise to Noon, Play of the Waves*, and *Discourse between Wind and Sea*.

But also in the much more limited realm of the piano, Debussy succeeded in producing entirely new, magical sound effects, as in the *Suite Bergamesque* which contains the wonderful *Clair de lune*, the *Arabesques*, the scintillating *Préludes*, and, finally, the enchanting *Children's Corner* with its rhythmically agitated climactic *Golliwog's Cake-Walk*, in which elements of jazz are already discernible.

The application of the impressionistic style to the Lied form has been accompanied understandably by happy results. Wherever the seemingly floating melody is supported by the verses of a congenial poet, the expression of the most mature and ultimate beauty, of the most delicate coloring, and of the profoundest wisdom of life has been achieved. The new style had been conceived in the art of Duparc, Fauré, and Hahn. Debussy carried it to its ultimate conclusion in *Fêtes galantes* and *Ariettes oubliées*—cycles based on the melancholy verses of Verlaine— *Five Poems by Baudelaire*, and the *Ballads of François Villon*.

In the course of his lonely creative life, Debussy went through many stages of inward development. It seemed as if his soul were forever roaming. It finally found a resting place in a far-off cultural milieu— that of Malay and Indonesia. Not that he ever traveled there in the flesh; but Javanese and other Far-Eastern groups of musicians could be heard in Paris from time to time.

The First World War filled the hearts of all artists with horror. Debussy retired to a quiet villa at the seashore near the Spanish frontier. For days on end, he would let his gaze rest on the waters. Then again, he would start to write feverishly day and night. He, the laborious producer, was tortured by the thought that many, many works were as yet unwritten and that he would not be able to complete them. For he realized that his body was wasting away from day to day. He died in Paris, in March, 1918, while the Germans were bombarding the city. One of the significant symptoms of modern art is that increasingly it loses its national characteristics. Just as the great cities of our century resemble each other because of a uniformly adopted style of building, so the musical styles of our era, too, quickly adapt themselves to one another. Modern technique with its railways, planes, and radio is largely responsible for that. The outer confines of musical tendencies no longer coincide with national borderlines, as was the case in the romantic century, when a clear distinction could be made between German, Italian, Polish, and Scandinavian music. The line of demarcation separating the various musical styles of the twentieth century runs between individual groups of the same country, so that, for instance, a French impressionist feels much more akin to impressionists in England, Spain, Italy, or Russia than, say, to the verists, expressionists, and neo-classicists of his own country. This development is also influenced by the fact that national characteristics, which to the romanticists were often all-important, are being eliminated by a great many composers as bases of artistic music. It will be shown, however, that these characteristics are once more essentially important in the development of budding American music.

Although it would not do to assert that Debussy had established a school, in the strict sense of the word, since he was too much of an individualist and kept too much to himself, impressionism nevertheless spread all over the world, as if it were the answer to an era's deep yearning.

Russia's contribution to impressionism was largely due to the interesting figure of Alexander Scriabin (1873-1915), but this Slav genius at the same time expanded the idea to the very limits of music itself. His inexhaustibly imaginative spirit, in which mysticism and fanaticism dwelt side by side with the characteristic melancholy and dreaminess of impressionism, was responsible for rather strange productions. *Prometheus* is generally considered his most characteristic work. In it, man is symbolized by the piano, while the orchestra represents the cosmos and a mixed chorus supplies utterances from the primordial depths of humanity. But sound effects alone did not satisfy the composer. His imagination suggested to him a blending of acoustic and visual effects.

He had a "Light and Color Piano" constructed, an instrument which, according to the tones produced, projected light and color effects on a screen. This strange instrument, widely discussed at the time, but never used again except in similar experiments made by Schönberg, plays a part in some of Scriabin's works, which are thus lifted from the realm of pure sound.

Another interesting work by Scriabin is significantly entitled *Poem of Ecstasy*. Here the composer tries to express by all the means at his command and a veritably all-consuming ecstasy that which lies slumbering in the primordial depths of existence, of the earth, and of mankind. Scriabin's piano compositions also reveal his flaming temperament. There are ten sonatas which fill the old form with an entirely new and revolutionary content, as indicated by the very titles of two of them: *The Black Mass* and *The White Mass*. For the first time, secret sciences, occultism, and magic are transposed into tone language. Of his etudes, the *Pathetic* was the one to become most widely known. Today, his works are almost forgotten, neither is there any trace of the considerable influence exerted by him on a following musical generation; on the young Stravinsky, for instance.

Let us return to France where, in the person of Maurice Ravel (1875-1937), we come face to face with not only the most remarkable of Debussy's successors but also with one of the greatest geniuses among the composers of our century. He felt drawn especially to the artistic dance, to the ballet. In partnership with the Russian choreographer, Sergei Diaghilev (1872-1929), he created a number of highly important dance poems. This renewal of a close contact between the two sister arts proved beneficial to both. It may have saved musical impressionism from the danger of ever increasing abstraction and inanimateness by supplying new impulses originating in the realm of rhythm. On the other hand, it induced the dancer to adhere more strictly to certain rules common to both arts and to discard some of the arbitrariness he had displayed for decades, if not longer, toward music, which he had come to regard as a necessary evil.

Thus came into being the enchanting ballet operas *Ma mère l'oye* and *Daphnis et Chloë*. But many others of Ravel's works were also inspired by dance rhythms, such as *La valse,* his portrait of the city of Johann Strauss, and the world-famous *Boléro* in which a simple theme, taken from Spanish folk music, is by the most ingenious use of the art of instrumentation carried from a delicate melody, in a continuous and most exciting crescendo, to a thundering climax. It is characteristic of all modern composers, children of a technical age, that they are masters in the use of the modern orchestra. Ravel was no exception, as proved by his instrumentation of Moussorgsky's *Pictures from an Exhibition*. A wealth of attractive sound effects is revealed in his opera *L'heure espagnole,* while in his many piano compositions, such as *Pavane pour une infante défunte, Valses nobles et sentimentales, Tombeau de Couperin* (an homage to the great clavecinist of the French seventeenth and eighteenth centuries), as well as in his beautiful string quartet and in his songs he continued to walk in the paths of Debussy's impressionism, although he never failed to sound a personal note of his own.

Some French composers plainly belong, at least in certain periods of their creative activity, to the impressionist school. In this group were Erik Satie (1866-1925), a man who somehow presents a connecting link with Stravinsky, and Albert Roussel (1869-1937), a pupil of Vincent d'Indy, who left to the world a number of important works: symphonies, a notable sinfonietta, chamber music, and a great many other compositions. Not least of all, there was Paul Dukas (1865-1935) who, like Debussy, wrote an opera to a text by Maeterlinck, *Ariane et Barbe-Bleu*, and, with his brilliant *Sorcerer's Apprentice*, created a truly inspired musical interpretation of Goethe's ballad as well as one of the most effective modern orchestral works.

Very close to the world of Debussy is an Englishman, Cyril Scott (1879-   ), whose finely conceived *Poems* for piano are comparable to some of his British contemporaries' aquarelles, with their exquisite coloring and their slightly foggy atmosphere. England! We have not spoken of music since Handel, and that is a matter of a century and a half. Mention should have been made of John Field (1782-1837), whose *Nocturnes* inspired Chopin to write his own. There are in fact some which are almost undistinguishable from those of the great Pole. But although, thanks to the orchestras, the excellent choruses, and the population's general love of music, England's part in the world's musical life never sank to the level of insignificance—proved by the fact that almost all the prominent composers of the romantic century maintained a personal contact with the British Isles—the country did not rejoin the circle of musically creative nations until the turn of the new century. Then came Edward Elgar (1857-1934) and Frederick Delius (1863-1934).

Elgar centered his attention on the large orchestra and the oratorio. For the former he wrote symphonies, symphonic poems (one of which, *Falstaff*, makes one think of Richard Strauss), and above all, the *Enigma Variations*, which has become an established item in the repertory of not only all English but also many North American orchestras. His oratorio, *The Dream of Gerontius*, a form of composition of great interest to the English ever since the days of Handel, is a fine specimen of this category.

Delius was one of the finest impressionists and one of the loneliest creators, lonelier than Debussy or Moussorgsky. To the text of Nietzsche's *Zarathustra* he composed his *Mass of Life*. Among his six operas, *A Village Romeo and Juliet* stands out especially, based on Gottfried Keller's profound novel. But he probably achieved his greatest stature in the idyllic, tender orchestral pieces inspired by nature, called *On Hearing the First Cuckoo in Spring* and *Song before Sunrise. Ap-*

palachia, a series of variations on a North American Negro song, and *Brigg Fair* must also be mentioned. Delius' life is shadowed in tragedy: he was crippled and he became blind. Despite this, the spring of melody always flowed inside him. *A Song of Summer* was written as a hymn to the sun, to light and life. How spiritually poor are men who believe that the artist must actually see and experience whatever he is to portray. The artist's world lies within himself. Self-sufficient, Delius never sought recognition from the outside world. It came to him only shortly before he died.

Elgar and Delius were not solitary figures in England's musical renaissance. They were merely outstanding composers, among a great many others of the period, from today's standpoint. There were, in the years at the turn of the century, such composers as the Irish Charles Villiers Stanford who wrote the *Irish Symphony, Irish Rhapsody,* and several operas; the Scotchman Alexander Mackenzie, who is closest to the late German romantic period and whose *Scottish Pianoforte Concerto,* sponsored by Paderewski, had a great success; the symphonies of Hubert Parry, and the successful composer Ethel Smyth who produced two operas. To write an opera in the England of those years took a large measure of courage since the chances of its being performed were negligible. That situation soon changed, however, and when we return to a consideration of English music we shall find that England has become one of the first countries in the world in the performance of music.

The homeland of Chopin gave us the impressionist Karol Szymanowski (1883-1937), whose work again bears out our contention that the music of our century has lost its national characteristics. While Chopin's music still drew its strength from his native soil, that of his successor was wholly international in its character. Like Chopin, Szymanowski spent the major part of his life outside his country. Most of his works came into being on the idyllic shores of Lake Geneva. Among them are three symphonies (one of them has a tenor solo and chorus), *Song of the Night,* a song cycle with orchestra accompaniment (the individual parts are entitled *The Siren Island, Calypso,* and *Nausikaa*), a string quartet, a great deal of chamber music, and many songs.

Ottorino Respighi (1879-1936) was the first symphonist from the land of opera. While his beautiful symphonic poems unmistakably bear the imprint of Debussy's influence, his melodies are just as unmistakably Italian. His most prominent, and at the same time most impressionistic, works are *The Pines of Rome* and *The Fountains of Rome,* veritable sound paintings depicting in all their glory and splendor the trees and fountains of the Eternal City, the brilliance of the rising sun, and the magic of the deep blue night. The voice of a bird is heard in Respighi's pines. The sweet melody rising above the soft rustle of the trees is so overwhelmingly beautiful that the listener uneasily holds his breath. No man-made instrument this, no human voice. . . . It is—every hearing makes us marvel anew at the simplicity and ingenuity of the idea—a recording of the actual voice of a nightingale. . . .

Manuel de Falla may well be called the greatest genius in the more recent musical history of Spain. True, he had absorbed many traits of Debussy and Ravel, but the essence of his style is nevertheless wholly his own. And strong though the influence of national folklore may be in his work, he has succeeded in imparting to Spanish music a fully artistic form and in raising it to an international level. In all the nervous confusion of our time and its countless stylistic experiments, Falla is a creative genius whose feet were firmly planted on the ground —the ground of his native land.

Manuel de Falla y Matheu was born in Cadiz, on November 22, 1876. His first musical impression was of a strange kind. In an old church of his home town, on every Good Friday, there was a performance of a Haydn string quartet which the Vienna master had dedicated to that house of worship for its exclusive use and to which he had given the title "The Redeemer's Seven Words on the Cross." The wonderful symmetry of the classic work, in which there was "not a single note too many, not one too few," as Falla himself expressed it, made a profound impression on him and instilled into him, subconsciously, that sense of symmetry and artistic economy which today is the possession of but a few. Of decisive importance for his artistic growth were Pedrell's instructions and the seven years of study in Paris. There he became friendly with Debussy, Dukas, Ravel, and Stravinsky and wrote his *Seven Spanish Songs.* The sketch of his piano concerto, *Nights in the Gardens of Spain,* was also completed when the outbreak of hostilities made him return to his native land. Only very slowly did he gain recognition there. The brilliant work of his youth, the ballet *La Vida breve,* has not been performed in his fatherland to this day. His way of composing was exceedingly slow, and he gave full attention to even the minutest detail. He was one of those who do an enormous amount of correcting and polishing before considering a work worthy of being released. In this manner he wrote *El amor brujo,* a ballet with vocal music, whose orgiastic-ritual *Fire Dance* is a well-known piece in today's concert music; *The Three-Cornered Hat,* based on the Corregidor theme, which the hapless Hugo Wolf had treated before him; the extraordinarily strange operatic work *El retablo de Maese Pedro,* a Don Quixote episode, in which living singers as well as marionettes are used; instrumental compositions, like the *Fantasia Baetica* or the *Cembello Concerto,* the first performance of which was given by Falla in the Pleyel Salon in Paris, a few days before that celebrated hall was turned over to a wrecking crew.

In 1939, Falla, whose sensitive artist's soul was profoundly affected by the happenings in Europe, sought peace in the New Continent and settled in the Cordoban Mountains of Argentina. But his health was so weakened that he was able to work but a few hours a day. That was not enough to finish the monumental oratorio *Atlantida,* intended as a hymn to that legendary submerged continent. A few days before he would have reached the age of seventy, Falla died in Alta Gracia, in the Argentine province of Cordoba, on November 15, 1946.

QUESTIONS

1. Is there any connection between Debussy's obvious concern with "water" music and the impressionism that characterises his work? Could you state the connection clearly?
2. Make a list of synonyms for "vague." Do you think the adjectives you have listed are suitable for describing impressionism? In what ways are they satisfactory? In what ways unsatisfactory?
3. Listen to your instructor play Scriabin's favorite chord: a dominant 13th with a flat fifth and major ninth (C F♯ B♭ E A D). How does the sound affect you? Compare and discuss this sound with that of traditional chords.
4. Listen to a piece by Debussy, and another by Ravel. Do you think these pieces could have been written by the same composer? Why? Can you recognize any difference in the musical atmosphere of these pieces? Can you describe what is mean by "musical atmosphere"?
5. If you were a music historian would you consider impressionism the end of the Romantic period or the beginning of the Modern period? Give your reasons.

COMPOSERS IN THEIR TIMES / 7

Twentieth Century *In 1940 the Second World War forced Béla Bartók (1881-1945) to leave his native Hungary and come to America to begin, as Halsey Stevens put it, "a new life in a new country." He remained in America until his death. Few composers since have remained uninfluenced by Bartók's music. Today, Bartók is recognized not only as the foremost Hungarian composer of our time, but also as a composer with unqualified international stature and respect. In the following essay Halsey Stevens, composer and teacher of composition at the University of Southern California, whose own works have been performed by the nation's major orchestras, presents an authoritative picture of Bartók's last years.*

bartók in america

HALSEY STEVENS

a FEW DAYS AFTER THEIR ARRIVAL, THE NEW
Friends of Music presented the Bartóks in Town Hall, in
the Sonata for Two Pianos and Percussion; three weeks later
they gave a duo-piano recital there, playing the Mozart Sonata in D
(K. 448), Debussy's *En blanc et noir*, four pieces from *Mikrokosmos*,
two contrapuncti from *The Art of Fugue*, and the Brahms F-minor
Sonata. On 25 November, Columbia University held a special convoca-
tion in the rotunda of Low Memorial Library, at which Bartók was
awarded an honorary Doctor of Music degree. Degrees were granted
at the same time to Dr. Karl T. Compton, president of the Massachu-
setts Institute of Technology; Sir Cecil Thomas Carr, English barrister;
and Dr. Paul Hazard, member of the Académie Française.

This was quite a ceremony [Bartók wrote]. As prelude, my measure had to be
taken, in yards, feet, and fathoms, the details of my head, shoulder, etc., size
to be sent. They dressed all of us in the university toga or cloak; then in pairs
we marched solemnly in, amidst the sounding of discreet organ music. The directions were precise: when my name was called, I must stand up; when the
chairman addressed me, I must take off the toga; when at last he reached the
proper words, I must go up to him so that he might bestow the diploma; on my
back would be hung the pink velvet ribbons of the music degree; then I could
go back and sit down. That is the way it happened. Fortunately for us and for
the ceremony, we didn't have to speak . . .

In conferring the degree upon Bartók, Nicholas Murray Bulter cited
him as:

. . . distinguished teacher and master; internationally recognized authority on
the folk music of Hungary, Slovakia, Romania, and Arabia [sic]; creator through
his composition of a musical style universally acknowledged to be one of the great
contributions to the twentieth-century literature of music; a truly outstanding
artist who has brought high distinction to the spiritual life of his country.

On 1 December Bartók left for a week in Cleveland, where there
was a festive evening in the Hungarian colony, 'with gipsy music and
palotás (!!). Hungarians here, Hungarians there, Hungarians everywhere, but we could not be very glad of this, because the second generation already uses the language only with difficulty.' Returning to New
York, the Bartóks moved into a fifth-floor apartment in Forest Hills,
twenty minutes from New York by subway, and began the process of

BARTÓK IN AMERICA from *The Life and Music of Béla Bartók* by Halsey Stevens;
copyright 1953 by the Oxford University Press, Inc. Reprinted by permission.

acclimatization before the appointment at Columbia took effect. In his letters Bartók describes the 'Americanization' of their living—'crackled-*wheat* (!)' for breakfast, the necessity of learning multitudes of new words (subway stations, names of streets), of becoming acquainted with complex transportation systems (they once spent three hours in the subway, 'traveling hither and thither in the earth; finally, our time waning and our mission incomplete, we shamefacedly slunk home—of course, entirely underground'). Their luggage, which had been taken from them in Spain on 16 October, reached New York only on Christmas Eve.

Before beginning work at Columbia University, Bartók and his wife made a transcontinental tour, playing recitals in St. Louis, Denver, Provo, San Francisco, and Seattle, and returning through Kansas City and Detroit. In some places he found the public better prepared than in 1928 to appreciate his music; in others there was only a perfunctory response. The works programmed were still mainly his own, though they were somewhat more varied than before, through the inclusion of a number of the pieces from the *Mikrokosmos;* in addition Mrs. Bartók joined him in the performance of duo-piano works.

In March he took up his appointment at Columbia. No restrictions were placed upon him in his choice of work, but Dr. Herzog suggested that he might like to investigate the large collection of records—nearly 2500 double-faced discs—made in Yugoslavia in 1934-35 by Milman Parry, professor of classical philology at Harvard University. No systematic study had been made of these materials, since the collector died shortly after his return. The great majority of the discs are devoted to the heroic epic songs of Yugoslavia; here was where Parry's interests lay, since his purpose in making the study was to discover relationships between the Homeric chants of Greece and present-day Balkan 'men's songs.' But among the others there are more than two hundred discs of Serbo-Croatian 'women's songs,' of lyrical character and musically more grateful; and it was this section that Bartók elected to prepare for publication.

Dr. Herzog placed a room at his disposal, and he worked there entirely without supervision; his time was his own. The Archives of Primitive Music (in the Department of Anthropology) duplicated the original discs to prevent damage in the transcribing process, and the Alice M. Ditson Fund made a further grant of $2500 to subsidize the publication of the study, without any claims upon the royalties which would accrue to Bartók.

Near the end of his first year as Visiting Associate in Music, Bartók described his situation in a letter to Zoltán Kodály:

It was entirely left to me what sort of work I choose to do—I have not to lecture. I chose the transcribing into musical notation of the Parry Collection— I am working now in a wing of the Columbia University, at the phonograph archive of Herzog's. The equipment is excellent. I almost feel as if I were continuing my work at the Hungarian Academy of Science, only in slightly altered conditions. Even the setting resembles its nobility. When I cross the campus in the evening, I feel as if I were passing the historic square of a European city.

Publication of the results of Bartók's study was delayed for several years. Although the preface of this book, *Serbo-Croatian Folk Songs*, is dated February 1943, it was not published until September 1951; another group of notations made during the course of his work have not yet been issued. These latter concern the heroic epic songs in the Parry Collection. Once having begun the study of these materials, Bartók was reluctant to leave it incomplete; in October 1941, as he was planning another trip to the Pacific Coast (for lectures at Palo Alto and Portland, and a conference at the University of Washington), he wrote to Mrs. Creel:

I prefer to *tell* you than to write about all our good- and mishaps (in fact a great deal of mis-, and tiny bits of good-). My intended letter was to be a very long and un-American letter—complaints and complaints (here one *must* always feel fine and excellent even if dying). The only bright spot in my work at Columbia University: studying Serbo-Croatian folk-music material from really unique records . . . But—*hélas*—this is only a temporary job and the work probably must remaine unfinished, so even there is mingled a bitter drop.

Realizing that the Columbia appointment could not be made permanent, Bartók cast about for other work. Concert engagements were difficult to obtain; for the 1941-2 season there were in prospect by late autumn only a single concert with orchestra, three duo-piano recitals, and four 'minor engagements' (solo recital or lecture). Bartók's younger son, Péter, had obtained a visitor's visa to come to the United States, but encountered difficulty in securing transit visas 'through the wild-beasts-land. But I don't know,' Bartók wrote, 'if it would not be more advisable for us to go back than for him to come over—that of course is only a vague idea.' In the meantime he was carrying on negotiations with the University of Washington, in case the Columbia appointment were not renewed; in August he wrote to Carl Paige Wood in Seattle that he hoped his appointment could be extended beyond June 1942, in which case he could come to Washington for the year 1943-4. It was not until the spring of 1942 that he was notified of a further extension of the Ditson grant, which assured him of an income until the end of December, and he notified the University of Washington that he would be available at any time thereafter.

Meanwhile the United States itself had been drawn into the war, and communication between Hungary and America was cut off. Bartók, his visitor's visa expiring, was compelled to go to Montreal and re-enter as a non-quota immigrant. Péter Bartók, somewhere between Budapest and New York, was not heard from for weeks, but finally arrived in Lisbon in February 1942. There were a few concerts, among them a two-piano recital in Chicago, about which Bartók wrote Mrs. Creel:

We plaid rather well, and got very bad criticisms. In fact, 1 was good, 1 rather lukewarm, and [a third?] as bad as I never got in my life. Just as if we were the last of the last pianists. So you see your choice of piano-teacher was a very bad one! . . .
And now the bad knews. Our situation is getting daily worse and worse. All I can say is that never in my life since I earn my livelihood (that is from my 20th year) have I been in such a dreadful situation as I will be probably very soon. To say dreadful is probably exaggerated, but not too much. Mrs. Bartók bears this very valiantly: the worse the happenings, the more energetic, confident and optimistic she is. She tries to do some work, teaching for instance. But how to get pupils or a job . . . I am rather pessimistic, I lost all confidence in people, in countries, in everything. Unfortunately, I know much better the circonstances, than Ditta does, so probably I am right in being pessimistic. Do you remember what I said just one year ago: I wonder if it is not too late (concerning war preparations). Now, I am afraid it is too late. And I wish only to be wrong in this my feeling . . .
Until know we had . . . two free pianos, a baby grand and an upright. Just today I got the news the upright will be taken from us. Of course we have no money to hire a second piano. So we will have no possibility to study two-piano works. And each month brings a similar blow. I am wondering and asking myself what next? With these dissonant chords, I finish my letter . . .

But Mrs. Bartók added a postscript to the same letter, saying, 'In spite of all the difficulties, I always am thankful for being here and I am thinking how sad it would be for my husband to be in his own country now . . .'

On 20 April, at the 231st Street subway station in the Bronx, Bartók unexpectedly encountered his son, who had left Budapest four months before. Although he had cabled from Lisbon, the name of his ship had been deleted by the censor. Péter Bartók's arrival was the occasion for a joyful reunion; but other events were far from reassuring. Bartók wrote to Mrs. Creel about his concern for his health,

. . . which is impaired since the beginning of April: since that time I have every day temperature elevation (of about 100°) in the evening, quite regularly and relentlessly! The doctors cann't find out the cause, and as a consequence, cann't even try a treatment. Is not that rather strange? Fortunately, I can do my work; only it may happen for instance this: in Oct. I had a lecture in New York at the Musicological Society. It was aggravated by a dinner and discussions: when I came home, I had 102.

During the whole year he was busy with his work at Columbia University, completing in October the book on Serbo-Croatian folk-songs, and also working on a collection of 2500 Romanian melodies he had amassed earlier, for which he provided an introductory study and notes in the hope of eventual publication. These works were written in English—his first work in that tongue. 'All this was a rather tiresome work (and my struggling with the English language) but very interesting indeed.'

At the end of December 1942, the appointment at Columbia was scheduled for termination, since the Ditson Fund could no longer be drawn upon for this purpose. Bartók was notified of this, and was quite naturally concerned, since the amount of the Ditson grant, small though it was, had made it possible for the Bartóks to live in reasonable security, especially when supplemented with occasional fees for concerts and lectures. Of course, such funds as might have accrued in royalties and performance fees in Hungary, together with the payments on his pension, were cut off with the entrance of the United States into the war. And with the constant threat of a physical collapse, there was cause for apprehension.

At Columbia I am 'dismissed' from Jan. 1 on. They seem to have no more money for me. This is annoying because little more than half of the work (connected with the Parry Collection) could be achieved during these 2 years; and I hate incompleteness. If it ever can be continued, Heaven only knows. But from Febr. on, I am invited to Harvard University to give there a certain number of conferences and lectures during the 1st [sic] semester. This gives us a respite until next fall (no possibilities with concertizing or lecturing; we have a 'unique' engagement in Jan. with the New Yorkg Philh. Society, but this is a 'family' business, the engagement was made through my friend Fritz Reiner who is guest conductor in some of these concerts. So we are living from half-year to half-year . . .

So, with my books and articles I am gradually advancing to the position of an English writer (I don't mean it seriously, of course); I never had an idea that this will be the end of my career! Otherwise, my career as a composer is as much as finished: the quasi boycott of my works by the leading orchestras continues; no performances either of old works or new ones. It is a shame—not for me of course.

On 21 January 1943, Béla and Ditta Bartók gave the first performance of his Concerto for Two Pianos (the reworked version of the Sonata for Two Pianos and Percussion) in a concert of the New York Philharmonic-Symphony Society. Fritz Reiner conducted. The audience was generally receptive, the critics antagonistic; one went so far as to wish that the concert had stopped at the intermission, so that he would not have had to hear the Concerto. It is curious to find the words 'arid and doctrinaire' applied to this glowing score, especially after the critic has acknowledged its complete sincerity, and admitted that it 'bears [Bartók's] stamp in every measure.'

This was Bartók's last public concert. During the first part of 1943, his health became conspicuously worse. In January and February there was a complete breakdown, with such weakness that he could scarcely walk from one room to another, and a temperature frequently four degrees above normal. He gave three of the scheduled lectures at Harvard, but was completely exhausted by them; and although he had had a continual series of medical examinations, without tangible result,

. . . the Harvard people . . . persuaded me to go through another examination, led by a doctor highly appreciated by them and at their expenses. This had a certain result as an X-ray showed some trouble in the lungs which they believed to be T.B.C. and greeted with cheers and great joy: 'at last we have the real cause.' (I was less joyful at hearing these news.) I went home, was kept in bed during weeks. Then came the ASCAP which got somehow interested in my case and decided to cure me at their expenses (though I am not a member!). They sent me to their doctors who again took me to a hospital. The new X-rays, however, showed a lesser and lesser degree of lung trouble, it appears to be a very slight one indeed, and maybe not a T.B.C. at all! *It does not account for the high temperatures.* So we have the same story again, doctors don't know the real cause of my illness—and, consequently, can't treat and cure it! They are groping about as in a darkness, try desperately to invent the most extraordinary hypotheses. But all that is of no avail.

From April on there were recurrent periods of lower and higher fever; from May, pain in the joints which made walking almost impossible.

The only thing on the credit side is that I gained 9 lb. during Apr. and May (having before the ridiculous weight of 87!). Unfortunately, the terribly oppressing New York heat in June took all my appetite, and I lost again 2 of those precious 9. —So you have a succinct picture of my ailments which makes a tedious and unexhilarating reading! —There is no hope of recovery, and it is out of the question to take anywhere a job.

The summer of 1943 was spent at Saranac Lake, in northern New York, at the expense of ASCAP. Before the Bartóks left the city, Serge Koussevitzky came to Bartók's hospital room to offer him a commission of a thousand dollars from the Koussevitzky Foundation, to write an orchestral work in memory of the late Mrs. Koussevitzky. Unknown to Bartók, the suggestion for the commission had come from Szigeti and Reiner; but the circumstances were concealed from him to prevent interpretation as a form of charity. Bartók was reluctant, even so, to accept, with the prospect of his being unable to fulfill the commission, but Koussevitzky left with him a check for half the amount, the remainder to be paid upon completion of the score, and the Bartóks left for the Adirondacks.

Until mid-August he spent his time reading, finding in the local library such things as Motteux's translation of *Don Quixote,* and being pleased because the seventeenth-century English did not give him 'particular difficulties.' As his recurrent fever abated, he found it possible to work 'practically day and night' on the work commissioned by the Koussevitzky Foundation (which he began on 15 August), and brought the score of the Concerto for Orchestra with him when he came to New York in October to hear—for the first time—a performance of his Violin Concerto. Late in November he met Yehudi Menuhin and heard him play the First Violin Sonata in his New York recital.

He is really a great artist, he played in the same concert Bach's C-major sonata in a grand, classical style. My sonata, too, was excellently done. When there is a real great artist, then the composer's advice and help is not necessary, the performer finds his way quite well, alone. It is alltogether a happy thing that a young artist is interested in contemporary works which draw no public, and likes them, and—performs them *comme il faut.*

Under the sponsorship of ASCAP, Bartók was sent—alone—to Asheville, North Carolina, for the winter of 1943-4, his wife and son remaining in New York. In the meantime, arrangements had been made by Victor Bátor with Columbia University for a resumption of Bartók's appointment there for another six months, with funds partially collected by Joseph Szigeti through solicitation of musical organizations, recording companies, and individuals. But again the details were kept secret from Bartók, who would have felt obliged to decline the appointment as a charity measure. The work was to be done between April and December 1944; Bartók hoped that his Serbo-Croatian study would be published during that period as well. He had given up hope of being able to publish the Romanian and Turkish material, and after the breakdown of negotiations with the New York Public Library, he deposited the manuscripts at Columbia University: 'there they are available to those few persons (very few indeed) who may be interested in them.'

In Asheville, the apparent improvement in his health continued.

At present I feel in the best of health, no fever, my strength has returned, I take fine walks in the woods and mountains—actually I climb the mountain (of course only with due caution. In March my weight was 87 pounds; now it is 105. I grow fat. I bulge. I explode. You will not recognize me.

With his renewed strength—to which he attributed his ability to complete the Koussevitzky commission 'or vice versa'—Bartók wrote during his Asheville sojourn a Sonata for Solo Violin, commissioned by Menuhin and completed on 14 March 1944. This was the last original score he was to finish. In the same winter he also busied himself with arranging and writing out fair copies of 2000 Walachian folksong texts, about which he wrote to Szigeti:

I believe that many interesting things will turn up in this . . . For example, that for the girl it is a much greater misfortune to be jilted than for the boy. This of course we knew before, but now it can be proved in black and white with statistical facts. Further, that girls (or women) are so much more vehement, more wrathful; there are many more texts about girls cursing faithless boys than vice versa. These cursing texts, incidentally, are exceedingly singular: what a Shakespearean fantasy is manifested in them, quite prodigious. Sorry that I can't quote from the Walachian, since you do not understand it. But we Magyars have an abundance of that kind, for example:

> May thirteen apothecary's shelves
> Empty themselves in thee;
> May nine cartloads of hay and straw
> Rot in thy bed;
> May thy towel throw out flames,
> Thy washing water turn to blood.

Or even:

> May God smite thee with bread bought with money,
> With bread bought with money, and a whore for a wife.

Bread bought with money—this the urban Americans would not understand, for doesn't everyone buy his bread? Quite so, but not the small-propertied peasant: he grows the wheat himself, bakes his own bread, and if the frost has struck his crops, then he has to buy his bread with money, but where does he get the money? . . .

And so these are the things that occupy me now—and I await the end of my exile.

Other things occupied him as well. There was so far little progress to show in the European war, and Bartók was depressed to see the entire civilization he had known still in peril of destruction.

But what most worries me is this lagging and slow procedure on the 'battle-fields.' There is no end in sight—and the destroying of Europe (people and works of art) continues without respite and mercy. Personally, I do not know how long I can endure the insecurity of this gipsy life. (But for 1944, at least, my living expenses are secured, no worry about that.) And the destiny of poor Hungary, with the Russian danger in the background—the prospects of the future are rather dark.

During all this time he could learn nothing of his family in Hungary —his son Béla and his wife, his sister Elza and her family; nor of the many friends he had left there, the Kodálys and all the rest. Péter Bartók, having passed his regents' examinations in New York, remained there for a time, but in February 1944 enlisted in the United States Navy and was stationed in Panama, after a six months' training course. And the promise of continued improvement in Bartók's health was not fulfilled:

You said in one of your letters that my recovering was a miracle. This is true only with some reservations: it was only a hemisemidemi-miracle. Of course, that lung-infection disappeared as mysteriously as it came. . . . There are, however—and almost continuously—some minor troubles which probably never can be completely cured and make a regular job or concertizing etc. impossible for me. So for instance, last April my spleen became rebellious. My Asheville doctor mistook it for a pleuresy. He would have quite gallantly treated me against it, but fortunately I had to come back to New York where the mistake was at once discovered, and my spleen punished by a rude X-ray treatment. Then it appeared there is a disorder in my blood-picture, so they poisoned me with arsenic. Shall I continue? I think better not.

A few weeks ago I said, 'Tell me, doctor, exactly what my ailment is! Choose a nice Latin or Greek word and tell me.' After a moment's hesitation he emitted: 'Polycithemia.' There we are again! Only, 2 years ago this meant too many red corpuscles, and now it means too many white ones.

Even with these difficulties, Bartók felt that he could by exercising care still do some work at home, teaching; but there were only occasional pupils, some who had studied with him in Budapest and came to him for a few lessons when they were in New York: among them were Dorothy Parrish Domonkos and Agnes Butcher. The Bartóks' apartment—at 309 West 57th Street in New York, a few blocks from Carnegie Hall—was too small, but with the shortage of housing they felt fortunate to have found even these two rooms.

In November 1944, Menuhin played the Sonata for Solo Violin in his New York recital. Bartók was present and was brought to the stage to acknowledge the applause of an audience that filled the hall to overflowing. The critics had little good to say about the work. Olin Downes reported the enthusiasm of the audience, which 'must have been rewarding to Mr. Bartók, who has had his share of the difficulties of the radical innovator'; but found the work itself 'a test for the ears, the intelligence, the receptiveness of the most learned listener . . . On initial acquaintance, we take none too kindly to the piece.' But Bartók himself was of another opinion:

It was a wonderful performance. [The Sonata] has 4 movements and lasts *ca.* 20 minutes. I was afraid it is too long; imagine: listen to a single violin during 20 minutes. But it was quite all right, at least for me.

A few days later Bartók was present for another triumph: the first performance of the Concerto for Orchestra, which Koussevitzky and the Boston Symphony played on 1 and 2 December.

We went there for the rehearsals and performances—after having obtained the grudgingly granted permission of my doctor for this trip. It was worth while, the performance was excellent. Koussevitzky is very enthusiastic about the piece, and says it is 'the best orchestra piece of the last 25 years' (including the works of his idol Shostakovich!).

This, the largest of Bartók's mature orchestra works, was to play a significant role in at last bringing his music to the eminence it now occupies. In 1948-9, American symphony orchestras played Bartók's music more frequently than that of any other composer of the twentieth century except Strauss and Prokofiev. In that season, American orchestras gave fifty-six performances of eight works by Bartók; there were more performances of Bartók than of such earlier composers as Berlioz, Liszt, Dvořák, Schubert, or Mahler; the level has remained nearly as high in the years since. Side by side with this, and with the cyclical performances of the six string quartets which contributed to the understanding of Bartók's work, came performances of *Duke Bluebeard's Castle, The Wonderful Mandarin,* and the first American performance of the *Cantata profana.* Simultaneously, the demand for his music has led to the recording of almost all the larger works and many of the smaller ones, and the reprinting of most of the out-of-print scores. From being one of the least accessible of twentieth-century composers, Bartók has become one of the best known.

At the end of 1944, Bartók wrote to Mrs. Creel that he was assured of a 'modest living' for the next three years. During that year he had received about $1400 in royalties and performance fees in the United States and Great Britain, as well as some other income; and he had just signed an agreement with Boosey and Hawkes which called for an advance of $1400 annually for the next three years in addition to income from sale and performance. ASCAP was still assuming responsibility for medical expenses.

In December 1944, Ralph Hawkes commissioned a seventh string quartet from Bartók; the following February, at Hawkes's instigation, William Primrose asked him for a viola concerto. Bartók was reluctant to undertake the latter.

He showed no great enthusiasm [Primrose wrote]; rather he seemed doubtful as to the success of such an undertaking on his part. As he was anxious to get some idea of the technical capacity of the viola [as a solo instrument], we arranged that he should attend a performance of the Walton Viola Concerto which I was to give the following week . . . Unfortunately he was too ill to attend this performance, but he listened to it over the air . . .

There was also a commission for a duo-piano concerto for Bartlett and Robertson; from almost complete obsurity, almost complete neglect on the part of performers, Bartók had suddenly become sought after. Had there been time, a whole series of major works was in prospect. But in March he became ill with pneumonia; thanks to recently-developed antibiotics, this was quickly conquered. Yehudi Menuhin invited the Bartóks to spend the summer in California, and Bartók, with his doctor's approval, gladly accepted, planning to leave New York in mid-June. Early in June, however, he had to write to Menuhin:

Regretfully I must tell you that we cannot come to California! I am not feeling very well, and—owing to a variety of things—now my wife has been ill for several weeks and has still not recovered. The whole thing is that we are afraid of such a long journey, which, especially, now, would be attended by all kinds of inconvenience. I hardly know how to say how sorry I am. I had so many plans for music in connection with my sojourn there. Now these have turned to naught . . . We must try next winter somewhere to talk about the final form of the Solo Sonata; the matter is not urgent . . .

Instead of California, the Bartóks went back to Saranac Lake. There at last they received news from Hungary. Zoltán and Emma Kodály were well, though they had lost their home and possessions; Bartók's son Béla and his wife, and his sister Elza and her family, had escaped. Both copies of his thirteen years' work of folksong notation had survived, carefully hidden; his own household goods were almost unscathed. But the situation of the country itself was far from reassuring.

More harm—at least spiritually—was done by the extremely bad news about Hungary. Direct news did not arrive . . . But there are regularly reprinted Budapest newspaper (each copy coming probably through the Russian embassy and reprinted in facsimile by a Hungarian language communist newspaper in N. Y.) There we read about Kodály and other musicians, artists, who seem to be (comparatively) well. Dohnányi is a 'war-criminal'! However, so much damage has been done to the country that Heaven knows if and when it can again somehow recover. The Germans were beasts, but the Russians do not seem to be saints, too.

But the summer was not without its rewards. Péter Bartók was discharged from the Navy and returned to the United States in August, stopping in New York and then going on to Saranac Lake to be with his parents. And Bartók found pleasure in the out-of-doors, watching the 'chickmucks' and calculating the number of vibrations per second of the wings of hummingbirds ('My result is about 90 or 100').

During the summer another commission was proffered; Bartók announced it cryptically: 'A turtle wants to order a 5-minute orchestral work from me. . . . Only it's too bad that the turtle makes no sound, so that it could be worked into the piece.' This is another instance of Bartók's punning: the 'turtle' was Nat Shilkret (*Schildkröte* is the German word for turtle), and the proposal was that Bartók collaborate in the musical symposium called *Genesis,* which ultimately brought together separate movements by such strange bedfellows as Schönberg, Stravinsky, Milhaud, Toch, and Shilkret himself. But Bartók could not agree to undertake the composition of such a work for a year, and in addition, because of his commitment to Boosey and Hawkes found participation in the project beset by complications. In the end (Bartók wrote), 'The turtle proved obstinate, he will do nothing at all.'

As for the summer's composition, Bartók divided his waning energies between the Viola Concerto, intended for William Primrose, and a new—and uncommissioned—Piano Concerto. It had been many years since he had worked simultaneously on two major scores; now his desperate activity seems to have been prompted by a realization of the gravity of his illness. On 8 September he wrote to Primrose:

I am very glad to be able to tell you that your Viola Concerto is ready in draft, so that only the score has to be written, which means a purely mechanical work, so to speak. If nothing happens I can be through in 5 or 6 weeks, that is, I can send you a copy of the orchestral score in the second half of October, and a few weeks afterwards a copy (or if you wish more copies) of the piano score. Many interesting problems arose in composing this work. The orchestration will be rather transparent, more transparent than in the Violin Concerto. Also the sombre, more masculine character of your instrument executed some influence on the general character of the work. The highest note I use is 'A,' but I exploit rather frequently the lower registers. It is conceived in a rather virtuoso style. Most pobably some passages will prove to be uncomfortable or unplayable. These we will discuss later, according to your observations.

The Viola Concerto was destined to remain unfinished. When Tibor Serly saw him on the evening of 21 September Bartók was working on the orchestral score of the Third Piano Concerto; Péter Bartók had drawn the measure bars for him, and with the manuscript scattered over his bed he was struggling to fill in the last few measures. Other manuscript pages under a clutter of medicine bottles proved to be the Viola Concerto, the completion of which, Bartók told Serly, was a matter of working out details and scoring. The next day he was taken from the tiny apartment on 57th Street to the West Side Hospital. There, on 26 September, Béla Bartók died.

After the last bar of the Third Piano Concerto, Bartók had written—prematurely—the Hungarian word *vége,* the end. For Bartók the man, this *was* the end: an end such as no man would wish for, in a strange land, far from home, family, friends, all that meant so much to him.

But for Bartók the composer, this was by no means an end. It is callous to say, as some have said, that recognition waited only for his death. Such a point of view implies the half-truth that a great artist creates only for the future, not for his own time. But Bartók created for his own time: the essence of that time is in his music, and there were many who during his life heard it with understanding and keenly perceptive enjoyment. It is tragic that Bartók could not have benefited from the wider acceptance he was able to foresee; when he stood upon the stage of Carnegie Hall on 26 November 1944, acknowledging wave upon wave of applause for a 'difficult' work, and when, a week afterward, he heard the tumultuous reception of his Concerto for Orchestra in Boston, he knew that he had written—and written well—for his own time and for the future as well. In the years since, with increasing opportunity to know Bartók's music, audiences everywhere have come to realize that here is a colossus among men. And in that sense, there is no longer *vége*, the end, but only *kezdete*, the beginning.

QUESTIONS

1. Can you suggest reasons why Bartók had such difficulty in America earning enough money to live on? Do you think what happened to Bartók in 1940 could happen today? Discuss your reasons.
2. Do you think the public ought to distinguish between a man's position as a creative artist and his political beliefs? Would you buy a ticket to a concert of a great pianist, violinist, or conductor if you knew he had been a Nazi or a Fascist in a war against the United States? Give your reasons.
3. In 1940 Bartók's musical compositions were relatively unknown in the United States. Yet today many of his works are recorded and in the standard repertory. Can you suggest reasons for this change?
4. Listen to any composition by Bartók. Do you hear anything that sounds like folk music? How can you tell? Give your reasons.
5. Bartók has been called a Hungarian composer. What makes a man a "Hungarian" composer? a French composer? an American composer? an "international" composer? Discuss this question and give your reasons.

THE EXPERIMENTALISTS *Peter Yates is a Los Angeles critic with an uncommon interest in all the arts. His book,* Twentieth Century Music, *seeks to persuade the average listener to listen to new music without prejudice—no easy task. "The unknown," Yates tells us, "is the antagonist, and the heroes are the exploring composers who by rightly making their way into and through the unknown are able to chart it for us and make it known. Instead of geographical charts, they give us works of art, that when we assemble them offer us a broad picture of the successive landscapes these explorers have passed through on their ways." Yates' essay, which follows, serves as a first-rate guide into the "unknown" territory.*

The Proof
of the Notation

PETER YATES

*U*NTIL NOW WE HAVE BEEN LOOKING AT MUSIC AS history, in retrospect; now we shall see it, in prospect, as a great wave rising.

What is a wave good for? It can only break on the beach. But much may happen while it is passing across the ocean surface. Most waves are similar, formed to a common pattern of place and time. Yes, but no two waves are the same, and the pattern changes constantly, influenced by time, tide, wind, a distant storm at sea, a seismic convulsion. A tidal wave, carrying its burden of potential destruction thousands of miles across the ocean surface, may be no more than a few feet high; such is the music of Erik Satie, of Anton Webern.

Is there esthetic worth in a destructive force? The art of tragedy affirms it. Nature and need do not value our categories of form and permanence. The oldest surviving creatures are not the powerful predators. Wind and water erode rock, shape cliff and desert; fire, storm, nature, and human nature destroy habitations and cathedrals; evolution involves constant destruction and replacement, not the survival of the fittest by overt competition but continual adaptation of that which survives to changing circumstance. No music of another period is heard today in the style or sound in which it was conceived.

"Compare a concept with a style of painting," Ludwig Wittgenstein proposes, almost at the end of his *Philosophical Investigations*. "For is even our style of painting arbitrary? Can we choose one at pleasure? (The Egyptian, for instance.) Is it a mere question of pleasing and ugly?

"What is most difficult here is to put this indefiniteness, correctly and unfalsified, into words.

"We find certain things about seeing puzzling, because we do not find the whole business of seeing puzzling enough." (Gertrude Stein wrote: 'What is strange is this.')

". . . It is the field of force of a word that is decisive."

Substitute a musical note: it is the field of force of a musical note that is decisive. What is a musical note?

Notation is the skill of expressing musical ideas in writing—or, as Busoni put it, "an ingenious expedient for catching an inspiration." Stravinsky speaks of the *Danse sacrale*, which, while composing *Rite of Spring*, "I could play but did not know how to write."

Most notational systems are imperfect, like systems of spelling and pronunciation. They may change decisively, bringing us unexpected and unprecedented knowledge and ability to think and say new things; this

The Experimentalists / Yates

has happened during the past century to our long-established mathematical systems. A notational system implies a corresponding system of interpretation, according to a traditional usage which is at once acquired by habituation and learned by rote (repetition of forms or phrases—and the dictionary adds, "often without attention to meaning").

Challenging our established system of musical notation we direct fresh thought to its substance, its significance as a language of signs; and, as it has happened in mathematics, we gain unexpected and unprecedented knowledge and the ability to think and say new things.

In the eighteenth century, musicianship was the ability to read notes, not simply as written but often by embellishing them with ornaments, by the addition of other notes, and by alteration of the notated rhythm, according to principles of learning and good taste: musicianship focused on the skill of the performer. During the nineteenth century, with the establishing of large orchestras, musicianship was divided between two contrary skills: the ability of any group of orchestral musicians to play the same written notes almost exactly alike under the direction of a conductor; and the ability of the conductor or solo player to interpret the notation in his own way, which resulted in excesses of applied demonstrative rhetoric. The conflict has not ended. Conductors still mime a ritualistic interpretation between orchestra and public—they are admired either because they do this or because they do not—to which the players give no notice, watching only for the downbeat. Soloists prove their expertise with note-perfect, mechanically expert renderings, which by their impersonal efficiency cease to be musical. "The young pianists all play exceedingly well," Virgil Thomson said to me, "and they are nearly all equally uninteresting."

By the early twentieth century, Arnold Schoenberg could write to a singer: "I am anxious to explain to you why I cannot allow any will but mine to prevail in realizing the musical thoughts that I have recorded on paper, and why realizing them must be done in such deadly earnest, with inexorable severity, because the composing was done just that way. I should very much like to do some thorough rehearsing with you, so that you should get to know the way to solve the musical picture-puzzles that my works constitute. . . ."

Can a "musical picture-puzzle" be "in deadly earnest"? The answer is, yes, of course—with some allowance for Schoenberg's humor. Stravinsky, at a later time, would be complaining that conductors failed to study his phonograph records to learn how they should prepare his compositions for performance.

Schoenberg wrote that the effect of a musical composition changes with each hearing, therefore one must study it in score. Today, a composer can write out his exact instructions on a worksheet in the language read by a computer, have these instructions fed on punch-cards into the electronic machine, which does none of his composing for him but works out his instructions in the sequence he has indicated; converter and tape recorder translate the numerical output into an analogous magnetic trace on tape, which can be translated into audible vibrations (music) when played anywhere by means of tape player, amplifier, and loudspeaker to an audience of any size. Where is the score? It is not the composer's worksheet; any musical "secrets" hidden there which are not audible on the recorded tape as the composer desired them reveal technological failure but no fresh understanding of the music. The musical thoughts have been realized "with inexorable severity," and the puzzles have been solved in the making of them, "because the composing was done just that way." The composer has decided the interpretation while composing it. Schoenberg was aware of this possibility, which he did not live to see realized.

Schoenberg repeatedly refused invitations to direct his music when ample time for rehearsal had not been guaranteed. Writing to Edgar Varèse in 1922 he was holding up the example of "something like 100 rehearsals" for *Pierrot Lunaire* in Vienna, "with everyone shivering and starving." About twenty years after this, when I brought a group of Los Angeles musicians to Schoenberg's home to discuss performing *Pierrot Lunaire* under his direction at Stanford University, he was still asking between sixty and a hundred rehearsals; the musicians gave up the project. At a later time, for a program of Schoenberg's music in honor of his seventieth birthday, we prepared the same work with no more than the usual number of rehearsals expected in this country; when Schoenberg heard a broadcast of the performance, directed by Ingolf Dahl, he praised it.

In today's economic conditions it is probably not possible anywhere in the world to afford rehearsal time for a performance on Schoenberg's terms. Preparation of the first performance of Ives's Fourth Symphony, a superlatively demanding, very large score, though scarcely more than a half-hour in playing time, needed eleven rehearsals—and a grant of money from the Rockefeller Foundation to pay for part of them.

Today, musicians who would play any but routined music must learn to read difficult compositions accurately at sight and work them out for performance with a minimum of rehearsal. The proliferation of chamber compositions for groups of solo instrumentalists encourages individual musicians to make this effort, and reflects their willingness to do so. One of the most admired, and the prime model of such compositions, is *Pierrot Lunaire*.

We may say that music consists of: (1) notation; (2) the score, the entire ensemble of notes, plus expressive indications; (3) a more or less exact translation of the notation into sounds; and (4) what the listener hears. Each of these, however anyone may insist otherwise, is a variable. Notation may be by other means than musical notes; a score may not exist. Even a performance by electronic means will vary with the equipment and acoustics.

The odd fact is that while most composers and lovers of music at the present time continue to believe that a notated composition should be performed exactly to the composer's notation and instructions, they question the musical worth of an electronic composition which dispenses with a live performer's interpretation. Is the beauty of a musical performance to be scored negatively, like that of a diving or gymnastic contest, according to the performer's errors?

Composers have written puzzle-canons in musical notation without consideration of the sound as music, because they did not intend that the canons should be performed. Schoenberg wrote a number of these; some are in performance "interesting" and some very beautiful. Notation as an art can exist without sound, as handwriting can be an art apart from its message, or a graphic musical score may be exhibited as a visual work of art. Music as an art exists to be realized in sound and silence.

Silence can be musical. Silence plus one note can be musical, but one note is not music. The most primitive music consists of at least two sounds in rhythmic relationship. Notation thus implies rhythm, and rhythm depends on dynamics (relative volume and timbre), which notation can but approximately indicate. A new notation to provide for these is possible. In a score for computer the composer must control each of these variables by writing out exact instructions. Even "indeterminacy" must be programmed in advance. The machine will not think for him like a musician; it will do only what he tells it to do. Is it desirable that an orchestra or a soloist should reproduce a score with a computer's exactness?

A note is, by contemporary agreement, the sign for a particular sound. With the continual rising of musical pitch during the nineteenth and twentieth centuries, a note written by Mozart will be played and heard today at a pitch perhaps a half-step higher than Mozart intended: in Mozart's ears it would be another note, the wrong one. The disparity is enough to intensify the brilliance of the note when played by a string instrument or sung, because the string will be more taut and the voice strained to rise higher, and the sonority will be correspondingly lessened. We give no thought to such disparity, which would assuredly have brought sharp protest from Mozart.

We perform today in equal temperament music meant to be heard with different pitch relationships in just intonation, or meantone or well-tempered tuning, and give no thought to the distinct changes in intervallic relationships and consequently in harmony which result. It is as if we played these compositions on a mistuned instrument. An eighteenth century musician hearing such performance would be convinced that we think music only in terms of notation regardless of its sound. (We may soon be able to record and perform Bach fugues and Beethoven sonatas by computer, adjusting the intervals to acoustically correct relationships not obtainable with a twelve-note keyboard. Some string quartets claim to do this at the present time. Would Bach and Beethoven prefer it?)

Even when playing older music on the correct archaic instruments, as many now do, we customarily tune these instruments to our higher concert pitch and equal temperament, so that the instruments no longer sound with their natural voices. The vocal *tessitura* of Beethoven's *Ode to Joy* is as high as Beethoven could risk; we force it still higher. Because we pay no attention to the rhythmic conventions, the eighteenth century musician would be doubly convinced that we think music only in terms of its exact notation, with no sense of the correct rhythm. (The same thing is already happening in our "musicological jazz.")

We accept as consonances or permissible dissonances such discords as the eighteenth century musician took care to avoid, calling them "the Wolf." Indeed, many composers seem to have lost understanding of the difference between dissonance and discord. Our extreme inconsistency of intonation leaves many notes and intervals in doubt. A great composer and a great instrumentalist have each complained to me: "Our orchestras today sound like mud." For an ear sharpened by the microtonal distinctions of electronic and noise music the confused spread of intonation in ordinary orchestral playing can be distressing.

A note is consequently, at the present time, the sign for an arbitrary pitch, generally agreed to be correct when produced by a well-tuned piano (unless originally for harpsichord, in which case a majority of the overtones will have been lost), less accurate when produced by a string instrument, and no more than approximate when produced by the thick, heavily wound lower bass strings of a piano, or a string bass or a tuba. A note differs also according to the timbre or overtone pattern, attack, decay, etc. (the *sound envelope*) of the instrument which sounds it.

Correct pitch or intonation is not the ultimate consideration. To play a melody as they believe it should be heard, musicians deviate above or below the correct pitches, if the instrument permits, with the result that voice or violin often do not sound the same pitches as an accompanying piano; the player alters the exact fall of the notes to shape a melodic rhythm by degrees which our notation cannot indicate. The rhythm of a melodic passage played on organ or harpsichord will need to be articulated by a more decided differentiation in the time-span of intervals notated as alike than when the same passage is played on a piano, because the organ and harpsichord cannot provide the dynamic shaping of piano tone. That is why the altered rhythm of eighteenth century organ and harpsichord music changed to the dynamically shaped rhythm of nineteenth century piano music, revising completely the fundamentals of musical interpretation.

Stravinsky wrote the keyboard obbligato of his opera *The Rake's Progress* to be played on a harpsichord, because of his pleasure in the sound of that instrument, but in piano style. He told me that he had at last solved the problem of balance by doubling the keyboard parts at the octave—thus creating in effect an instrumental quality which belongs neither to harpsichord nor to piano. Several composers, among them Frank Martin and Elliott Carter, have written concerto-type compositions for contrasting solo harpsichord and solo piano, after the example of C. P. E. Bach's concertos for the two instruments. Bach's harpsichord and piano sounded very nearly in the same volume and register, focusing the stylistic differences between the two instruments, which shape and color every phrase. In the works by Martin and Carter the disparity in volume and register between a large modern harpsichord and a large modern piano are very great, but the stylistic distinction has been lost; the contrasting sound of the two instruments, however well managed, is too often obscured—certainly in a large concert hall—by the lack of balance. Amplifying a harpsichord by electronic means to increase the volume distorts the tone quality. We are so accustomed to amplifying records of harpsichord music beyond the normal sounding of the instrument that many do not recognize the distinction, but a good harpsichordist knows it: a strident brilliance replaces the natural coloring of the intonation. The question arises: Does the modern composer of an ensemble work including harpsichord intend that the harpsichord tone should be amplified, and that the consequent brilliance, unnatural to the instrument but not to our contemporary hearing, should be its *correct* intonation for his composition?

Ivor Darreg in Los Angeles has built a steel-strung clavichord, with iron and steel tangents, and electronic pickup at three different sounding-points on each string, like the different plucking-points of a harpsichord. These give a timbre resembling that of a clavichord, a second timbre approximating that of an early piano, and a third related to the timbre of a clarinet. The instrument retains useful characteristics of the clavichord, for example the vibrato; it permits a variety of coloration and control of individual tones which, if developed, could make it an adequate foil for a concert grand piano, whereas a true clavichord would be inaudible. Lou Harrison has adapted the so-called *tack piano,* having thumbtacks in its hammers, used sometimes as a homemade substitute for a harpsichord, to furnish a new quality of pitched percussive tone which he has used with notable effectiveness in several compositions.

In the music of Webern and much of Stravinsky the field of force of a single note in relation to the other notes around it may be decisive. In Schoenberg's music and in Alban Berg's a note is usually decisive not for itself alone but because of its place within a larger melodic pattern of intervals; the field, as in J. S. Bach's music, is that of the entire melody, the melodic consistency remaining coherent, with a unified texture of continual melodic, not analytic, variation. (Compare Webern's little pieces for violin and for cello with piano and Berg's pieces for clarinet and piano or Schoenberg's piano pieces, opus 19.) With Bartók, the field of force of the single note diminishes as the melody enlarges, but Bartók will often contrast this melodic tonal expansion against a single tone constantly reiterated; analytic variation of the melody by the addition of new notes and percussive sounds embroiders the contrast. In Messiaen's music a group of notes does the work of a note, the field of force of the single note being so much the less decisive. In several of Henry Cowell's youthful compositions and some of Bartók's middle period, as well as in earlier instances by Ives, a *tone-cluster* (an extraharmonic clump of notes sounded by fingers, fists, or forearm, or in the *Hawthorne* movement of the Ives *Concord Sonata* by a fourteen-inch rule) may do the work of a note; the harmonic field of force will be increased, but not the fineness of discrimination.

John Cage demonstrated with his compositions for *prepared piano* (screws, bolts, nuts, rubber strips, or other objects placed at measured points between the strings sounded by some keys of a piano, altering the pitch and timbre) that a note (as written) may be read as instruction to strike a certain key of the piano keyboard, the sign having no other relation to the quite unexpected tone (pitch and type of sound) the instrument may produce, transforming the piano into a percussive instrument of microtonal variability. Lou Harrison in one work indicates by notation the identity of the note and by a mathematical figure above it the exact pitch frequency he wishes. Partch frequently notates in this manner.

A note intended to be played by a percussive sound-producer of indefinite pitch may have a distinct timbre like a snare drum, or an indeterminate clangor like a cowbell, a thump or thud like a bass drum, or a knock. The snare drum functions as a solo instrument in Ives's *Putnam's Camp* for orchestra and Lou Harrison's *Song of Queztecoatl* for percussion group. Cage and Ben Johnston have composed interesting works made of the various timbres to be obtained by knocking on the piano frame or strings.

The Experimentalists / Yates

Stravinsky employed a battery of indeterminate sound-producers with the four pianos in *The Wedding;* the rich spread of imprecisely focused pitches accentuates the polytonal motor of the pianos, creating by simple means a consistency of sound-atmosphere which colors the dramatic variety of vocal styles. The great tapestries of abstract instrumental and percussive sound which Edgar Varèse created divorced still farther the expected sound from the notated sign. Cowell, Milhaud, Gerald Strang, Carlos Chávez, and other composers explored in various ways the tonal freedom of such percussive media, with and without instruments of determinate pitch.

In the later 1930s, John Cage, with Lou Harrison and William Russell, created a new extratonal percussion orchestra and a percussion literature, strongly influenced at the start by the Indonesian *gamelan* orchestra and by the melodic-rhythmic proportions (*raga* and *tala*) of Indian music. Harrison composed a large number of percussion pieces in an increasingly melodic and polyphonic style, the intervals relative to the arbitrary pitches and timbres of the sound-producers. Among these are a Concerto for violin and a wide range of percussion including flowerpots, one-pound coffee cans, and metal bucket, and *Concerto in Slendro* (a five-note scale) for violin with two tack pianos, celesta, tympani, and two garbage pails. The seemingly arbitrary and unmusical sound-producing objects become, in these settings, distinctly musical, each unsual timbre exerting a distinguishable field of force. Percussion groups playing the percussion literature now exist in several universities and cities; and composers are steadily adding new compositions.

After these developments, it is only going a step farther to substitute for the twelve-note scale any microtonal scale or pattern of intervals, or any note or tone-cluster selected by chance means (as in Cage's *Music of Changes* for piano—the name and the idea are from the Chinese *Book of Changes, I Ching*), or indeed any sound or noise, however indeterminately arrived at or produced, for an instrumental tone. Substitute words for notes, and there is a lecture; substitute actions, and the result is *theatrical-performance music.*

Nothing is wrong with these substitutions, except the temporary incapacity or unwillingness of the audience to accept them.

The consequences of these logical decisions, resulting from no arbitrary waywardness but inherent in the current evolution of music, as I have tried to demonstrate, are rapidly changing our conception of music as an art, while increasing our skill to use sound musically and our knowledge of its creative potentialities.

During the present century, musical notation, as a result of the composers' efforts to adapt it to a continually changing and enlarging scope and opportunity of music, has been constantly adopting more refined and elaborate and also cruder means, depending on what the composer expects of the performer. If the composer looks to the performer for an exact reproduction of his notated message—the notated composition is not in reality the music but an instructive message to the performer telling him what to do—the composer is hampered by the inadequacy of any notational convention to convey his message in sufficient detail. Paraphrasing a statement by Roger Reynolds: Interest in the independence of sounds (their right to a full life and freedom of individual movement) is the cause of many notational problems: free pitch-alteration in time; differing and changing tempo references for each voice; decay times of sounding units made up of instruments having different modes and periods of attack and decay (this is most crucial and difficult). The effort to resolve these problems is clearly evident in Reynolds's beautifully notated scores, each desired effect carefully but economically described.

Some composers (among them Morton Feldman, Christian Wolff, Karlheinz Stockhausen, Earle Brown, Bo Nilsson, Sylvano Bussotti, Morton Subotnick), but not in all compositions, provide merely a rough chart of their intentions, leaving it to the performer to decide the specific interpretation, or the assembling of parts, or the order and grouping of the notes, or the types and kinds of sounds. The resulting composition is both new and old, since it revives for example the Italian white-note convention or the jazz convention, where the notation serves for the basis of an improvisation, the player supplying by choice out of an agreed idiom the notes or sounds he performs. In such case, notation will be diagrammatic or graphic; a large quantity of such music, substituting actual graphs or diagrams for much or all of the notation, is already in existence. The permanent value of such music, as much as survives, will be comparable with that of a white-note keyboard composition by Alessandro Scarlatti (which scarcely anyone at present can perform correctly), or a written composition by one of the already historic jazz composers who didn't expect his music to be played like it looks, or of any ensemble music requiring realization of the continuo accompaniment (for which players today substitute common chords and passing notes).

J. S. Bach and Schoenberg held in disdain any "keyboard-rider" who composed at the piano. Wagner's Bechstein piano held a writing desk, and Stravinsky unabashedly composes at the keyboard. L. M. Gottschalk admired Beethoven's orchestral compositions but not his piano sonatas, which in Gottschalk's opinion lacked the modern refinements of piano playing added by Liszt, Thalberg, and himself. Gottschalk held in low esteem any mere performer of other men's music, if he did not also improvise, compose, and vary his compositions in performance. As to that opinion, J. S. Bach, Mozart, and Beethoven would have agreed with him. But Mozart despised in Clementi the type of piano playing which became the virtuosity of Liszt, Thalberg, and Gottschalk, while Chopin, who admired Liszt's piano playing, thought poorly of his compositions. David Tudor, the pianist whose creative skills and ingenuity have contributed largely to realizing the more oddly notated and unpredictable piano compositions of the last fifteen years, is a collector and profound admirer of the piano works by Gottschalk.

It is possible that generations of pianists will follow David Tudor in inventing, to the composer's indications, their own performing versions of such music by indicia as John Cage's *Winter Music,* for which any sound obtainable on, in, or by means of any part of a piano is valid, the notation consisting of isolated clusters of notes in irregular location on a page; or Stockhausen's composition by assembling pages of separately notated parts; or a wide variety of compositions written out as graphs or by graphic or pictorial devices. Students may begin exploring, with a new sort of musical pleasure, combinations of game and dramatic action with musical performance, such as Robert Ashley's *Maneuvers for Small Hands* in notes, graphic indicia, and brief verbal instructions on one hundred separate cards. Roger Reynolds's *The Emperor of Ice Cream* dramatizes a choral and instrumental performance of Wallace Stevens's poem with pistol shot, bursting paper bag, graphic indicia, and variously written sizes of verbal text, as well as notes. Malcolm Goldstein graphs a vocal score by the rise and fall, size, and visible convolutions of the handwritten text, the vocal pitches rising and falling indeterminately with the graphic line within the normal vocal span.

The argument does not by any means all run in one direction. The goal is not total or anarchic freedom. Earle Brown came to music through the mobiles of Alexander Calder, the later paintings of Jackson Pollock, and the writings of Gertrude Stein. Brown writes: "The greatest single misinterpretation of our time is the general feeling that my kind of work is intended to be 'free' of art, choice, responsibility, beauty, form, content, or *anything.* From the very beginning I have been attempting to intensify and expand the composition-performance potential of responsible, sensitive, contextual, human-artistic *choice,* choosing within an intentionally ambiguous environment of generalized potential, on the basis of the given 'programme' and the 'feed-back' effect inherent in human awareness, spontaneity, memory, accepting, rejecting, liking, disliking, and just plain activity in relation to the particular materials I have given and the alternatives I have permitted in each composition.

". . . One does not diminish the amount of 'meaningful' control within a work but seeks to create the work as an entity, a quasi-organism, and to 'programme' a life for it within which it comes to find its shape, extensions of meaningfulness, and its multiple formal identities of its basic nature [composed] through its programme of process potential." Is the performer, after he has assembled and completed his performing version, or worked out the graphic instructions, the real composer? If so, David Tudor is one of the most potent composers of the new era of sound. One man serving many different composers, he asserted and reiterated the new possibility, transforming the perishable nature of incompletely specified musical intention to give it validity. But Tudor, like most of those who perform this music, still credits the composition as the work of the composer. Say rather that the composer creates new opportunities for the performer, instead of the customary final statement of his idea completely predetermined in notation, and the performer in turn shares what he has accomplished with his audience. This is the significance of Cage's spontaneous reply, "Composing's one thing, performing's another, listening's a third. What can they have to do with one another?" The creative-imaginative opportunity is distributed among all participants.

Composers, that is to say, are breaking down the three components of the esthetic experience as we have known it, composition, performance, audience reception, into an indefinite number of distinct experiences. Instead of the notated composition as a completed structure or texture, there may be a succession of individual or composite sounds heard each for itself. Cage writes of his audibly radical String Quartet: "The composition, a melodic line without accompaniment, employs single tones, intervals, triads, and aggregates requiring one or more of the instruments for their production. These constitute a gamut of sounds." An earlier example is Cage's Suite for Toy Piano, using a gamut of nine somewhat arbitrarily pitched tones. The melodic consistency of the tone-row, which Cage had rejected, is replaced by an indeterminate consistency of notated tones. When the line ceases to be melodic, does it cease to be a consistency? At what extreme does this occur?

Cage tells us: "A sound does not view itself as thought, as ought, as needing another sound for its elucidation, as etc.; it has no time for any consideration—it is occupied with the performance of its characteristics: before it has died away it must have made perfectly exact its frequency, its loudness, its length, its overtone structure, the precise morphology of these and of itself." A sound therefore need not be melodic; it may be still a note or a combination of notes; it may be, instead, a sound which is not a note: a noise, a scrape, a spoken word, an electronically generated or altered pitch or noise, anything indeed which can be heard, or a silence which not being heard is musically resonant or filled with chance sound-events.

On one occasion when I was listening to such a composed, prepared, enacted silence, during a concert given in a small church, the silence was filled from outside the hall, too eloquently, with the songs of mockingbirds.

Cage's *Concert for Piano and Orchestra* consists of: a piano composition of separate sheets to be assembled by the pianist, which may be heard alone; an orchestral composition of instrumental parts (nonconsecutive figures on separate sheets, to be played in any order), which is to be performed according to predetermined rules by an indeterminate number of musicians, preferably at least twelve or as many as a full orchestra; an aria for vocal soloist (a variety of voice techniques in five languages and eleven styles from coloratura song to barking dog) which may be performed separately accompanied by the taped composition, *Fontana Mix,* both or either of which may be included in the *Concert:* the length of the performance is indeterminate, to be decided in advance of the occasions. One sees that the work when fully assembled is indeed more like a concert than a concerto.

The resulting auditory complex is no more complicated, if listened to quietly and without dismay, than traffic at a busy street corner, where more different things may be expected to be going on at one time than at another; where the volume and direction of the sound alter with each change of traffic lights (marking chronological time, as in Cage's *Concert,* instead of metrical time as in Beethoven); where all events are indeterminate in arrangement but determined by the shape of traffic flow; and the cop at the corner knows the score but does not direct the play.

Such a composition is a rational extension of Schoenberg's "picture-puzzle" . . . in "deadly earnest." However elaborate the choices he provides, Cage, like Schoenberg, "cannot allow any will but mine to prevail . . . because the composing was done just that way." The *Concert* is a completely ordered and structured formal composition, the ordering and structure determined in detail by indeterminate means. Cage knows when the musicians play wrong notes or disobey his instructions; he knows when the composition has been well or incompetently played.

Oh but! one may exclaim, this is farce, satire, parody, not music, antimusic! Pierre Boulez said to me that after the pieces for prepared piano Cage went "outside the musical continuum." (Stravinsky had said, apropos of Boulez's discontinuous *Polyphony X,* that music cannot exist without continuity.) Boulez's criticism resembles Hindemith's complaint that the tone-row destroys the sense of musical space by denying the gravitational uprightness of harmony. Quite true, one might reply. That's what it does. To emphasize his point, Boulez rapped on the wood frame of the piano. Cage wrote his *Wonderful Widow of*

Eighteen Springs (text from James Joyce's *Finnegans Wake*) with accompaniment of knocking by fingers and knuckles on the piano frame, a highly sophisticated primitive music.

"Is it," in Wittgenstein's words, "a mere question of pleasing and ugly?" That is an argument the critic by polemic seldom wins. (Such criticism exposes the inadequacy of the critic but not the inadequacy of the work which is his subject.) Though the intrusion of indeterminacy in both composition and performance may seem to deny the facts of order and structure, it does not really do so, since the resulting performance, however different on each occasion, will be ordered by the rules of the game—as gamblers play by strict rules—, the composite structure is clearly stated, and the composition presents itself in terms subject to exact description, as much as a game of chess or football or a yacht race.

Cage's descriptions of his works, in the catalogue published by C. F. Peters, are, in each instance, or unexceptionable lucidity, overcoming the difficulty of putting "indefiniteness, correctly and unfalsified, into words." The compositions, so stated, are not indefinite, not haphazard, not nonsense, and therefore, unavoidably, compositions. Anyone may concede that much, as of Beethoven's *Great Fugue,* and still dislike the music. But it is very unwise if, disliking the music, one explains that Beethoven could do no better because he was deaf.

A haphazard noncomposition may exist; musical literature is crowded with haphazard compositions in traditional idiom and formal layout, which have no validity except habitual practice. A *happening* is one name for a haphazard noncomposition; happenings are, generally, inadequate noncompositions seeking a false justification in disorder, though some may be amusing. Anarchy, however plausible in generalities, fails too often in the instance.

How to distinguish the one from the other? How distinguish a good from a bad fugue? Creative activity does not offer its products for the purpose of enabling critics to sort them into good, mediocre, or bad. The generation of composers from Debussy to Stravinsky—except Ives —believed in the created composition as an absolute and labored to make it so; the present generation has been much influenced by the improvisatory practice of jazz, in which the performance is relative to the occasion and to the skills of the participants. In this way perhaps more than any other, true jazz has influenced the more seriously composed music. Between, there is a broad area of fully composed music which seeks to convey, with more determinate order, the freedom of jazz improvisation—for an example, *All Set* by Milton Babbitt.

The determinate-indeterminate composition, determinate in conception but indeterminate in execution, or designed to impede or distract the audience from grasping it as a unit, has come into full existence. Causality has not been excluded but made indefinite in time-sequence. A computer can carry such invention much farther, but the broad band of causality in time-sequence has not been done away with; it still begins with the composer and proceeds to the performance.

The proof of the notation is in the reading. Most of the notational systems which are being devised and experimentally tried today are too complex to be practical, too individual or specialized to be of general application, and inadequate to serve the composer's needs. Abundant performance has proved that Cage's notational systems, though specialized each to its occasion, do not impede performance and may present modifiable types, capable of wider applications; these have been widely and variously imitated.

The established system of twelve notes in the octave is being pulled out of orbit by the new potentiality of sound. (It is still of course perfectly reasonable to compose twelve-note music with a twelve-note octave in any appropriate style.) The technical inconvenience of the established body of instruments (a much smaller number than the thirty-five families of instruments which were counted during the fourteenth century in the music room of Rheims Cathedral), to which a musician may devote a life's labor yet never graduate from a back seat in the orchestra, is already resulting in a scarcity of professional string players, with a corresponding increase in the number of amateur orchestras across the American continent. The instrumentalist does not cease to be a lover of music or wish, any more than in the past, to cease playing his instrument; he chooses to play for pleasure, according to the degree of skill he can maintain without great effort, and has no desire to make his living by this means. The symphony orchestra as we have known it, in which a few musicians play all the solos while the remainder drudge through season after season of unenlightening routine, may give way to amateur orchestras, in which the back-seat player can take part to the best of his ability, and to smaller groups in which all the players are skilled soloists. (One amateur orchestra, the St. Louis Philharmonic, has been in existence since 1860; the members pay a small fee for the privilege of playing and give four concerts a year.)

At this point music-lovers become frightened: What shall we do to preserve our high standards of performance, our Beethoven, our Brahms, our Berlioz, our operas, our ballets, our beloved symphonic and solo repertory? Are our standards really so high, or are they merely rigid? Do players in large orchestras play at all times to the best of their ability, right through to the back seats, or as slackly as they can get away with? In updating our repertory, as we do in any case periodically, do we lose more than we gain?

The change will be gradual, and our ears and minds will make it by necessity—no use worrying about it. The symphony orchestra will not disappear tomorrow; the opera will be around for quite a while. Only a small part of the audience has learned to appreciate the higher skills and standards of soloistic playing in chamber music. But the change is occurring. The ballet is changing already under the influence of contemporary dance, the new dance art created in this century by American women from Isadora Duncan and Maud Allan to Martha Graham, influenced again from abroad by Mary Wigman and combining with the more traditional European dance from Pavlova to George Balanchine. It is an art not of soloists and a great, static *corps de ballet* but of individual dancers in well-led cooperative groups, a model of what is also happening around us in music. Connoisseurs and dilettantes are always afraid of what they may be losing, devoting themselves to perpetuating the past instead of looking about to discover what is coming to pass.

Temporary certainties vanish. Medieval and Renaissance music, using a notation we read but do not correctly interpret, is being rediscovered, widening and increasing our musical awareness, contributing to the fresh creative synthesis that is already occurring, not a Hegelian but a revolutionary synthesis. Oriental, Indian, Indonesian, African music, of many periods and kinds; the cumulative influence of our recent perception of the true nature of folk music; the new experimental music of Europe which responds to the American experimental tradition; the music now coming out of Central and South America and from the Caribbean countries: all these contributions to fresh modes of conceiving and of hearing music are coming together like a great wave gathering, urging music forward.

Technical problems, notation among them, will solve themselves as the new musical period we have entered, like it or not, gains impetus. We are at the inception of a new musical orientation, like the change from polyphony to harmony at the start of the seventeenth century, with new content, new idioms, new styles, new instruments, and new routines, combined with new experiences that will sharpen and increase our musical perception. Amateur musicians may again become as skilled as the amateur singers and instrumentalists of the madrigal period. Our pleasure in music is our ability to share in it; skills of performance follow the composer but often begin with the rise to prominence of a new instrument: the organ, the violin, the computer. Comprehension follows listening. This is an extraordinary time in an art which by custom and habituation clings to its traditions. Today as never before, certainly not since the later sixteenth century, tradition is being reassessed and much of it rejected. Composers are trying out new, expedient means to catch an inspiration. And in some cases, to judge by the technical literature, the importance of the means seems to be greater than that of the inspiration. In Charles Ives's words, "manner breeds a cussed cleverness."

QUESTIONS

1. Yates asks, "Is there esthetic worth in a destructive force?" What is meant here by "destructive force"? Look up the word "nihilism." How does it refer to certain twentieth-century experimental music?
2. The musical symbols for "loud," and "soft," are *f* and *p*. A good question may be *how* loud? *How* soft? Can you think of a way to indicate *degrees* of loudness and softness so that the performer will know what the composer has in mind? Is this an important problem? Why?
3. Why do any but first-rate performers avoid "new" music? What are the connections between the musical experience of the performer and the experience of the listener? Discuss these.
4. Look up the following terms in a music dictionary: "equal temperament," "just intonation," "well-tempered," and "wolf-tone." What do we mean when we say someone is playing or singing "out-of-tune"? What do we mean when we say someone is either "flat" or "sharp"?
5. Do you think that sticking thumbtacks into the hammers of a piano is a "legitimate" device for creating "new" sounds from the instrument? Why? How is this technique different from electronically amplifying musical instruments? What is the esthetic effect? Can this be measured? Why?

MUSIC OF SHOW BUSINESS / 1

*Leonard Bernstein's talent and imagination have
brought him to the highest places in at least two
musical worlds—the world of the Broadway musical,
and the world of the concert stage. His fame on
Broadway (to take these worlds alphabetically) has
been solidly established by* On the Town, *his first
successful show, and* West Side Story, *his best.
His serious work includes the Jeremiah* Symphony
and the one-act opera, Trouble in Tahiti. *Bernstein
dislikes being called versatile, but, call it what
you will, he has further distinguished himself
as the permanent conductor of the New York
Philharmonic Orchestra and as a popular television
music educator without peer. This last distinction,
together with his magnetic appeal and his engaging
appearance, has given him a reknown usually reserved
for home-run kings and movie stars. In his essay he
referees a bout between Broadway and the classics.*

Whatever Happened to That
☆ Great American Symphony? ☆

LEONARD BERNSTEIN

(**T**he following, not properly a conversation, is an exchange of documents between L. B. and Broadway Producer, henceforth known as B. P., a man who interests himself, curiously enough, in some facets of art generally unknown to his calling. A born gentleman of average producer height; chin framed by a luxurious Persian-lamb collar which adorns his fifty-per-cent-cashmere evening coat; a man with an emerald tie pin and a wise, sweaty look—a man, in short, who carries his five feet two with pride and power.)

I. Via Western Union

B.P.
HOTEL GORBEDUC
NEW YORK
VERY SORRY CANNOT ACCEPT KIND OFFER SHOW BASED BURTON'S ANATOMY MELANCHOLY SPLENDID IDEA WISH YOU ALL LUCK WITH IT REGRET UNABLE BUT DEEPLY INVOLVED WRITING NEW SYMPHONY GREETINGS

L.B.

II. Via Post

L.B.
Steinway Hall
New York City
Dear L.B.:

My associates and I were very much disappointed to receive your refusal by wire yesterday of our offer to collaborate with us, and with many other artists of outstanding merit and importance, on our new project for this season. I have long felt (and now feel corroborated by my associates in that opinion) that Burton's *Anatomy of Melancholy* would one day serve as the basis of a great work in the musical theater. We think that you are just the man to write the music for it, thereby enriching our stage which this season cries for such a work. Instead you tell us that you are writing a new symphony, a commendable enough

---

WHATEVER HAPPENED TO THAT GREAT AMERICAN SYMPHONY? from *The Joy of Music* by Leonard Bernstein; copyright 1954, 1959 by Leonard Bernstein. Reprinted by permission of Simon and Schuster, Inc.

enterprise. But if you will allow me to take a few minutes of your time, I should like to point out a few facts which you may not have taken into account in making your decision.

I begin with a question: why? Why continue to write symphonies in America for a public which does not care one way or the other about them? Can you honestly name me two or three people in all America who actually *care* whether you or anybody else ever writes another symphony or not? Do not answer this too hastily, or too defensively. The more you consider the question, the clearer will come the answer: that nobody, with the possible exception of some other composers and some critics who live by denouncing or flattering new works, will be any the sorrier if you or any of your symphonic colleagues never writes a symphony again. There seems to me to be no historical necessity for symphonies in our time: perhaps our age does not express itself truly through the symphonic form; I really am not in a position to know. I am a simple man, and know mainly through intuition whatever it is I know. I think I have my fingers on the pulse of the people, and believe me, L.B., it is not a symphonic pulse that I feel.

So there you are, writing music for which there is no historical necessity, probably; for which there is no public demand, certainly; and from which, if you will pardon me, there is no economic gain. Perhaps now you can see more clearly why I asked: why? Now let me ask: why not? Why not give of your talents to that sector of musical art in America where there is hot, live, young blood—the theater? Here you will find the public waiting for you, and you will be complying with the demands of history. All art, in all times, I believe, has been created to meet a public or private demand, whether it be the art of building Gothic cathedrals, or of painting the portrait of a wealthy patron, or of writing a play for the Elizabethan public, or of composing a Mass. Or, if you will again pardon me, the art of writing a symphony. Haydn and Mozart and Brahms surely didn't write their symphonies in a vacuum; their symphonies were expected of them. Nobody today really *expects* a symphony of anybody. Our American composers have an obligation to the theater, which is alive and which needs them. Won't you think seriously about it again?

Faithfully,
B.P.

P.S. How had you planned for this new symphony to feed, clothe and house your charming wife and baby (to whom warmest personal regards)?

B.P.
Hotel Gorbeduc
New York City
Dear B.P.:

I have read and reread your most interesting letter of yesterday, and I am impressed. I say *impressed* rather than *convinced*, since I cannot honestly report a change of heart as a result. But I have rarely met a producer operating in the Broadway area who has given so much sincere and deeply felt thought to a situation which basically does not concern his immediate livelihood. I am further impressed with your legal style, which is persuasive to a point where, if I were not more closely acquainted than you with the facts of the case (which is only natural), I might yield to your arguments. But the facts stand, and I feel obliged to report them to you.

There has never in history, by statistical record, been so great an interest in the symphony and in the symphony orchestra as is at this moment manifested in the United States. There are orchestras everywhere, in every small city, in every university and high school, in even some of our most provincial areas. How can you speak of "no public demand" when the latest figures of the League of Symphony Orchestras shows xx orchestras of major proportions now operating in the United States, as against xx orchestras of similar size in 19xx? The League further reports xx orchestras of smaller proportions now professionally active. Everywhere there have arisen festivals to which the public flocks in unprecedented numbers—and they are festivals which emphasize contemporary music almost as much as the standard repertory. Summer concerts have become as great an attraction as canoeing once was; and the winter seasons of our major orchestras are enjoying a lively increase in both attendance and interest. Community concert services send out great numbers of artists to cities large and small from coast to coast, where they are heard by audiences that a decade ago would not have dreamed of attending a concert.

I am sorry to bore you with statistics this way, but these facts are a matter of record. And think of all the new works being commissioned by such agencies as the Louisville Orchestra. xx works this year alone! And then think of the prizes, fellowships, awards of various kinds, all of which encourage the writing of concert music. Think of the enormous increase in the sale of records: why, it amounts almost to a craze. No, you cannot say that the public is indifferent to concert music. As to your reference to historical necessity, I simply do not understand you. And when you speak of economic gain, you are right; but economic considerations cannot enter into this area. One is an artist by necessity, and there are other ways of making money.

As you know, I love to write for the theater: I have done it before, and hope to do it often again. But this is a moment when other things come first. Thank you again for having asked me and for having taken the trouble to write.

Sincerely,
L.B.

IV. Via Post

L.B.
Yaddo [An artist's retreat]
Saratoga Springs, New York
Dear L.B.:

Forgive me for breaking into your privacy again, but in the week that has elapsed since I received your letter I have given a lot of thought to the subject we have been discussing, and have even done some reading to back me up. Besides, your letter was so incredibly solemn, and, were it not for its obvious sincerity, so *dull*, if you will pardon me, that I am intrigued. I cannot believe that a young fellow like you, grown up in America, with the sense of fun that you have exhibited in some of your works, can possibly be such a fuddy-duddy. This letter is written partly to find out, and partly to acquaint you with my more recent thoughts about the symphonic form. I have given up the idea of trying ·to persuade you to do our show with us, and we are now negotiating with another composer. But you have awakened in me, by your refusal and your reasons for refusing, a real interest in this whole subject. I now have what might almost be called a theory. I explained it yesterday to our mutual friend P., who was in town for a day, and he found it silly. But what can you expect of a poet? As you know, he is also up at Yaddo for a month, working on his new volume, *Greaves of Brass,* and that's how I knew where to write you. Please avoid discussing my theory with him when you see him; his sense of historical necessity is appalling, if I can judge by the two poems from *Greaves of Brass* that he showed me yesterday.

Well, then, the theory. All music must begin in the theater, historically speaking. Does that amaze you? Just think about it. The origins of music are mostly folklore, comprising songs and dances of prayer, of work, of celebration, of love. This means that music first arises attached to words and ideas. There is no folk music, to my knowledge, that is abstract. It is music for working to, or for dancing to, or for singing words to. It is always *about* something. Then, as it develops, music becomes more sophisticated, more complicated; but it is still attached to concepts, as it is in the theater. Where music really grew up was in the church, wasn't it? The greatest theater of them all! (If ever there was theater music in the truest and best sense it was simple plain-chant.) Now we find little operas beginning to emerge, in Italy and in Germany and in Austria. The little operas (or masques, or singspiels, or whatever they were) become bigger operas—and we have Mozart. While in the church, little motets have grown into large requiems and cantatas. Now is the moment when the big switch can happen, and not until this moment. Now musical idioms have become familiar; and the procedures of Western music are enough alike so that the music can be *separated* from the words or the ideas or the concepts—that is, from the theater—and can exist for the audience in its own right. Now that there is a Mozart opera, there can also be a Mozart symphony. (But never forget that the symphony, as my books tell me, came from the opera overture!) And now that there are Bach Passions, there can also be Bach preludes and fugues. (But remember that the preludes and fugues were first of all reverie-pieces used in the church service!) In short, the audiences had grown up *with* the music in the theater, and had reached the point where they could relate to the music *without* the theater. Their ears were ready for abstract sound: F-sharps and E-flats had become in themselves interesting and moving, without benefit of words to tell why they ought to be. But it had taken the audience a long time to reach this point.

Does all this sound like nonsense to you? I hope not: I'm banking on that solemnity of yours. But now to the meat of the theory.

The point I want to make with all my might is that America right now seems to me to be, musically, just about where Germany was around the seventeenth century. Deep in the singspiel. (We mustn't talk about present-day church music: that must be traditional, and has all been inherited.) But our secular music is just about where German music was fifty years before Mozart. Only *our* singspiels are called *Oklahoma!* and *Can-Can*. This is a period we must pass through before we can arrive at a real American symphonic form, or a real American style of whatever kind of concert music. It may not be the symphony as we have known it: we may produce something very different. But the musical language it will speak must first be created in our theater; then one day it can be divorced from "meaning" and stand alone, abstract. Do you see what I mean? For all our technical mastery and sophistication we are not really ready yet to produce our own concert music. As a result, all the stuff that is being turned out by the mile every day for concert performance in American halls is really European, and *old* European at that, with perhaps some American spice added by way of cowboy tunes or blues harmonies or jazz rhythms. But the music remains essentially European, because the whole notion of the symphonic form is a German notion, and don't let anybody tell you anything else. All the Russian symphonies are really German ones with vodka substituted for beer; and Franck's is German with some cornets making the difference; and Liszt's are German with nothing making the difference, and so are Elgar's and Grieg's and Dvořák's. Whatever national touches have been added, it's all German deep down, because the line of the symphony is a straight one smack from Mozart to Mahler.

Now here we are, remember, a brand-new country, comparatively speaking, a baby only a hundred and seventy-five years old. Which is nothing at all when you think of the old empires that produced that straight line I just mentioned. And actually we have been writing music in this country for only fifty years, and half of that fifty years the music has been borrowed clean out of the pockets of Brahms and Company. Of course we have the disadvantage here of having been born already grown up, so we don't start with folk dances and prayers for rain. We started with the leavings of the European development, handed to us on an old cracked dish. But then, we have an advantage after all: we have jazz. Which is the beginning of some other straight line which will grow here as certainly as the symphonic line grew out of another folk-strain for about a hundred years in Germany. Whatever jazz is, it's our own folk music, naïve, sophisticated, and exciting. And out of it has been born something we call the musical comedy. Well, 175 years isn't very long for that to have happened (and it really took only the last fifty years) compared to the centuries it took for the singspiel to arrive. And here we are at the point of building that singspiel into real opera—or, in our terms, developing *Pal Joey* into whatever American music is going to become. We are all ready and waiting for the Mozart to come along and just simply do it. That's why I'm in the producing business: I want to be there when it happens, if I live that long. I'm taking bids on the new Mozart. Any comers?

Well, there you have it. Very rough, not really thought out, but as plain as day to me. What I would love to make plain as day to you is the difference that arises out of all this between Europe and America as they relate to concert music. A new Brahms symphony to a Viennese of that period was of consuming interest to him: it caused endless speculation about what it would turn out to be, how it would differ from the last one, and all the rest, just as we speculate now about a forthcoming Rodgers-Hammerstein show. It made table-talk the next morning; it was everybody's concern; it was part of daily living, the air breathed, food taken. As a result, the Viennese or German of today has inherited some of that possessiveness about the Brahms music: it is almost as though he had written it himself. The same is true of the relation between Italians and Italian opera. But in America the listener cannot share these feelings, no matter how wildly he loves the music of Brahms or Verdi, and no matter how much talk he makes about music being a universal language. There will always be the element of the museum about this repertory for him—the revered classic, always slightly remote. It can never be his private property, so to speak. And since he doesn't give a damn about whether anyone is writing new symphonies or not, there is no real vitality for him in our concert life, except the vitality of a visit to the museum. Q.E.D.

This has been a really long one, and I hope you will forgive my going on and on. But I was excited about this when it occurred to me and I wanted you to hear it all right away, even if you are trying to write that long, useless piece up there in your retreat. My best to P., and whatever you do don't let him talk you into setting *Greaves of Brass* to music. You're being abstract now, remember: you're committed.

Faithfully,
B.P.

V. Via Air Mail

B.P.
Hotel Gorbeduc
New York City
Dear B.P.:

It is a month since I had your last long, astonishing letter, and I apologize for my lateness in answering; but I have been to Yaddo and back to New York and then here to Milan all rather quickly. I had to suspend work on my symphony temporarily to fill this engagement conducting at La Scala, and now that the rehearsals and first performance are over I finally have a chance to answer you.

I must admit that I see to some extent what you mean about the sense of possessiveness toward music. Here in Milan people are still spending their time and energy at parties and luncheons arguing loudly about which is the greater opera, *Rigoletto* or *Trovatore*. As though it had all been written yesterday, hot off the presses. These Italians (or at least these Milanese) really own that music; and as you say, they seem to think they have written it all themselves. And you are right when you say that the wildest music-lover in the States can never relate that closely and familiarly to the same music. I am reminded of people at similar parties and luncheons in New York who will talk for hours about the relative merits of two hit musical shows, and even get excited or angry or hurt as they attack or defend them. All that part of your letter is perfectly true.

But I must take issue with your historical survey. It all sounds so easy and slick as you put it; and I admire you enormously for going into books and digging out all those facts and making them into ideas. Perhaps your main idea has some validity, but there are remarkable holes in your reasoning. What of the Frescobaldi *ricercare*, and the whole seventeenth-century school of organ music? What of Froberger and Pachelbel, who preceded Bach? Oh, all right, I'm being solemn and dull again, and I won't go into a lot of boring musicology. But you don't say the most obvious fact: that even if America is now in a period analogous to the singspiel period in Germany, she is at the same time equipped with the foreknowledge of the next 250 years. What a difference that makes, after all! Don't you see that the greatest development of German music was dependent on its very naïveté in its early stages? American composers can never be that naïve now, writing as they are after the world has already known Mozart and Strauss and Debussy and Schönberg. Perhaps they are condemned after all to be epigonous, and to follow in the line handed them by an already over-developed Europe. It may not be so exciting to compose now as it must have been in 1850; perhaps this is all very sad, but perhaps it is true. And anyway, what would you have all these serious American composers do? Go *en masse* into the shoe business? They are writing out of some sort of inner necessity, so there must be a real validity to it, whether or not it is explainable by your new theory.

I have a matinee today and so I must leave this and run to the theater. How is your show coming? Have you found a composer yet? I wish you luck and hope that whoever finally writes it will turn out to be your Mozart, in spades.

Sincerely,
L.B.

VI. Via Transatlantic Cable

L.B.
SCALA
MILANO
SHOE BUSINESS GOOD IDEA LETTER FOLLOWS GREET-
INGS

B.P.

VII. Via Air Mail

Teatro alla Scala
Milano, Italy
Dear L.B.:

Hooray! You are a dead duck! You have obviously been convinced of my theory, and that makes me very happy. Your letter clearly shows that you have no real, sensible rebuttal. Of course what I said was full of holes; what do you expect from a brand-new musicologist? What do I know about Pachelbel and Frescobaldi and that other guy? But what I know I know on all twelves, and at this point I am more certain than ever that I am right. Why, I went to the Philharmonic concert the other night, just to see what is happening in your thrilling concert world. There were empty seats everywhere. People were sleeping on all sides, some noisily, and I do not exclude one or two critics. It was all as dull as it could be, and the applause was polite and seemed intended more as something to start people's circulation going again after their nap than approval of the music. Dull, dull, dull! After the concert the audience shuffled out in a stupor, not talking much about it or about anything; and I shuffled to Sardi's for a double stinger. It was like waking up. The theater, the theater, on all sides: people arguing, recalling scenes and jokes with gales of laughter, people singing snatches of tunes to each other to prove some point, everyone alive. Alive, I tell you!

Sure, there are some American composers who will have to go on writing their symphonies which may get heard twice with indifference. They may even be geniuses. I wish them all the luck in the world, and I hope they make it. But I have a sneaky feeling that they will continue to do symphonies because they *can't* do music for the theater. Don't think it is so easy to be a theater composer! In some ways it's harder: there is a discipline of the stage. You're not your own boss; it is the whole work that counts. A composer of symphonies has all the notes in the rainbow before him: he can choose as he wishes; not the theater composer. He really has to *work!* A great theater composer is a rare thing: he must have the sense of timing of a Duse, a sense of when to go easy and when to lay it on, a preknowledge of what the audience will feel every second of the work. He must have lightness and weight, wit and sentiment, pathos and brilliance. He must know his craft and everyone else's as well. Don't disparage him. I listened to *Tosca* the other day, and what a wallop it gave me! That man knew theater. And that man does not exactly languish in dishonor.

I tell you again: what is alive and young and throbbing with historic current in America is musical theater. And I tell you another thing:

228   *Music of Show Business / Bernstein*

you know it as well as I do! You know in your heart that the real pieces of importance and interest to America now are not X's Fourteenth Symphony and Y's Flute Soliloquy, but *Finian's Rainbow* and *Carousel* and maybe even *Wonderful Town,* though I doubt it, and *South Pacific.* And all your long lists of dead statistics and all your Pachelbels put together cannot make you feel otherwise.

I want to thank you for giving me the push to go out and investigate all this stuff I have never been so glad or so proud to be a producer of musical theater on Broadway. We are going ahead with our show at full speed, as soon as we find the right composer, and I can't wait to begin. I want to be part of this big new line that is forming to the right in the musical history of America, and I want to watch it take its place in the musical history of the world.

Faithfully,
B.P.

VIII. Via Transatlantic Cable

B.P.
HOTEL GORBEDUC
NEW YORK
PLANS CHANGED HAVE DECIDED ACCEPT YOUR SHOW
STILL DISAGREE HEARTILY YOUR THEORY HOME NEXT
WEEK WARMEST REGARDS

L.B.

QUESTIONS

1. Can you name any composers, in addition to Leonard Bernstein, capable of writing both a symphony and a musical comedy score? Can you suggest the kind of training and experience necessary to this combination?

2. Do you agree with the statement, "There seems to be no historical necessity for symphonies in our time?" Give your reasons. Do you believe there is, in our time, a historical necessity for musical comedies? What, exactly, is "historical necessity?"

3. If Richard Rodgers is essentially a composer of Broadway musicals, why was he selected to compose the music for the TV documentary *Victory at Sea?* Do you think he needed the money? the prestige? Suggest reasons why Rodgers accepted the assignment.

4. Look up the names of Vladimir Dukelsky, Kurt Weill, and Gunther Schuller. What are their accomplishments? What do these men have in common?

5. What is Bernstein's point in making up these letters? Is there any special significance in having one of the writers be a Broadway producer? Are the questions Bernstein poses controversial? If a composer could earn a good living composing symphonies would B.P. still have an argument with L.B.? Discuss these questions.

MUSIC OF SHOW BUSINESS / 2

Jazz is the comprehensive name for a variety of specific musical styles: New Orleans style, Pre-Swing, Swing, Bop, Cool, Thirdstream, and such regional, self-styled types as Chicago jazz, Kansas City jazz, and West Coast jazz. Jazz is a way of playing, a manner of performance. It is not characterized by song titles. There is no jazz unless there is an attempt by the jazzman at creative improvization; and the quality of the jazz then produced is determined by the degree of creativity. For this reason, there is jazz that is great or mediocre or poor—categories that may also be found in classical music. The jazzman attempts to improvise on a theme that may be melodic, harmonic, rhythmic, or any combination of these. In the following essay from The Anatomy of Jazz, *the author discusses early jazz criticism and its effect on the general reader.*

jazz: some early difficulties

LEROY OSTRANSKY

*A*S RECENTLY AS TEN YEARS AGO, TECHNICAL jazz analysis had been given little serious or systematic thought. The prime reason for this lack of thoughtful analysis may be found in the analyses and evaluations made by jazz writers who apparently had difficulty in making themselves understood. The language of jazz was coined, for the most part, by jazz musicians with little regard for the written word, or by well-meaning writers with little technical knowledge of music in general, or—and worst of all—by a small but influential school of semiliterate enthusiasts whose main interest seemed to lie not in furthering jazz itself, but in merchandising the adjuncts of jazz: records, horns, bop berets, and tired stock arrangements. Aimed at adolescents and jungle intellects, the language of this last group jangled with nouns and verbs that carried little meaning and adjectives that, while scarcely descriptive, were on the whole redundant. Unable to make even an attempt at straightforward musical analysis (or, for that matter, to write a straightforward sentence), they adopted a gibbering prose calculated to hide the thinness of their analysis and evaluation.

With the establishment in 1934 of *Down Beat*, a jazz magazine, there was hope for serious discussion of the subject, a hope soon betrayed, for the editors aimed their publication at adolescent jazz fans and conceived their function to be that of serving the jazz industry as movie magazines served Hollywood. Until the swing era, there was little mention of jazz in popular magazines of national circulation, and whatever notice jazz received in the daily press was—its scantiness notwithstanding—pejorative and a little absurd. Jazz buffs therefore welcomed the new publication sight unseen, only to find its critical writing a disappointment. Serious jazz students, who had little to choose from among the writing on jazz before *Down Beat*, soon learned not to expect much of *Down Beat* either. Nat Hentoff, a former associate editor of *Down Beat*, summed up the magazine's twenty-five years of publication when he said:

> *Down Beat* is especially shallow and is apparently geared for less advanced high school sophomores. . . . Critical and historical jazz writing does appear to be slowly improving, but fervid amateurism is apt to be predominant for some time, because the fan-writer is well entrenched. As long as *Down Beat* remains

JAZZ: SOME EARLY DIFFICULTIES from *The Anatomy of Jazz* by Leroy Ostransky; copyright 1960 by the University of Washington Press. Reprinted by permission.

the "bible" of the field, the writing will be of a caliber more appropriate to revealed religion than to responsible criticism.

Because of their inability to write on jazz as music, writers for most of the popular jazz journals turned their hands to grinding out deadline record reviews and uncovering sensational biographical data that were then translated into trite but shocking headlines; or they concocted diffuse, sophomoric think-pieces intended to show why the jazz musician is a nice guy or a bad guy or simply a misunderstood guy who never got the breaks until the writer discovered him in a tired but happy moment.

The language problem is one thing, but wrong-headed intolerance is another. For some time now there has been a tendency among jazz writers to look down upon anyone who doesn't "dig" jazz. Their attitude toward the uninitiated layman has often been one of indifference. But their attitude toward classical musicians has been one of intolerance —not just a passive intolerance, but an active one. In its most primitive form, this intolerance manifests itself in simple name-calling; in a somewhat higher form it appears in the condescension apparent in the following items. The first compares the musical intelligence of the classical musician to that of the jazzman.

CAT ON KEYS

New York—Drummer Osie Johnson was telling of the time a group of classical musicians were gathered in a jazzman's home, and the latter put some Charlie Parker records on the phonograph.

After a few seconds, one of the classical men protested: "Come on now, fix the machine. That motor's obviously going too fast. Nobody can play that many notes so fast." The jazzman took great and obvious delight in proving that there was nothing at all wrong with the machine.

The second is a three-column headline of an article on recording studios which reminds its readers: "Classics Recorders Just Discovering Something Jazz Fans Found Out Early."

Square or classical musicians, finding themselves patronized by the self-appointed defenders of jazz, were unlikely to seek to overcome their feeling of alienation from jazz. The tone of *Down Beat* helped cement many of the squares into four-square blocks of antagonism toward all jazz. It is a happy circumstance that many serious musicians are able to disregard the rather obvious insinuations of petty jazz writers who, to retaliate for fancied snubs, attack with their fists flying in the name of defending jazz. There are many first-rate musicians who believe it is possible, and even desirable, to study, understand, and enjoy the work of Mozart as well as the work of Thelonious Monk. Such musicians (and it would seem that jazz has need of many) may be amused at the ineptness of undistinguished jazz reporters, but they are less likely to be amused when a critic of André Hodeir's reputation and sensitivity asks a question such as this: "Isn't it true that those who prefer the Beethoven work [*Ninth Symphony*] confess implicitly their inability to understand Stravinsky's masterpiece [*Le Sacre du Printemps*]?"

If Hodeir means to imply by his question that there are musicians who prefer Beethoven to Stravinsky, or that there are musicians who believe there is something unnatural about any music that is not German, then he should say so. No one will question this. If, however, his question is to be taken at face value, it seems to indicate an inability on Hodeir's part to recognize the distinctions between comprehension, appreciation, and enjoyment. A respectable number of classical musicians understand fully the nature of Stravinsky's work, but nevertheless prefer Beethoven's *Ninth Symphony* to Stravinsky's *Le Sacre*—and if not Beethoven's *Ninth,* then a Bach suite perhaps, or a Mozart divertimento, a Schubert song, a Chopin étude. Moreover, there can be no doubt that many musicians, and laymen as well, not only do not prefer *Le Sacre,* but do not understand it; neither is there any doubt, in my mind at least, that there are a good many who prefer Beethoven's *Ninth* and don't understand *it,* either. The fact remains that it is not necessary to understand a work in order to like it; or, to put it another way: a musician may have a comprehensive understanding and appreciation of a work—jazz or otherwise—without liking it. The failure to understand this principle—perhaps the guiding principle in critical evaluation— is part of the reason for the apparent schism between some well-known jazz critics and contemporary classical musicians who evince an interest in jazz.

Jazz has reached an important stage in its growth. In the past decade it has finally attracted a number of men of literary taste and musical perception, and this favorable climate must be maintained. Jazz needs the aid and interest of historians, theorists, composers, estheticians— anyone willing to lend his support, knowledge, and experience to the task of establishing jazz as a significant part of music. Jazz is an important branch of music, of American music especially; as such, it must be allowed to flourish, cultivated by respectful consideration and intensive study. Much has been done in the past ten years toward this goal: the inauguration of jazz study groups and institutes, for example, and the recognition of jazz as a subject for study in institutions of higher learning. Of the highest significance, also, is the probing look backward by men of appropriate intellectual habits, men who feel the compulsion to take the study of jazz out of the shadows of semiliterateness and anti-intellectualism and place it in the light of serious and searching study.

Jazz has at last become respectable. But in order to understand the origins of its present-day problems—semantic and otherwise—it is necessary to survey, however briefly, early jazz criticism. As long ago as 1946, Winthrop Sargeant wrote: "There has been a great deal of dubious and highly confusing writing around the subject of jazz. Probably no musical movement in history has been made the subject of more leaky speculation. . . ." Many critics have since echoed, in more or less detail, Sargeant's view. In order to show the scope of the work still to be done, I have listed the following representative statements, which, I believe, pose the most important problems faced by present-day jazz writers and theorists. Morroe Berger, a Columbia University fellow in sociology, wrote in 1946:

The origins of jazz and the story of its spread, as well as the careers of its players, are all subjects about which there is still considerable question. The importance of these matters is, in addition, not limited to music itself, or to the interest of collectors or to the reputation of musicians; they are significant, also, for the problems of the origins and diffusion of culture, and racial interaction, which involve other arts as well as some sciences.

In 1955 Keepnews and Grauer commented on the growing importance and complexities of jazz in America:

Perhaps the truest measure of the validity of jazz is that it can be all things to all men: a mild form of amusement; an emotional or an intellectual stimulant; an art form; a social commentary; a cult; something to like, love, or even hate for a wide variety of esthetic, emotional or social reasons. Thus jazz is both simple (no more than the combinations of notes you hear) and incredibly complex (as complex as human beings and as the world we inhabit). And thus it is a fit subject for all the analysis, history, biography, criticism, and written what-have-you that has been built up alongside it.

In 1956 Jacques Barzun emphasized the difficulty we are concerned with:

It [jazz] ranks with sports and philately as the realm of the self-made expert and of the controversialist as well, for musicology has not yet settled all the historical, stylistic, and biographical problems that have been raised about it.

In 1957 Shapiro and Hentoff summed up the question: "Since jazz musicians are notoriously inarticulate verbally, a good deal of analytical and creative writing about jazz during the past three decades has been speculative, fanciful, romantic, and wrong."

Shapiro and Hentoff's statement brings us back to the semantic problem. It is sometimes easy for us to forget how new the language of jazz is, and quite frequently how subjective the meanings are of even its most established terms. "One of the difficulties of describing an elusive music like jazz," Whitney Balliett has said, "is a made-at-home terminology that includes such aimless and largely inscrutable brand names as 'swing,' 'be-bop,' and 'Dixieland.' "

To say nothing of "jazz." Although the word "jazz" was undoubtedly in use for a good many years before 1914, it was not until then, according to Nick La Rocca, founder of the Original Dixieland Jazz Band, that "jazz" appeared in an advertisement. "The Original Dixieland Jazz Band," he wrote to Nicolas Slonimsky, "was the first band in the world to be called a Jazz Band. Our first billing was in the year of 1914, month of March, place Boosters Club, Chicago, Illinois, Manager Harry James." Two years later *Variety* wrote, "Chicago has added another innovation to its list of discoveries in the so-called 'Jazz Bands.' " According to Slonimsky, this may be the first mention of the word "jazz" in print. A year after the *Variety* item appeared, the Victor Company issued their first jazz record (March, 1917), and in 1918 the Columbia Phonograph Company issued its first jazz record, *Darktown Strutters Ball* and *Indiana*, played by the Original Dixieland Jass Band.

Conjecture on the derivation of the word "jazz" (or "jass") has ranged widely. The term has been variously considered as a corruption of "Charles" by way of "Chas," "jass," "jazz"; a diminution of "jaser," that is, to exhilarate; and some linguistic scholars claim to have traced its origins to West Africa. In the early days of jazz writing, it may have seemed more profitable to seek the linguistic origins of jazz than to try to define it. Once it was out of its infancy, however, little could be said of its linguistic origins that had not been said before, and critics—the apt and inept alike—set about defining, or not defining, jazz.

Many of those attempting to define jazz took advantage of the elusiveness of the term by using jazz as a springboard for sociological, psychological, and anthropological speculations, without recognizing that jazz is music; nevertheless, many of these critics have made some contribution to the understanding of jazz. Before we attempt to search out the musical aspects of jazz, it might be well to acknowledge the work of those social critics who had a hand in creating the image of jazz still dominant in the minds of many people. These are the critics who have, in the main, produced the miasmatic atmosphere in which jazzmen often have had to perform. These are the critics who have stamped their opinions and attitudes upon the jazz-uninformed reading public and have made it difficult, and sometimes impossible, to convince the uninitiated of the worth of jazz, or to persuade them to accept the analysis of jazz as a serious and worthy enterprise.

For the social critics of jazz and the people they have influenced, the years between 1920 and 1929 were the crucial years, the years when all good men strode onto the field of Armageddon, pen in hand, to conquer the evil forces of jazz. It is therefore natural to search for the corpus of social criticism of jazz in the writings of Jazz Age critics—not because its critics were unmusical (or, in some cases, not even American), but because their criticism reflects the literate viewpoint of sincere writers and jazz-innocent readers at the time when first impressions of jazz were being formed.

In 1920 Harold Spender, a representative critic of American mores and author of *A Briton in America*, was led to believe that many of the jazz tunes he had heard were African in origin. This caused him painful concern. If we were not careful, American musical tradition might be "submerged by the aboriginal music of the Negro," and, if we insisted on stomping along such "semibarbaric paths," heaven knows where we would end up. But Harold Spender, the Englishman, was a mild fellow indeed compared with a critic whom I shall call "The Amazing American." That author, who preferred to remain nameless, wrote a provocative study ingeniously entitled "The Amazing American," in which—and his lack of comprehension did not deter him a bit —he spoke of jazz, among other evils. The place of America in the future spiritual scheme of things was, he opined, assured. Any nation capable of producing the "nigger minstrel, rag-time music, and the tango dance," was close to the top. His indictment of jazz, however, is spiritless compared to his brilliantly indiscriminating castigation of American culture in general. In 1925 he wrote:

In deathless page, in song, in art, America has contributed but little to the world's treasury. If that land were to cease to be tomorrow, its most flattering epitaph would be the sign of the dollar chiselled in the stone. . . . It is a land of flesh-pots, with no great national aim speaking through a national art. . . . The general attitude of the American mind is in deadly opposition to culture.

Outbursts of this sort were not uncommon even among authors who signed their work. At about the same time, the distinguished writer Aldous Huxley had a go at us. He said much the same thing as the others, but with more style. Here, in jazz prose, is a sample from his book. *Jesting Pilate: An Intellectual Holiday:*

Jazz it up, jazz it up. Keep moving. Step on the gas. Say it with dancing. The Charleston, the Baptists. Radios and Revivals. Uplift and Gilda Gray. The pipe organ, the nigger with the saxophone, the Giant Marimbaphone. Hymns and the movies and Irving Berlin. Petting Parties and the First Free United Episcopal Methodist Church. Jazz it up!

If laid end to end, all the jazz-inspired, pointed-finger, stream-of-licentiousness pieces of the twenties on the debilitating effects of wine, women, and jazz would span the distance from New Orleans to New York—by way of Memphis, Kansas City, and Chicago—and back again. Jazz, for critics in the twenties, was a social manifestation, not a musical one. For anyone interested in jazz as music, the critical climate promised little sunshine.

The slow progress in jazz analysis is probably due chiefly to the confusion of jazz with commercial popular music. It is scarcely credible nowadays that certain writers of the Jazz Age were unable to recognize that jazz is a manner of performance rather than a collection of Tin Pan Alley tunes. Nevertheless, such was the case, and this confusion resulted in establishing men like Paul Whiteman, George Gershwin, and Irving Berlin at the top of the jazz hierarchy. By now, of course, their place in jazz is clear; their place in popular music even clearer. But in the twenties the confusion—even in the minds of otherwise acute writers—enabled Whiteman to attain the unchallenged position of King of Jazz. For the general public the songs of Berlin and Gershwin, as played by the Whiteman band, had enough characteristics in common with whatever fragments of jazz they knew to seem to be much the same thing. Those who heard genuine jazz occasionally—the music of Armstrong, say, or Fletcher Henderson—heard these men and their groups play tunes with the same titles used by Whiteman, and they naturally assumed they were hearing a poor version of Whiteman's music. To their conditioned ears, Whiteman's "jazz" was smoother, richer, cleaner, and more civilized. In 1926, at the height of the confusion, Henry O. Osgood wrote *So This Is Jazz,* a book Whitney Balliett has happily described as "a triumphant and fascinating failure." In this work Osgood showed how it was possible to write a book on jazz without actually considering the Negro's position in jazz. Here is the premise on which Osgood's book was based:

> Nowhere have I gone into detail about Negro jazz bands. There are so many good ones, it would be hard to pick out a few for special mention. None of them, however, are as good as the best white bands, and very rarely are their best players as good as the best white virtuosos. Their playing makes up for what it may lack in smoothness and finish by abandon, dash, spirit and warmth. There are fewer trained musicians, consequently more of the improvisations and variations which characterized early jazz.

Osgood was not alone in his beliefs; other, more astute writers than he made the same mistakes. In 1923, Gilbert Seldes, then a brilliant young critic with unrestrained interests and perpetually *au courant,* set about answering another critic who believed that jazz was on the way out. "Jazz, for me," Seldes wrote, in *Dial,* August, 1923, "isn't a last feverish excitement, a spasm of energy before death. It is the normal development of our resources, the expected, and wonderful, arrival of America at a point of creative intensity."

Now, that was an enthusiastic, patriotic, moving, even poetic statement, except for one thing: Seldes had little notion of what jazz was in 1923. He made the fashionable mistake of thinking that certain pieces of sheet music were jazz—good or bad—and others were not; that certain songwriters were better jazz composers than other songwriters; and that the notated melodic, harmonic, and rhythmic structure of a piece of music determined its jazz quality. Seldes is a good man to have on your side in any literary battle, but in 1923 he was not writing about jazz; he was writing about popular music. He was not yet aware that the jazz quality of a piece is determined by the manner in which it is played. Jazz is not a piece called *Tiger Rag, St. Louis Blues, Wang Wang Blues,* or *Yes, We Have No Bananas.* The title determines nothing; Whiteman's recording of *Wang Wang Blues* had about as much to do with jazz as his performances of *Song of India, By the Waters of Minnetonka,* or *Oh Katherina,* with its *Ach Du lieber Augustin* introduction. Seldes, apparently unaware of this, made an extraordinary effort to show that Irving Berlin was a great jazz composer. "Mr. Berlin's masterpieces . . . in jazz," he wrote in the same article, "are *Everybody Step* and *Pack Up Your Sins.*" Other of Seldes' favorites were *I'm Gonna Pin My Medal on the Girl I Left Behind* and *Someone Else May Be There While I'm Gone;* he admired these tunes because they were equally good played slow or fast. "Berlin's work," he added, "is musically interesting, and that means it has a chance to survive. I have no such confidence in *Dardanella* or *Chicago.*"

Seldes then went on to distinguish between white jazz and colored jazz, and it is here that he missed the riverboat entirely. About the future of American music, he wrote, "I say the Negro is not our salvation because with all my feelings for his desirable indifference to our set of conventions about emotional decency, I am on the side of civilization." Words like these from a man of Seldes' unquestionable intellect and sensitivity helped delay the unprejudiced, thoroughgoing analysis of jazz a good many years. As long as critics of Seldes' caliber and reputation continued to write about "emotional decency" and whatever it is that is not "on the side of civilization," jazz continued to seek its laurels along skid road.

In 1929, or shortly before the release of Ellington's *Wall Street Wail,* P. F. Laubenstein, a serious music critic, made an attempt to present the prevailing position of jazz in an essay in the *Musical Quarterly.* Trying manfully to be objective—but not always succeeding—Laubenstein was not especially sympathetic to jazz. His essay did, however, summarize certain significant aspects of jazz and recognized certain problems of the future at a time when many hoped that jazz had no future. Here, from "Jazz—Debit and Credit," is Laubenstein's summation:

The musical historian of the future will doubtless find his *bête noire* in this inescapable task of evaluating jazz. Indeed, many of its contemporaries there be who execrate the "stuff" as inebriate, doggerel, degenerate, ghoulish, vulturine, etc. *ad infinitum*—music, or as not music at all, bearing inherent frailties which spell its own ephemerality. Its enthusiastic devotees see in its local generation and popular cultivation the very best attestation of its truly representative American character, and from its study would derive invaluable leadings as to the direction which a national music should take. Those holding a middle ground discover in it some elements of permanent value and certain developments which must be counted as real contributions toward the progress of music.

Critical onslaughts in books, journals, and magazines were, of course, the bulk of jazz criticism. In addition, the daily press, acting as if it were woefully certain that jazz would flourish under any circumstances, offered little sympathy or understanding. Until recently, jazz news consisted mostly of unfavorable criticisms by names in the news and self-styled watch and ward societies. The subject of jazz, with its popular connotations, could usually be counted on to make provocative and lively news copy. What the general reader read in the newspapers about jazz was what he wanted to believe; and what the press published reflected his opinion. He knew nothing about jazz as music, but he had a firm opinion that the men and women of jazz were degenerate and unwholesome. The average reader received (and still receives) great comfort in believing that there were people to whom he could feel superior. And much feature writing was intended to reinforce the reader's opinions. With few exceptions, it is not an easy task to find a news item of the twenties on jazz that does not speak of jazz with tongue in cheek, as a kind of drollery always good for a chuckle, if not a laugh. Overseas items, from France particularly, were always welcome and in the twenties were usually offered with heavyhanded merriment. The following headlines from the *New York Times* reflect the general public's attitude toward jazz in the Jazz Age:

> Fails to Stop Jazz, Is Arrested Later [July 7, 1922]
> French Police Stop Jazz Band Burial; Dead Man Wanted It in Procession, but the Mourners were Foxtrotting [October 18, 1923]
> France Orders Our Jazz Players Expelled [May 31, 1924]
> Isadora Duncan Plans Greek Temple for Nice; She is Reported to Have Bought the Theatre Promenade des Anglais, to Fight Jazz [May 1, 1925]
> Ford Wars on Jazz; Gives Party for Old Time Dances, Seeking to Revive Their Popularity [July 12, 1925]
> American Dancer Jazzing the *Marseillaise* Angers Friendly Audience in Paris Music Hall [January 31, 1926]
> Church Jazz Wedding Utilizes Saxophone [November 14, 1926]
> Damrosch Assails Jazz [April 17, 1928]
> French Find Our Jazz Too Soul-disturbing [February 3, 1929]

From these headlines, it would seem that nobody in the twenties dared say a kind word for jazz. By the thirties, however, the jazz initiate could sense that some changes would be made. The Roosevelt administration's early efforts to lift the nation out of the Great Depression looked as if they would work, and everything, jazz included, suddenly seemed brighter and more useful. Many intellectuals sought, and found, rewards in studying America's popular culture, and folk songs and jazz came in for a good share of the spotlight. In 1933, the repeal of Prohibition and the subsequent opening of many night clubs and dance halls led to the employment of more jazz musicians and to a wider audience for jazz. It is possible also that the general unrest caused by events in Europe helped create a small musical nationalism, much of which may well have been fostered by the reports in the daily press of various actions and pronouncements against jazz in European countries. On March 15, 1933, the National Socialist head of the Berlin Rundfunk forbade the broadcasting of "Negro jazz," and on January 7, 1934, a headline in the *New York Times* read: "Ban against Jazz Sought in Ireland." (A week before, an Irish antijazz group had paraded in Mohall, Ireland, with banners and posters bearing the slogan "Down with Jazz and Paganism." The unruly antijazzists had been aroused by the actions of their finance minister, Sean MacEntee, who had stood by while jazz bands broadcast their wares over the state broadcasting system.) On October 12, 1935, Eugen Hadamowski, director of the German broadcasting system, issued an order banning broadcasts of jazz in order, as he put it, "to do away with the last remnants of the culture-Bolshevistic Jew."

By the time these items appeared in the press, the swing era was under way, and swing—or jazz—was beginning to enjoy unprecedented popularity in the United States, and Hadamowski was no longer talking about the music of a handful of people, but the music of millions. Americans, generally speaking, were not particularly curious about their own culture. As long as they regarded jazz as something they were permitted to take or leave alone, they left it alone—it seemed socially more prudent to do so.

However, once swing as a popular movement surged forward, and they learned that other nations saw jazz as a threat to their way of life, many Americans began to see in jazz a symbol of their own freedom, and foreign pronouncements condemning jazz became something to ridicule and defy. There were no great public refutations or demonstrations, of course (unless one so considers the crowds flocking to the New York Paramount Theater, Randall's Island, and Carnegie Hall swing concerts), and the thought that jazz was a symbol of anything was for the most part left unsaid. Altogether, though, there was increasing public support for jazz as something American. And this was all to the good. Pronouncements like those issued by the Nazis may not have sent anyone into a fit of righteous rage, but perhaps such items made it possible for people—some of them public figures—to feel less queasy about defending jazz, in whatever aspect.

In the late thirties, swing burst forth and reached all parts of the nation. Radio and admen—agencies responsible for much of its growth —were becoming powerful and influential; a shrewd promotion of swing, big white bands in particular (with Benny Goodman's name leading the rest), resulted in making swing a suitable, if controversial, topic for conversation however genteel. Since respected figures occasionally spoke up for swing, tongue-in-cheek press notices diminshed (to increase again after World War II, with Dizzy Gillespie and his early high jinks) and became serious, objective, and sometimes even sympathetic reports. And on May 5, 1937, the New York Times reported that "Dr. Carleton Sprague Smith, head of the Music Division of the N.Y. Public Library, championed 'swing' music tonight, terming it an 'appropriate' musical expression which must receive serious consideration."

During this same period, however, the opposite point of view continued to be expressed with varying degrees of violence. The president of the Dancing Teachers Business Association, for example, in a talk to his associates reported by the New York Times on July 7, 1938, said that swing music was a "degenerated form of jazz," and its devotees were "unfortunate victims of economic instability." He went on to predict hopefully that "the popularity of swing will fade with the return of economic stability." Furthermore, if people wished to dance, there were plenty of suitable and proper tangos, rumbas, and waltzes. On May 22, 1938, an exhibition of "degenerate music" opened in Düsseldorf. Nazi Germany wished to prevent the spread of jazz and atonal music—"the microbes of musical decomposition"—and to wipe out all music that showed "Marxist, Bolshevistic, Jewish, or any other un-German tendencies." And, finally, Dr. Harry D. Gideonse, then head of the economics and social science department of Barnard College, stated in the New York Times of November 2, 1938, "Swing is musical Hitlerism."

Altogether, it is not difficult to understand why so little serious work on jazz was accomplished in the twenties and thirties. Add the confusions, misunderstandings, disagreements, and misconceptions of those sincerely interested in jazz to the rantings and bitterness of those opposed to jazz, and you have the main reason why jazz analysis was delayed until we were well into the swing era. By the middle forties, serious attempts to analyze jazz as music became more frequent. Most critics began to recognize the need for emphasizing proper jazz analysis and evaluation and de-emphasizing the social import of jazz and attempts to tie jazz in with sociology became less and less rewarding. Freed of its social shackles, jazz in the forties finally became a fit subject for serious study, and students of jazz were now able to ask, "What is jazz?"

QUESTIONS

1. What enables "fan" magazines of all kinds—jazz, movies, sports, television—to flourish? Discuss the subject matter of these magazines. On what level are the subjects treated?
2. Clarify the distinctions between "comprehension," "appreciation," and "enjoyment." Relate their meanings to jazz and to classical music.
3. Do you think it is possible for one person to understand and enjoy both jazz and classical music equally? Give your reasons.
4. Do you agree that "Jazz has at last become respectable?" What, exactly, does that statement mean? Was there a time when jazz was not respectable? When? Why?
5. In the history of jazz criticism, why are the years 1920-1929 important? Compare the criticism of that era with present criticism. What are the likenesses? the differences?